P9-CEJ-835

The very Healthy Cat Book

By the same authors—

How to Have a Healthier Dog

The *very* Healthy Cat Book

A Vitamin and Mineral Program
for Optimal Feline Health

by

Wendell O. Belfield, D.V.M.
and Martin Zucker

With a Foreword by
Dr. Linus Pauling

McGraw-Hill Book Company
New York St. Louis San Francisco Bogotá Guatemala Hamburg Lisbon
Madrid Mexico Montreal Panama Paris San Juan São Paulo Tokyo Toronto

Copyright © 1983 by Wendell O. Belfield and Martin Zucker

All rights reserved. Printed in the United States of America. Except as permitted under the Copyright Act of 1976, no part of this publication may be reproduced or distributed in any form or by any means, or stored in a data base or retrieval system, without the prior written permission of the publisher.

1 2 3 4 5 6 7 8 9 F G R F G R 8 7 6 5 4 3

ISBN 0-07-004367-1
ISBN 0-07-004354-X {PBK.}

LIBRARY OF CONGRESS CATALOGING IN PUBLICATION DATA

Belfield, Wendell O.
The very healthy cat book.
Includes bibliographical references and index.
1. Cats—Food.   2. Vitamins in animal nutrition.
3. Minerals in animal nutrition.   I. Zucker, Martin.
II. Title.
SF447.6.B44   1983   636.8'089328   82-22887
ISBN 0-07-004367-1
ISBN 0-07-004354-X (pbk.)

Book design by Janice Willcocks Stern

To Marlene and Rosita,

who were patient and wonderfully supportive

Contents

Acknowledgments

Thanks to Laneen Firth, a cherished client, whose keen interest, abiding faith, and intelligent observations have helped me to help her cats and thence the cats of other breeders; to Carolyn Bussey, for sharing her vast practical knowledge of feline nutrition and illness; to veterinarians Robert and Marty Goldstein of Yorktown Heights, New York, and Carvel Tiekert, of Bel Air, Maryland, whose clinical experiences with nutrition greatly enhanced the depth of this book; to veterinarian Alfred Plechner of West Los Angeles, for generosity once again in sharing his unique knowledge of food-related pet sensitivities; to Thea Sutherland, a scholar of cat nutrition, for helping fill some gaps in our understanding of cat nutrition; to breeders Gerri Raicevich, Ann Ransom, Laura and Dennis Dayton, and Susan Ironside for supplying real-life dramas and background about cats helped by better nutrition; to Dr. Irwin Stone, whose knowledge of ascorbic acid is virtually unbounded; to Wayne Harris of Hillestad Corporation in San Jose for help in locating information on pet nutrition; to Susan Goldstein, whose Lick Your Chops Shop in Yorktown Heights is the first health-food pet store in the country, for some valuable information on consumerism; to Nancy Stephens and Pat Tedford, those endearing and enduring pillars of the Bel-Mar Veterinary Hospital who, among other services both little and great, helped jiggle a veterinarian's memory; to Marie Stephens, the mother of my assistant, for a superfast typing job; to a number of knowledgeable people inside and outside of government who provided time, insight, and patience in explaining the ways of the pet-food industry.

The authors owe a special debt of gratitude to Miss PJ Haduch, their editor at McGraw-Hill. From start to finish, she has been totally interested, totally helpful, totally positive, totally professional. Thanks, PJ.

The authors also want to thank Patrick Delahunt of the Richard Curtis Agency, who has been a most efficient, wise, and thoughtful agent.

Foreword

The Food and Nutrition Board of the National Academy of Sciences' National Research Council issues periodical recommendations about daily allowances of vitamins and minerals for human beings and also for domesticated animals. The scientists, physicians, and veterinarians who make these recommendations address one primary question: What amount of each of these nutrients is needed in order to keep a person or animal from dying of the corresponding deficiency disease? For instance, the disease associated with a deficiency of vitamin C is scurvy, that with a deficiency of B_1 is beriberi, and that with a deficiency of niacin is pellagra. In regard to preventing these deficiency diseases, the Food and Nutrition Board and the other authoritative agencies have given good recommendations about the necessary amounts.

There is, however, another question that can be asked. The question is, what amount of each of these nutrient substances is needed in order to put the person or the cat or the dog in the best of health; what amount will decrease most effectively the incidence of disease and common aches, pains, and ailments; and what amount will be of the greatest benefit in the treatment of disease?

There is a difference between minimum amounts that prevent the classic deficiency diseases and optimal amounts that promote optimal health. Compared with the many years we have recognized the value of vitamins to humans and animals, it has been only recently, however, that optimal intakes of these nutrients have been recognized as being much greater than the intakes needed to prevent death from deficiency diseases.

In an earlier book on dogs, Dr. Belfield discussed the question of the amounts of vitamins and minerals that could maintain canines in the best of health, and also the way in which these substances can be used in the treatment of disease. Now Dr. Belfield has done the same for cats.

Cat breeders, cat fanciers, and the owners of cherished house pets will learn how vitamins and minerals can develop the maximum health in felines and make them highly resistant to disease.

To Dr. Belfield goes great credit for the discovery that massive doses of vitamin C, as great as a half gram of sodium ascorbate intravenously per pound of body weight twice a day, have significant effects in the treatment of viral and other diseases in dogs and cats.

Vitamin C is indeed an extraordinary substance, somewhat different from other vitamins. The difference is this: Animals of most species synthesize, that is, produce their own ascorbic acid (vitamin C) in the cells of either the liver or kidney, with humans and a few other animal species being exceptions. Accordingly, most animals do not die of scurvy when they are completely deprived of vitamin C in their diets. On the other hand, the other substances that humans require for life—that is, the other vitamins—are also required for life by essentially all animal species.

An idea of the amount of vitamin C needed for good health is provided by analyzing the amount of this substance made by various animal species. The amount made is approximately proportional to the body weight. The average animal weighing 16 pounds produces between 200 and 2,000 milligrams of vitamin C per day, with animals of some species making less and others more. Dogs and cats are in the first group. A 16-pound dog synthesizes only about 200 milligrams of vitamin C per day. A 9-pound cat will make only about 160 milligrams. Cats and dogs thus make only about one-fifth as much as animals of most other species. It is probably for this reason that a large amount of supplementary vitamin C is beneficial for the development and preservation of optimal health in cats.

This book by Dr. Belfield provides a good deal of information that should be of practical value to every owner of a cat.

—Linus Pauling
Palo Alto, California

PART 1

*Why Your Cats
Need Extra Vitamins
and Minerals*

1

Preventive Veterinary Medicine:
Getting to the Heart of Problems

Cats are becoming a "national mania," proclaimed the cover story of *Time* magazine on December 7, 1981.

"Plain or fancy, pampered or ignored, barn mousers or apartment pets, cats have captured the American imagination," said the magazine.

So much so that the cat population was making rapid gains on the canine majority. By *Time*'s count, there were 34 million cats residing in 24 percent of America's households, an increase of 55 percent during the last decade. In the meantime, dog ranks were holding steady at around 48 million.[1]

The current trends in pet demographics reflect the way we humans are living. In the past, when most people lived primarily on farms or in one-unit dwellings with plenty of romp room, dogs were the preferred pet. They were trained as hunters or watchdogs. They were loyal companions. They played with the kids. If a cat was in the picture, it was chiefly for its natural talents as a mouser.

However, in today's urbanized age of condo and apartment living, the desire for animal companionship is being neatly and increasingly fulfilled by cats.

Cats are self-cleaning. Give them a litterbox and they do it all right there. If you go away for the weekend, leave a little extra food and water and the cat will care for itself.

Dogs require much more attention.

It used to be that when a cat became sick it would seek out a dark corner of the barn or slip away into some foliage to die, or recover, without any notice. Today, with cats in closer contact with their owners, illness is usually noticed immediately.

The "apartmentization" of cats has meant the loss of a natural outdoor habitat and natural food sources. Electric light has replaced sunlight. Mice and birds have been replaced with the impure and chemical-ridden mishmash called commercial pet food. Pure air and grass have been replaced with polluted air and synthetic fiber carpets.

All these factors place a burden of stress on modern cats that weakens their resistance to disease.

Furthermore, there are more and more cat fanciers today housing and breeding expensive, purebred animals. These cats appear to be considerably more sensitive and susceptible to disease than robust outdoor cats of mixed blood.

Thus, the cat boom, the new style of living, and the popularity of purebreds have resulted in a buildup of feline traffic at the veterinary hospital. Years ago in my practice the dog-to-cat ratio was 70–30. Now it is 50–50.

When I attended veterinary school in the early fifties, cats were accorded little attention in the curriculum. Livestock and farm animals were regarded as the most important, then dogs, and, way down the list, the cats. It has only been in recent years that the veterinary profession has turned serious attention to cats. The first comprehensive book on feline medicine was not published until 1964!

As *Time* magazine accurately noted, there has been so little attention and research devoted to cats in the past that "dog cures were often simply transferred to cats, sometimes to no effect."[2]

Today there is specialized medical care and even veterinary practices dedicated solely to cats.

Still, there is a lot we do not know about cats.

Veterinarians are seeing many very sick cats and many cats die. We are seeing many cats ravaged by the feline leukemia virus. They are brought in hardly able to lift their heads to drink water. The veterinarian grabs at straws, trying any combination of drugs or ingredients that might magically pull the cat out. But nothing seems to work. There may be improvement for a day, for a few hours, but the cat generally declines, falls into a coma, and has to be euthanized. I have worked through many a lunch hour and weekend trying to cure such cats—mostly without success.

Among cat owners in general and cattery owners and breeders in particular, the appearance of leukemia or feline infectious peritonitis (FIP), another viral disease, is cause for panic.

I will never forget the case that dramatically changed my dismal luck with these highly contagious cat killer diseases. It happened one fall afternoon in 1976.

I had just returned from lunch when I received a rather frantic phone call from a cat breeder in Southern California. This woman had been a successful cattery owner for ten years but now was having a serious problem with leukemia and FIP.

There wasn't then, nor is there today, a known therapy for these conditions. They are so contagious and deadly that an animal testing positive for one or the other organism, even if there are no outward symptoms, will often be put to sleep. It will surely not be used for breeding, because of the high risk of transmitting the virus to the offspring.

This breeder had consulted with a leading California veterinary school. She explained the extent of the problem—the stillbirths, the inability to breed, the sickly kittens—and had her cats thoroughly tested. She hoped the experts could provide some saving recommendations, some new promising research, some encouragement.

Instead, she received the worst possible news. The experts suggested the cattery be closed.

Dismayed, the woman decided to call me. I was her last resort. She had read a magazine article describing my treatment of viral distemper with vitamin C. She hoped my method might work on her cats.

I quickly told her I hadn't had much success treating leukemia and FIP with vitamin C. However, if she was willing to try it, so was I.

She was desperate enough to try anything, and so she drove up with one of her animals who was extremely ill with infectious peritonitis. I then began what was essentially a distemper treatment based on massive doses of vitamin C intravenously. Unfortunately, the cat was too far gone. The treatment brought no positive results. I felt I had no choice but to put the animal to sleep.

Even though we lost the battle, I feel we won the war. I had given the woman a multivitamin and mineral formula I was using in my practice for dogs. I told her to administer the supplement to the other animals in her cattery and see if it helped the situation.

Several weeks later she phoned to say there were positive changes in her cats. They seemed to be more vigorous and healthy.

Over a period of several months we kept in contact, and she reported a lessening of her leukemia problem.

This was one of the first indications to me that a nutritional program of any sort could have an effect on a viral condition as serious as feline leukemia.

In about six months the leukemia problem had virtually been eliminated in this particular cattery. The owner, of course, was elated. Cats previously tested positive for leukemia were now testing negative. This meant that the cattery had a new life. Breeding could be resumed.

All the animals in the cattery were maintained on the supplement program. With time it became clear that good, healthy offspring were being produced from a good, healthy breeding stock.

The cattery owner realized the importance of maintaining kittens on the program. Each time she sold a kitten, she gave the buyer a vitamin and mineral supplement and strongly recommended the animal be kept on a lifelong program.

I was elated, too, but not totally surprised. I had already by this time been experiencing many good results with vitamin and mineral therapy in my practice.

Beginning in 1967 I began using high doses of vitamin C to treat dogs with distemper. There were no reliable vaccines at the time. No known cures. There was nothing my veterinary training had taught me that could help. The textbook said to put down dogs with distemper.

I had read a medical-journal article about the work of Dr. Fred Klenner, a North Carolina physician, who used big doses of vitamin C to cure people of polio, hepatitis, and other serious viral conditions. He had been achieving remarkable results back before the potent vaccines were developed.

I followed Klenner's lead and applied vitamin C to distemper, also a viral condition. It worked. In time I found it was equally as effective on a whole range of viral and nonviral diseases. I was successfully treating and preventing kennel cough, allergies, and common skin problems. Large-breed puppies put on a vitamin C program were not being stricken with hip dysplasia, a common puppy crippler thought to be a genetic condition. Bitches were whelping healthier puppies in half the normal delivery time and with fewer signs of stress.

To really appreciate what was happening you have to understand that physicians and veterinarians are essentially taught to treat diseases with drugs and surgery, not with vitamins. To have used nutritional methods ten or more years ago was to invite ridicule by medical colleagues practicing more conventional medicine. And I certainly got my share of criticism. Today, vitamins and minerals are more fashionable in the medical community, but practitioners accentuating nutrition are still considered mavericks.

My success with vitamin C was not only a pleasant surprise but somewhat of a shock. The results seemed to be contradicting scientific fact: most animals, including dogs and cats, produce their own supply of vitamin C through a biochemical reaction in the liver. Only the guinea pig, a few species of birds, the apes, and we humans lack this ability.

What's more, I learned that when subjected to stress or when their bodies are invaded by a virus, most animals can manufacture many times more vitamin C than normal. Vitamin C is an extremely important chemical produced by the liver to keep the body's immune system strong.

I later learned why treating and supplementing cats and dogs with extra vitamin C is so effective—and so important. I will explain why in Chapter Three.

My early work with vitamin C and canine distemper was so positive I began applying it to cats, primarily against feline distemper. Over a period of time, I began to use other nutrients such as vitamins A and E, the B complex vitamins, zinc, and other minerals. With more and more feline patients in my practice, I was seeing the same kind of positive effects on cats I had previously seen with dogs.

It is unlikely that anyone has ever advised you to buy vitamins and minerals for your cats to treat or prevent disease or health problems. But that is precisely my message to you if you want to see your animals active and happy and enjoying maximum health for as long as possible. Based on hundreds of cases in my practice, with alley cats and champion cats, I have seen just how big a difference extra vitamins and minerals can make in improving the quality of an animal's life. At one time I felt I was a "Lone Ranger" in emphasizing nutritional treatments for veterinary problems. Now there is a growing number of veterinarians doing similar things, and they, too, are reporting the same kind of good results. Some of them have been kind enough to share their experiences with me, and I will be reporting their findings in this book along with my own.

Whatever your relationship with your cats, this book is for you. It contains new, important, and practical information about an effective way to make your cats optimally healthy. Whether you own a gray domestic your neighbor gave you or a Persian kitten of champion stock with a $2,500 price tag, or you have converted your garage and house into a cat-breeding enterprise, the health of your animals is a matter of fundamental importance. Cats often live in close proximity to members of the household. They are, in fact, often cherished members of the household themselves. A sick cat can readily pass on its organisms to its human family or to other cats in the cattery. A whole house of valuable breeding and show stock can—and often is—thus wiped out.

A simple, easy-to-administer vitamin and mineral program can prevent these things from happening. Over the years I have developed such a program to successfully prevent and control many of the serious conditions in small animals. I have developed a prevention program with vitamins and minerals that my clients have used to keep their animals in the best of health.

The same advice I have given to my clients I now want to give to you. You and your pets can benefit just as my clients have done. This program applies equally to sensitive purebred cats and to the hardy hybrids—the street and outdoor cats. All cats are rendered healthier.

This book has big news about a way—finally—to eliminate the problem of viral leukemia, the number one cat killer. Millions of dollars have been poured into veterinary research to find an effective vaccine against this dreaded virus which is involved in many fatal disease processes. As yet, no effective vaccine has been marketed. But over the last five years, a simple vitamin and mineral program that I have developed has proven highly successful against leukemia and is currently used by some of the leading catteries in the country.

This book has big news about how the common urinary tract disorders of male cats can be prevented or minimized.

This book has big news on the many common respiratory diseases and nagging skin problems.

I will show you how to enhance queening and nursing and how easy it is to maintain the good appearance of your female during the stress of pregnancy and lactation.

I will show you how young cats can be protected against FIP and how old cats can be rejuvenated.

I will give you a program that eliminates litter runts and the ever present threat of sudden kitten death.

In Part Three of the book I will lay out my general prevention plan and show you how easy it is to follow. The plan is divided into cycle-of-life sections that tell you what, why, and how much supplementation is needed at certain periods of your cats' lives. I will also advise you how to select and how to use the supplements.

In Part Four I will discuss the cat-killer diseases—leukemia and FIP—and how vitamins and minerals can be used to keep your cats free of them.

In Part Five I will cover some of the other common feline conditions.

The purpose of this book is not to take the place of your veterinarian. Neither you nor this book can replace a skilled animal doctor trained to deal with animal disease. However, I can show you how to enjoy your animals more and save you unnecessary veterinary bills. I will show you how to use inexpensive vitamin and mineral products readily available in drugstores, health-foods stores, pet stores, supermarkets, and at your veterinarian's office.

By following my instructions and by taking the few seconds every day to supplement your animals' diets, you can save yourself considerable worry, money, and time. Just as my clients have done.

Laneen Firth, a top Persian breeder from San Jose and a client of mine since 1975, says that a solid vitamin and mineral program has meant big savings to her in cat medical bills.

"I handle much of the routine health care of my animals, as do many other breeders," she says. "But even with the considerable amount of nursing that breeders do, it is common to have an average expenditure of $100 or more per cat per year. This is because of such things as urinary blockage problems, cesarean sections, weak or dying kittens, and testing for leukemia and FIP.

"My vitamin and mineral program is uncomplicated and simple to administer and it eliminates these problems. I have no blockage, no C-sections, no sudden death or sickly kittens. I never have peritonitis or leukemia in my breeding stock, so my testing is at a minimum. Where this has occurred in animals purchased or traded, we have consistently been able to cure the problems with a diet change and the introduction of a vitamin and mineral program.

"My veterinary costs have been dropping every year. In 1981 the bill came to $11.65 per cat."

PREVENT—DON'T WAIT TO TREAT

Although I have used the nutritional approach in dealing with the killer diseases, I have frankly had little success in trying to save a deathly ill animal. But I have had great success in prevention—the by-product of my therapeutic efforts.

Cats are very private and independent animals. Sometimes they are not very cooperative with the veterinarian trying to treat them. They may scratch and bite and refuse to hold still during treatment. Furthermore, they have small veins that often elude the veterinarian's needle. In short, it is a whole lot easier to prevent disease in the first place than to treat it.

I believe that prevention is what medicine should really be about. Doesn't it make more sense to prevent the disease from happening rather than waiting around to treat disease once it strikes and does damage?

Medical and veterinary schools, however, are almost totally geared to disease. My entire training was dedicated to treating sick animals. There are no courses in "wellness" that teach doctors to make people and creatures optimally healthy.

It is said that among the ancient Chinese the people paid their healers only to keep them healthy and never paid for treatment of illness.

And it was Hippocrates, the father of medicine, who wisely said some two thousand five hundred years ago, "Let thy food be thy medicine and thy medicine be thy food."

The modern practice of medicine shows little influence of Chinese or Hippocratic thinking. Medical school graduates know much more about heart transplants and coronary bypasses than they do about nutrition, which is the basis of health. And yet doctors will often tell you not to waste your money buying extra vitamins and minerals because if you eat an adequate diet, you get all the vitamins you need. They don't even know what an adequate diet is!

The situation in veterinary medicine is perhaps even bleaker.

When I attended veterinary school, the curriculum called for only a single course on nutrition—and that was livestock feeding, because veterinarians were trained then to deal primarily with large farm animals. There was nothing on small-animal nutrition. Basically, we were taught how to diagnose and treat the classic vitamin-deficiency diseases. That was the extent of our nutrition education.

The late Dr. Lyle Baker, a California veterinarian who dedicated his career to livestock nutrition and preventive medicine, described the extent of his training thusly: "During my eight years of college, I was taught virtually nothing about nutrition and prevention of disease. As a matter of fact, the slightest mention of the possibility that something you ingested might exert some control over any disease was justification for branding one an oddball, out of step with the times."[3]

Although our knowledge of nutrition has improved over the years, the teaching of it has hardly changed.

In 1978, Dr. Robert Wilson of Washington State University's Department of Veterinary Medicine told a Senate committee that nutritional education in veterinary medicine is an "impoverished area" because of the emphasis on diagnosis and treatment.

Wilson said that veterinarians are psychologically geared to acting in emergency situations like the old family doctor and "we seem to find less satisfaction in preventing problems."[4]

In this unfortunate vacuum, the veterinarian and pet owner alike receive much of their nutritional education from the pet-food industry. As nutrition scientist Dr. Paul M. Newberne of Massachusetts Institute of Technology so aptly puts it, much of the information on how best to feed your pet is "misleading and primarily designed to sell a product."

He adds, "The pet-owning public and, in many cases, the veterinary profession has thus been at the mercy of mass media advertising, often to the detriment of the health of the animal and increased cost to the client."[5]

How, out of this kind of background, can we veterinarians advise clients about nutrition, which is obviously so essential to the health of their animals? How can we diagnose the low-grade and subtle symptoms of nutritional deficiencies when all we were taught was to recognize the unmistakable terminal symptoms?

We couldn't do it when I graduated in 1954, and the truth is that the young graduates today can't do it any better either.

At my San Jose animal hospital, I perform standard veterinary procedures. I diagnose and treat disease. I do spays and neuters and other surgery. I am proud of the fact that two surgical techniques I developed are widely used today in small-animal veterinary practice. I give immunizations. I treat the wounded warriors of cat fights. I set broken bones. I also administer drugs.

Drugs, of course, are necessary to the medical practitioner. They relieve symptoms and acute distress. But drugs don't eliminate the cause of symptoms. They don't cure.

Drugs are powerful foreign substances introduced into the body. They have side effects. You may eliminate the headache with a drug but often create another symptom in the process. Meanwhile, the cause of the headache is still at bay and bound to reassert itself.

As an example, steroids are drugs used routinely in veterinary practices to reduce swelling, itching, and stimulate appetite. However, they also suppress an animal's immune system and weaken his ability to fight disease. While useful, and often necessary, they leave the cause of problems untouched and create the potential for complications.

To get at the heart of problems, I do something that most veterinarians don't do. I put my animals on a vitamin and mineral program.

My concept of preventive veterinary medicine is easy to understand. It follows the philosophy of orthomolecular medicine, a new branch of human medicine founded by Nobel Prize winner Linus Pauling.

Orthomolecular means "right molecules in the right amounts." The idea is to provide optimal amounts of substances that are normally present in the body to achieve optimal health conditions or to treat disease. Vitamins and minerals are such substances. Drugs are not. They are not found in the body naturally.

Vitamins and minerals transact with other internal ingredients in an endless number of known and unknown biochemical processes that run the machinery of body and brain. However, because of stress, poor diet, aging, and environmental and genetic factors, they often become depleted and thus are not available in sufficient quantity or quality. As a result, you have less than optimal health or varying degrees of unwellness and disease.

Orthomolecular medicine provides these natural substances in the form of vitamin and mineral supplementation. The entire body receives this supplemental form of nourishment. All systems are strengthened, revitalized. The basis for an optimal level of health is created. If disease is present, the body's immune system is bolstered to fight the disorder and get on with the business of healing.

This concept applies to pets just as it does to humans.

Unfortunately, I can't assure you that a supplement program will entirely eliminate all disease, but what it doesn't prevent it will minimize. My clients tell me they have animals living longer and almost disease free. They tell me the supplements are bringing out the maximum in their cats.

Whether you were the recipient of a free kitten or you paid handsomely for a blue-blooded cat, you have an investment of love in your animal. You want a healthy and happy pet. And if you are a breeder or pet-shop owner you are concerned about the health of your animals because you have a reputation and business on the line. For these reasons, going to the minimal expense and minimal trouble of administering supplements to your animals is going to bring maximal rewards.

Often a client will question the idea of vitamins and minerals for an animal.

"Doctor, does my cat *really* need vitamins and minerals? Doesn't he get all he needs in his food?"

"No," I answer. "Your cat can survive without supplements. It is only a matter of how you want your animal to survive. Do you want a cat without upper respiratory disease when you go away and board him for a week? Do you want it protected from leukemia? Do you want your pet shedding all the time? Full of fleas?

"According to the pet-food manufacturers, your cat is supposed to be getting all the basic nutrient requirements in his prepared food. Yet what I have seen over the years is that supplementation makes the difference between a sickly or apparently healthy cat and an optimally healthy cat. What kind of a cat do you want?

"Remember that we live in close contact with our cats. We love them. Hug them. Kiss them. Some people even allow their cats in bed. Many elderly people in poor health enjoy the close companionship of cats. Bacterial and viral infections can be easily passed between people and cats at this kind of close range. A weak or stressed cat is going to be more susceptible to infection and disease. That means more risk and more medical bills for you, the owner. So what I am talking about is a program that will not only protect the cat but also the cat's owner."

We humans have the free will to do something about the quality of our health. If we want, we can smoke a pack of cigarettes a day and eat junk food and pollute our water and air and pave the way for disease. Or we can take responsibility for our health and make lifestyle choices that are more attuned to the laws of nature. We have the choice. Our pets do not. They have to eat the man-made food we give them (more about this in Chaper Two). They have to live in the environment we create for them. They are forced to breathe the air we thoroughly pollute. We have domesticated the cat, and it is very dependent despite a reputation for independence. By itself the cat cannot prevent disease. But you, the owner, can do something about it. And that is what my book is all about—helping you help your dependent animals.

There is much about cat nutrition that veterinarians don't know. We are taught very little about it. This book contains lessons I have learned from twenty years of clinical experience and also some precious insight other nutritionally oriented veterinarians have shared with me. There is obviously so much more to be known about the subject. But whatever the shortcomings, I hope this book will in some manner stimulate the veterinary medical establishment to begin looking at nutrition as the source of optimal animal health.

Recently a step in this direction was taken with the formation in February 1982 of the American Veterinary Holistic Medical Association, a group of veterinarians from around the country with a common interest in animal nutrition and preventive medicine.

Interested veterinarians and lay persons can apply for membership by writing to the American Veterinary Holistic Medical Association, 2214 Old Emmorton Road, Bel Air, MD 21014.

Cat owners can obtain the names of holistic practitioners nearest to them from this organization. Be sure to enclose a stamped, self-addressed envelope with the request.

2

What the TV Commercials
Don't Tell You About
Cat Food

The next time you are stocking up on your favorite cat food in the supermarket, take a moment or two and have a good look up and down the pet-food aisle.

What you are seeing is big, big business. Americans now shell out nearly $5 billion a year to feed their pets. Pet-food sales topped coffee in 1973 to become the largest-selling category among dry grocery commodities. People spend four times more on pet food than on baby food, twice as much than on cereal, macaroni, and flour products and, in England, even more than they spend on their beloved tea.

Look closely at the ingredient lists on the labels. They are monotonously alike. To convince you otherwise, that indeed "ours is better than theirs," the manufacturers spend more than $160 million a year in television commercials alone. They pitch you with trick photography, meaningless nutritional claims, and such inventive names as "Thrive" and "Crave" and "Meow Mix" and "Good Mews" and "Bright Eyes" and "Fish Ahoy." And, as if cats could really care, they even offer kitty snacks in the shape of fish.

Increasing sales for an increasing pet population are certainly good for the health of pet-food companies, but I'm doubtful about how good commercial pet food is for the health of pets. For thousands of years before Morris the Cat made his TV debut, cats were thriving on and craving food that never saw the inside of cellophane pouches or metal cans. Were cats better off then with rats, mice, birds, berries and other plants? Or has their existence improved with man-made kitty stews of tuna and kidney, or dry nuggets of ground yellow corn, wheat, meat, and bone meal, animal fat preserved with BHA, and artificial color?

Today, corn is the number one ingredient in many cat-food products. Yet, as veterinary nutritionist David Kronfeld points out, the cat was domesticated about three thousand years ago as a protector of granaries precisely because it refused to eat grain.[1] It has only been the last twenty years that the cat has been eating grain, ever since food manufacturers discovered that if you camouflaged corn by coating it with animal fat, a cat will eat it. Corn is cheap and in plentiful supply, a fact which no doubt motivates the manufacturers. As for evolution, well, that's a thing of the past anyway. I have to wonder if there is any analogy with the human experience. We are eating a lot of things our ancestors didn't eat. And we seem to be a whole lot sicker with chronic degenerative diseases too. I believe that just as today's diet has something to do with the poor state of modern man's health, so too does the cat's manufactured diet bear some responsibility for problems of feline health.

Jean Burden, a popular pet columnist, has written that "the domestic cat today is trying to adapt to our environment by eating man-made food, but it doesn't always wholly succeed. Sometimes its teeth fall out at an early age; sometimes it gives birth to stunted kittens. All because of poor nutrition."[2]

Cats are primarily outdoor roamers and hunters, but the average cat today may never set a paw outside. So we take away the natural environment and then we feed our cats food that is cheap and convenient to store and administer.

On its own, the natural cat has instinctual intelligence for its nutritional needs. The first course of food after the kill is the innards. The abdomen is opened. The cat eats the liver, the kidneys, the spleen, and the intestinal matter of undigested vegetable matter. These visceral parts are rich in vitamins and minerals. It is unlikely the cat would have anything to do with gristle, hooves, claws, beaks, and other tough body parts that are routinely ground up and incorporated into commercial pet food.

The industry claims the food it makes covers an animal's nutrient requirements. Does it really?

I have seen many a cat in varying states of unwellness and traced the problem directly to nutrition. I see diet involved frequently as the cause of diarrhea, scratching, skin problems, and other disorders.

Does commercial food create an optimally healthy cat? No way.

In 1972, *Consumer Reports* magazine conducted a critical test of commercial cat food. The investigation was prompted by letters from readers "telling us of illnesses and even deaths that they and sometimes their veterinarians have attributed to the commercial cat food," the magazine said.

Of the twenty-two cat foods tested, only five rated as an acceptable total diet for growing kittens. Four brands were not acceptable, and thirteen rated inconclusive.[3]

It was in part because of the shortcomings of commercial pet food that I developed a vitamin and mineral supplement program for animals. And a growing number of veterinarians are doing the same— prescribing supplements along with a better diet.

Says Robert Goldstein, a nutritionally oriented veterinarian who practices in Yorktown Heights, New York: "I see many problems caused by commercial food. When we take cats off their regular store-bought diets and put them on better, preservative-free food or on home-made diets, the whole image changes. Problems disappear. Coats begin shining. The changes are dramatic."

Many breeders are similarly aware of the deficiencies of commercial food and abundantly supplement with vitamins and minerals and special menus to bring their animals to maximum condition.

Carolyn Bussey, the proprietor of the New Dawn Cattery for Persians and Exotic Shorthairs in Olympia, Washington, is a longtime student of cat nutrition. "I use commercial food only as a base," she says. "Alone, it doesn't do the job. It simply doesn't have enough in it. You have to add or you are going to be in trouble, especially with breeding colonies of cats. I have found that many of the problems we have in cat breeding are due to poor nutrition, and most people don't know it."

I don't expect the average cat owner to enroll in feline nutrition classes, if such classes were to exist at all. We are all convenience-minded, and for this reason there is a practical dependence upon commercially available food. My message to you in light of this is caveat emptor! Let the buyer beware! For many people, the TV commercials are the sole source of nutritional information and believe me they don't tell you what's wrong with a product.

I may shock you, but that is not my intention. I just want to make you more aware of the flaws in commercial food, which in many cases is entirely what people feed their cats. If, for convenience sake, you rely on commercial food solely, I want to show you how to compensate—easily and simply. I want to share with you some of the conclusions I am drawing after more than two decades of seeing sick cats in my practice. The animal hospital, you see, is the front line of battle. This is where veterinarians see and treat the casualties of commercial diets.

"COMPLETE AND BALANCED"

You have surely seen products that carry the claim to be "complete and balanced." What this means is that such products comply with the nutrient requirements as defined by the Subcommittee on Cat Nutrition of the National Academy of Sciences' National Research Council (NRC). The subcommittee is composed of veterinary nutritionists who meet, review, and publish updated information every several years relating to nutritional requirements. Other subcommittees do similar work with other species, including humans. The opinions of these groups are expressed in terms of the RDAs which you hear so much about. RDAs are the recommended daily allowances.

As far as RDAs for cats are concerned, veterinary scientists have a long way to go in divining what is good and what is enough. In 1962, the NRC said flatly that it was impossible to describe how much of which nutrients cats needed. It was only able to offer estimates for protein and fat and nine vitamins, along with the comment that several additional vitamins and unspecified minerals were also required.[4] Remember that for a long time we veterinarians were concerned primarily with large animals and dogs. Only recently have cats gained some equality.

In its 1978 revision on the nutrient requirements of cats, the NRC made considerable progress. But, by its own admission, the NRC said that the present level of knowledge was still inadequate.

"It was the judgment of the panel that the available data are inadequate to set minimum nutrient requirements . . . but the levels established are presumed adequate to support maintenance and growth of the cat," the NRC said. "It is probable, but not certain, that they will also support reproduction. These recommendations are intended only as guides and may need to be modified as circumstances and experience warrant."[5]

What could be clearer? The best veterinary nutrition minds in the country aren't sure yet about the minimum—I repeat, minimum— levels of nutrients for cats.

In the words of Stanley N. Gershoff of Harvard's Department of Nutrition and a leading researcher in animal nutrition: "What is known about cats' nutritional requirements? The answer, unfortunately, is that, compared with many other species of domesticated animals, little is known."[6]

Given this background, doesn't it seem presumptuous and misleading for pet-food companies to advertise their products as "complete and balanced"? We can't even agree on what is a "complete and balanced" human diet, and we know much less about cat nutrition than we know about human nutrition.

And just how well the companies are policed to maintain the NRC levels in their "complete and balanced" line is another gray area to me. My impression from talking to various government officials familiar with pet-food-industry practice is that independent control is lax. Products that claim to be complete are essentially taken at face value.

"Complete and balanced" pet food is fortified with a wide range of vitamins and minerals. This is because the natural ingredients do not come up to the nutrient requirements of the NRC. Moreover, a substantial loss of vitamin potency occurs during processing and storage as a result of nutrient sensitivity to heat, moisture, light, and oxidation. The most sensitive are the B complex vitamins and they are critical to animal health. Both researchers and veterinarians in the field have traced serious problems in animals directly to insufficient B vitamins in the diet. Hyperactivity and aggressiveness in dogs and cats can sometimes be corrected by supplementing animals with B complex vitamins.

The degradation of vitamin content occurs both in the natural ingredients and in the fortified nutrients. One of the major suppliers of vitamins to the pet-food industry has tested commercial products and shown that these vitamin losses can be substantial. In order to compensate, the producers are urged to fortify their products with amounts of vitamins above the NRC levels.[7]

But overage or not, a sack of dry food is going to be considerably less fresh and nutritious after being opened a dozen times than when you first bought it from the store. A big sack may be more economical than a small sack, but it is also going to be stored longer and opened more often. The result is dwindling nutrition. You save money but maybe at the cost of your animals' health.

Products that do not make the "complete and balanced" claim have only limited nutrient fortification. They do not meet NRC nutrient standards and are primarily formulated to serve as supplemental variety to a more comprehensive diet.

Read labels. And keep in mind that "complete and balanced" is a very relative term, applicable to products based on uncertain minimum requirements. Products not making the "complete and balanced" claim are obviously offering even less in the way of nutrition.

The University of Pennsylvania's David Kronfeld, writing in 1980, noted that the largest pet-food manufacturer disdains using the "complete and balanced" claim because "the completeness and balance of all of its products should be taken for granted—but, 'Meow,' one of its premium mixes, induces retinal degeneration."

Major manufacturers have made products deficient in thiamine and taurine, an essential component of protein, he said.[8]

My interest is in optimal health, not adequate, not minimum. My advice, therefore, remains fast and firm, no matter which food you buy. Put your animals on a vitamin and mineral program!

ARE YOUR PETS GETTING QUALITY?

Cats have a higher protein requirement than dogs. Commercial cat food provides the higher percentage from a mixture of meat, fish, and vegetable sources. Higher percentage yes, but what about higher quality?

There are no government ingredient standards for cat food. There are only industry and individual company standards, and self-regulation. Some companies may have strict standards. What about those that don't? The question is well worth raising.

A main source of protein is meat and bone meal from beef, and if you think it comes from healthy, prime-grade USDA-inspected stock, you are very mistaken.

After graduation from veterinary school, I spent seven years as a veterinary meat inspector for the Department of Agriculture and the U.S. Air Force. Then and now, condemned parts and animals that are rejected for human consumption are routinely re-routed for use in commercial pet foods.

The same holds true for animals that are classified as 4-D. These are animals that are dead, dying, diseased, or disabled and never make it to the human-food slaughterhouse but are processed straightaway for pet consumption. Note that I did say "dead."

Here is what goes on. If an animal dies in winter and freezes up or is placed in refrigeration fairly soon after death, it doesn't undergo much decomposition. In such a situation, an animal can be boned out and sold as muscle meat or various other fleshy constituents, primarily for canning operations. On the other hand, if the death has occurred during the hot summer and the animal is pretty rank, it is rendered and made into meat meal.

In this scheme of things, diseased tissue, pus, hair, sundry slaughterhouse rejects, and animals in varying states of decomposition are put through chemical, heat, and pressure procedures to render it all commercially sterile. Then, in one form or another, these ingredients find their way into the brightly colored sacks, boxes, and cans that you pick off the shelf. Surely a cat, among the most discriminating of diners, would not eat such fare out in nature day after day after day.

From a cat's standpoint, the best quality of protein is unprocessed mammal or bird muscle meat. These are also expensive forms of protein, and in the highly competitive pet food market, cost overrides quality. Less than ideal ingredients are mixed together in an attempt to produce equivalents of higher-quality protein and then are subjected to crafty processing techniques designed to make the finished product taste and look good.

Dr. James Corbin, professor of animal science at the University of Illinois, cites some of the goodies that are used in cheap canned foods: "Gristle, hair, lungs, pigs' feet, tails, cheeks, udders and intestines. . . . Meat byproducts can be anything from pig snouts to condemned hog livers."[9]

Alfred J. Plechner, a West Los Angeles veterinarian who specializes in immunological and food-oriented pet problems, gives this blunt evaluation: "The overprocessed dry and semi-moist products are the easiest forms of food for the manufacturers to blend and hide all that poor protein in. They pressure it, cook it, flavor it, color it, dehydrate it and often blow air into it to get bigger surface particles so it looks as if you are getting bigger chunks for your money. All this means change and multiple degradation to protein that is already poor to start with."

The advertisements and commercials extoll the virtues of high protein. The higher the protein the better. But to me, the amount of total protein inside the package is not the important thing. What's important is the amount of utilizable protein. How much can the cat actually use? A product may have 30 percent protein, but a good deal of it exists in a form that cats cannot digest.

An authority on cat nutrition once estimated that only about 50 percent of the protein in "good" diets is actually utilized."[10]

All the extra protein and harsh ingredients place an added burden of stress on the internal organs that have to do the processing: the kidneys, the liver, the bowels. Often we veterinarians see loose stools, gassy bowels, direct irritation to the intestinal tract, and undigested protein coming through into the feces. These are symptoms indicating a daily chipping away at an animal's health.

THE CHEMICAL ONSLAUGHT

Cats surely did not evolve on butylated hydroxyanisole, propylene glycol, red dye 40, and sodium nitrite. For the last twenty or thirty years, however, this is what the species has been getting on a daily basis. These and other chemical additives are used in pet food to flavor, to color, to preserve, and to protect against bacteria, mold, and other undesirable elements. Thus commercial pet food, like commercial human food, has its unnatural array of chemical condiments.

The late Dr. Benjamin Feingold, the well-known expert on the relationship of food additives to hyperactivity, maintained that additives affect every part of the body. From him we have learned that two commonly used additives in commercial pet food cause behavioral difficulties in sensitive children and impair their learning ability. The two additives are butylated hydroxyanisole (BHA) and butylated hydroxytoluene (BHT). I will discuss hyperactive and aggressive pets in Chapter Eight, but here I will mention in passing that veterinarians are sometimes able to resolve this problem by taking hyper pets off of commercial food. Putting an animal on an additive-free food or adding vitamin supplements, or doing both, can be an effective solution.

BHA and BHT are chemical antioxidants. They are used to prevent the fatty contents of the food from becoming rancid, which can happen as the products sit in warehouse storage, on store shelves, or in your kitchen pantry. The fats are subject to oxidation and break down into substances that can be harmful to an animal.

BHA and BHT are being investigated by the FDA following animal tests showing adverse kidney, liver, reproductive, brain, behavioral, and allergic reactions. These additives are actually banned in some countries. In 1977, the FDA removed BHT from the GRAS list—Generally Regarded As Safe—but its continued use is permitted pending more study on health effects.

More recently, a Japanese study with BHA yielded a positive association with cancer and prompted the restriction of this preservative in Japan. In May 1982, I was told that the FDA was reviewing the Japanese findings.

Cats require animal fats in their diet. The problem is that unless these fatty substances are preserved, or eaten by the animal in the fresh state, they become rancid and dangerous to eat. The use of preservatives eliminates an acute health threat and seems to replace it with a lesser threat. Every expert I have talked to has not been able to rule out the possible risk to health that these preservatives pose over the long run.

I am not sure how necessary BHA or BHT are to shelf life. Some companies do not use them in their products. My advice is to stay clear of those that do.

One manufacturing practice I consider highly questionable is the use of coloring additives. Why questionable? Cats are color-blind and see colors only as various shades of gray. The coloring additives, namely red dye 40 or sodium nitrite, are added largely for cosmetic appeal to the owner. Without them, the complexion of the food may disgust buyers who would then resort to feeding table scraps or fresh meat, and that would be bad for business.

An article appearing in the *FDA Consumer* magazine says it all: "They (coloring additives) contribute nothing to nutrition, taste, safety, or ease of processing. And some consumer advocates argue that food is often made to look more appetizing at the risk of increasing health hazards."[11]

Sodium nitrite is used to prevent fading of colors and make meat products look vigorously blood-red. The labels say "to retain color." Sodium nitrite also serves as an antibacterial factor. Since 1962, scientists have known that nitrite can combine with food, agricultural, and digestive chemicals to form nitroso compounds, many of which cause cancer in laboratory animals.

Dr. William Lijinsky, director of the Chemical Carcinogenesis Program at the Frederick Cancer Research Center in Maryland is one of the world's foremost experts on these compounds. I spoke to him and asked him about the risk to small animals, even if the level of sodium nitrite is based on industry-accepted standards.

Referring to the use of sodium nitrite in canned products, he noted that many pets live almost entirely on canned food, exposing them to the additive for years. "My feeling is that sodium nitrite in food poses some risk," he said. "There is a risk to people and there is a risk to animals. It doesn't mean that it would cause cancer, but it might increase the risk."

Red dye 40 is one of the most widely used food colors. In pet foods, it contributes to a fresh, meaty appearance. But are your cats paying a price for this chemical deception?

Red dye 40 is suspected of causing cancer and birth defects. It is banned in Canada, Britain, France, and most other European countries. It is under FDA investigation but still in use in the United States.

This dye belongs to a family of artificial coloring agents derived from coal tar. Marshall Mandell, a prominent Connecticut physician who specializes in allergies associated with food, chemical, and other environmental factors, says these dyes can trigger many different symptoms in people, both subtle and acute, and should be removed from the diet. "They are substances foreign to the human body and manufactured in a chemical laboratory," he says. "They are not a part of man's natural food supply."[12] And certainly not the cat's.

Another iffy ingredient in that chemical feast called semi-moist is propylene glycol. This chemical, constituting about 10 percent of the total contents, is used to help keep the product soft, pliable, moist (but not too moist), and free of microbes.

Researchers have recently discovered that propylene glycol can have an effect on the red blood cells of cats. They aren't sure yet what this means, whether there is any medical significance; however, they report observing irregular substances in the blood that are associated with oxidative injury to hemoglobin, the oxygen-carrying part of red blood cells. Propylene glycol is said to increase the number of irregularities observed.

Perhaps one good thing to be said about semi-moist products for cats is that they do not seem to have the high sugar content of the semi-moists for dogs. This is because dogs, unlike cats, have a sweet tooth. For canines the sugar serves to enhance the palatability of the product and also acts as an antimicrobial factor in the mixture. But the sugar content for semi-moist dog food is as high as 25 percent of the total amount of the food! This may be creating some real health problems among dogs fed regularly on this product. It is certainly creating canine sugar junkies. In the semi-moist cat food, the propylene glycol does the job of the sugar.

According to MIT's Paul Newberne, "The cat does not accept or tolerate preservatives and humectants used in the semi-moist foods as well as the dog does."[13]

I know veterinarians who are vehement in their opposition to semi-moist products. Dr. Carvel Tiekert of Bel Air, Maryland, says he sees many cats on semi-moist diets with dry coats and skin problems. "The first thing I do is get them off that garbage," he says.

Dr. Robert Goldstein says he sees many cats that are puffy like a ball, overweight, with diarrhea, itchy skin, and dull coats and that are on semi-moist food. "We take them off that kind of food, put them on a wholesome diet, and in two months they are like new animals," he reports. "They have lost weight and their coats are shiny again."

In my practice I have also noticed quite a few animals with skin problems who were eating largely semi-moist diets. Switching them to better diets has similarly resulted in healthier-looking animals.

Pet foods also have their share of synthetic flavors. In fact, according to *Consumers Digest,* "few foods are so liberally laced with artificial flavors as pet foods." The magazine cites a source in the additive industry as saying that the addition of phony flavors is the only way to get pets to eat the quality-poor food.[14]

Whatever the reasons for putting them in there, the amount of chemicals in commercial cat food represents a risk to an animal's health. Consumer polls have shown that people are becoming increasingly sensitive about the matter of chemicals in the food they eat. What about the cats that eat the food that people buy? Cats can't read labels, but you can. If you see a label that looks like a chemical Who's Who, stay away from that product. There are others available that have fewer additives or none at all.

Medical science cannot keep pace with the rapid progress of profit-motivated food science. Safety testing is generally conducted by the individual manufacturers themselves and not by independent researchers. Can objective findings be expected? I doubt it. Moreover, the tests are normally conducted on a short-term basis because of the expense—not for a long enough period to determine possible chronic effects.

Industry usage of additives is inadequately controlled by government. There seem to be as many loopholes as there are additives— and there are thousands of additives. In their book *Eating May Be Hazardous to Your Health,* Jacqueline Verrett and Jean Carper reported that the GRAS additives—those "generally regarded as safe"—are indeed considered "so safe they are unrestricted and can be used in any amount in any food." The authors said that these additives "were not supposed to have detrimental information (to man or animal) against them in the medical literature, although as it was revealed later, few of the medical authorities consulted by the FDA even made a search to find out."[15]

It is very difficult for clinical veterinarians to pinpoint specific additives that may be causing problems. We don't have the research facilities, the funds, or the time to investigate. But we see sick cats on a daily basis and after a while we have our suspicions. We acquire a "dossier" on which products seem to be causing problems. And we advise our clients accordingly. What we can't do is scientifically prove that BHA or sodium nitrite or propylene glycol is the reason for your cat's failing health. Cats are exposed to a lifetime of chemicals not only in the food, but in the air, in the environment, in the medical drugs. A whole multitude of factors can influence the disease process. From my experience, however, commercial food is a likely source of health erosion. I suspect that the combination of chemicals and impurities in the food is contributing to a weakening of an animal's strength and immune system, a deterioration that invites disease.

While we are discussing chemicals in commercial pet foods, consider this as well: Many head of cattle die on the range each year from toxic agricultural chemicals—the pesticides and herbicides. The corpses do not go to waste, however. They are processed for pet food or livestock and poultry feed, toxins and all.

An FDA veterinarian toxicologist I spoke to about this situation expressed concern about the potential health hazard. "Nobody knows how much of the toxins are coming through the processing [into the pet food]," he said. "We don't have the adequate means for evaluation. The sterilization will take care of the microbes and nothing else, but most agricultural chemicals will survive the high temperature involved in processing.

"Even if the toxins are not present in appreciable amounts in the muscle tissue, and we are not sure of that, I have a great deal of concern about the visceral parts where larger amounts of the toxins may be present. These internal organs accumulate toxins that the body had been unable to excrete and thus contain the actual chemicals that cause the death of thousands of animals. Certainly these are not the type of ingredients that should be in animal feeds."

THE LEAD DANGER IN CAT FOOD

Some two thousand five hundred years after the poisonous properties of lead were first described, we know today that lead is everywhere, that it is present in small quantities in most any material, and that very tiny amounts can do very large damage to living cells. Both humans and animals are exposed to many sources of lead in the environment. Much of the hazard has been created as a by-product of man's industrial progress over the years.

Lead forms 5 percent of the particulate matter in the air near large cities, mainly because of the use of lead in gasolines. Lead in pesticides has also increased the level found in agricultural soil and thus contributed to lead entering the food chain.

Organ meats and bone meal used in pet foods can carry relatively higher amounts of lead than other animal tissue, since this metal tends to accumulate in the liver, kidneys, and bones.[16] Grease, paint, print-er's ink, and solder are other sources of lead that might inadvertently contaminate pet food during the manufacturing process.[17] The solder, of course, is an added exposure for people or animals who eat canned food, because the lead used to weld the side seam of food cans "leaks" into the contents.

Lead has always been a health concern because of its toxicity. Peeling paint and plaster and lead-laden dust in slum-type dwellings have been frequent sources of lead poisoning in children. In small animals, the most common cause of acute lead intoxication has been the licking or chewing of painted surfaces, particularly by puppies. But cats, too, have become poisoned through exposure to paint dust on hair and from automobile fumes.[18]

It is not so much the acute forms of poisoning that I am concerned with as the possible long-term effects.

In both man and animals, lead affects the nervous system, the kidneys, red blood cells, and the enzyme systems. It can cause anemia. Studies have shown that lead reduces the resistance of mice, rats, chickens, and rabbits to disease-carrying microorganisms. In short, it weakens the immune system. Prolonged low-level intake of lead from inhaled air or ingestion of contaminated water or food has been cited in cases of hyperactivity, mental impairment, and nervous system disruption in children. And if that's not enough, lead is also suspected of causing cancer.

In 1975, researchers at the Connecticut Agricultural Experiment Station found that some canned cat foods contained nearly four times the 0.3 milligrams that is considered a hazardous daily level for children. The researchers purchased thirteen samples of canned cat food at local food markets. Based on a typical six-ounce serving for a cat, all but four samples had more lead than the 0.3 level. The lead-perserving range was 0.15 for a meat by-product and liver sample up to 1.19 milligrams for a can of chicken by-products.

Although the precise amounts of lead that may cause biochemi-cal changes in a cat's body without showing overt symptoms are not known, the researcher felt that the potentially toxic level of lead could approximate that of a small child. Clearly, they said, there were "potential risks to pets ingesting low levels of lead from pet foods."[19]

Subsequent investigations have confirmed the presence of lead in cat food.

The year after the Connecticut revelations, veterinarian researcher James G. Fox of MIT published an analysis of commercial pet food. In it, he expressed concern that many of the products expose animals to "potentially toxic cumulative lead intakes," adding to the burden of lead they already absorb from the environment.

Fox analyzed forty-six samples of feline products from ten different manufacturers. Two (unnamed) popular companies consistently rated the highest in lead concentrations.

"This finding is of special interest," he said, "when one considers that . . . pet cats develop preferences for one type of commercial food."

Fox calculated that an average ten-pound adult cat would consume anywhere from one-tenth to more than four times the level of lead considered hazardous for children. Moreover, he felt, the feline burden of lead to body weight would be much higher than a child's because even a two- or three-year-old child weighs considerably more than an adult cat.[20]

The issue of lead in pet foods, as in human foods, has become controversial in recent years. The pet-food industry has steadfastly claimed that commercial levels and even experimentally higher levels present no danger to animals.[21]

I have spoken about this matter with Dr. Loren Koller, associate dean of the University of Idaho Veterinary Medical School and one of the country's leading experts on the relationship of lead to animal immunity. He says that even at extremely low dietary levels, lead has the ability to significantly suppress the immune system of hardy laboratory rats. Animals with suppressed immune systems are more susceptible to infectious agents and more apt to succumb from a really contagious disease, he points out.

The dietary lead-immune connection has potentially more dramatic importance, Koller suggests, in light of the current scientific debate over whether a suppressed immune system renders you more prone to cancer.

Koller has not studied the lead response in cats, nor was he aware of any such studies, but he felt that immune suppression similar to that in rodents could occur.

Cats are extremely sensitive animals. They are generally more sensitive to pollutants than dogs. My belief is that the constant absorption of lead from food and other environmental sources may contribute subtly and accumulatively to a weakening of the cat's immune system.

Why don't the pet food companies eliminate the lead from their products, you may be asking. There is no doubt that it can be removed. Major companies producing laboratory animal chows have guaranteed minimums of lead. However, economy is a prime consideration for consumers and the price of eliminating lead from commercial food would probably pass on to the buyer. As one FDA official told me: "These controls cost money, and what are people willing to pay to feed their pets? Whatever the cost to the company, it would clearly be felt by the consumer in higher prices."

It would be unfair to say that food processing alone is responsible for all the lead in an animal's diet. Sure, it adds to the burden; more is introduced during the stages of processing. But keep in mind that many of the original animal parts used in the food mix, such as liver and kidney, already contain some lead. Even if you feed your animals raw liver or kidney, there is lead in the tissue. The truth is that we really can't get away from lead. But we can do something to reduce its potential harm.

WHAT YOU CAN DO

Despite industry claims that pets live long and healthy lives on commercial pet food, we veterinarians are routinely faced with contradictory evidence in the form of sick animals. We frequently encounter acute reactions such as diarrhea and vomiting and skin lesions. Most often, though, we are witnessing symptoms of deteriorating health, of diminished efficiency of bodily functions and organs, of kidneys failing in middle age due to excessive protein, of weakened immune systems and allergic reactions. We are seeing the cumulative effect of all those additives, toxins, lead, and the very questionable source of the natural ingredients.

Veterinarian Alfred Plechner, in an article on food-related disorders, summed up the situation thusly: "Today's food, designed for today's pet, is becoming more inadequate daily. Unfortunately, the theme of today's pet food market is not what food is best to feed, but rather what food will cause less problems."[22]

If all this bad news about pet food seems overwhelming, take heart. There are some simple and effective steps you can take to protect your animals.

1. Supplement your cat's diet with vitamins and minerals. Supplements are necessary for optimal health. Vitamins and minerals have the ability to neutralize the possible harm that can be done by impurities and toxins present in a cat's food or environment.

Take lead as an example. By regularly supplementing your cats' daily diet with vitamins and minerals, including the high doses of vitamin C that I recommend, you can neutralize the effects of lead intake. Fortunately, lead is a slow poison and you can thus prevent possible harm. As I will explain later, vitamin C is a marvelous detoxifier of harmful metals such as lead and cadmium, which is also present in pet foods. Vitamin C has the power to grab hold of these metallic poisons and escort them out of the body. Zinc, iron, calcium, and magnesium are also part of a good supplement program and they have similarly been found to reduce the toxicity of lead.

Remember that cats evolved on raw meat. Commercial food, of course, is highly cooked, and cooked meat and animal protein is not the same as raw meat and raw protein. The big difference between the two as far as cats are concerned was discovered during the 1940s by Francis M. Pottenger, Jr., a California physician.

Pottenger was maintaining a colony of cats for medical experiments and observed that the health of his animals was deteriorating. He had a serious problem with weak and dying kittens, difficulty in queening and lactation, irritability, skin lesions, and allergies. Pottenger traced the problem directly to cooked food. When he substituted raw meat for cooked meat, the health of his animals improved dramatically. After a ten-year study involving some nine hundred cats, Pottenger concluded that cooking renders protein and minerals less easily digested and injures or destroys enzymes, vitamin C, and the B complex vitamins. He said cooking alters the physiochemical state and could render foods imperfect for the maintenance of health.[23]

Today's highly cooked commercial foods are supplemented with vitamins and minerals, in varying degrees, in an attempt to make up for the nutrient loss during processing. I haven't found that it is enough though.

Some people will supplement their animals' diets with raw meat. Some supplement with cooked meat. Some just feed good old commercial food by itself. Whatever your preference, supplement with vitamins and minerals. They will ensure against possible dietary deficiencies and provide extra nutrition in times of stress. They will help create optimal cats. As we will see in the following two chapters of the book, vitamins and mineral supplements can do many things for your animals.

2. Be choosy when buying commercial pet food. Read labels. Choose foods that have a minimum of additives or none at all. Be on the alert for BHA, sodium nitrite, propylene glycol, artificial coloring, and artificial flavoring. Your cats do not need any of these. Avoid the semi-moist products, which are highly unnatural and loaded with chemicals.

Most products contain preservatives and other additives. They may be unnecessary ingredients, however, if the increasing number of additive-free products on the market is any indication. I have seen pet foods with ten or more additives and others with none. You can choose, so be choosy.

Pet shops and health-food stores stock pet-food products that are free of additives. I suggest you look in these stores if your regular outlet doesn't carry any such items.

Remember, the fewer additives your animals eat, the less risk there is to their health.

As your veterinarian for advice on what products he or she has found to be the most problem-free.

3. Feed your cat table scraps. I have always been an advocate of this. By table scraps, I don't mean sugar and sweet stuff or cakes and cookies. I mean meat and vegetables, salad and cooked cereal. My assistant, Pat Tedford, feeds cooked whole-grain oatmeal to her Balinese, and they love it.

The pet-food industry has tried to discourage people from feeding their animals from the table, probably because they don't want anything cutting into their sales. The manufacturers want you to believe your animals are getting all the nutrition they need out of the bag or can. But that's not so. I have seen too much disease and minimal health to accept that. Table scraps can help animals get a little extra nutrition and also add some variety to their diets. Some cats won't have anything to do with variety, however, so table scraps won't apply to them.

4. Too much fish in the diet can be harmful. Cats eating a substantial amount of tuna or other fish on a regular basis can develop a vitamin E deficiency condition called steatitis. Such diets should be supplemented with vitamin E. I will talk more about this in the chapter on adult cats.

5. Don't feed cats dog food. Dog food, whether dry or canned, is deficient in taurine, an amino acid (component of protein) that a cat must obtain in its food. A diet of dog food can result in retinal degeneration and subsequent blindness.[24] Some commercial cat foods are also deficient in taurine. When reading labels, look for this important element.

PART 2

*Vitamins and Minerals
and Their Functions*

3

Vitamin C and the Cat

For years, my practice of treating small animals and preventing disease with vitamin C has branded me as something of a maverick in the veterinary ranks. This is because one of the sacred cows of veterinary medicine is the steadfast belief that cats and dogs do not need extra vitamin C. Like most animals, they are presumed to produce all they need through a biochemical process in the liver.

Tests conducted in 1950 failed to show a need for vitamin C in the diet of cats. These old tests, along with the belief in vitamin C self-sufficiency, are the reasons why you do not find this vitamin included in the nutrient fortification added to commercial cat food.

The National Research Council's Subcommittee on Cat Nutrition, the arbiter of nutrient requirements for cats, recognizes the need for many vitamins and minerals but not for vitamin C. Referring to the 1950 tests, the subcommittee states that "successful growth and reproduction are routinely experienced with commercial diets containing no supplemental ascorbic acid."[1] Ascorbic acid is the scientific name for vitamin C.

I agree that successful growth and reproduction are routinely experienced with commercial diets containing no supplemental vitamin C. But I contend that unsuccessful—and I repeat, unsuccessful—growth and reproduction are also routinely experienced with commercial diets containing no supplemental vitamin C. Nearly twenty years of clinical experience, involving hundreds of cases, has taught me that cats definitely benefit from extra vitamin C.

One of the aims of this book is to show you, in fact, how the addition of vitamin C in your cats' lives can make the difference between radiant health and so-so health.

Cat breeders supplement their animals' diets with the whole alphabet of vitamins and minerals, A to zinc, but usually with the notable exception of vitamin C. Why the exception? Because of the belief that cats produce all the vitamin C they need. Yet with all the supplementation they have been doing, they still have problems with the killer viral diseases, weak and dying kittens, and cats with poor coats.

Breeders who add vitamin C to their supplementation program begin seeing phenomenal changes: they control the killer diseases, urinary tract blockage in males is nonexistent, and kittens are healthier.

The long and short of what I hear from breeders who have added vitamin C is that their animals are healthier. There are fewer problems.

Vitamin C works preventively and therapeutically. I have reported this in a number of published papers and now I am pleased to see other veterinarians becoming believers by observing these same good results. One East Coast veterinarian told me he now uses vitamin C in all infectious processes and in all his feline urinary-problem cases.

When I first began using vitamin C, I was not altogether clear about why it was working; I only knew that it *was* working. Later I met Dr. Irwin Stone, who gave me a solid education on this remarkable substance.

Stone, a retired biochemist, is a walking encyclopedia on the medical uses of vitamin C. He began a lifetime of work with ascorbic acid back in 1934. He has patented techniques for the synthesis of ascorbic acid and for its use in stabilizing foodstuffs. For over three decades, he has been a tireless researcher of, and advocate for, the medical applications of vitamin C. His 1972 book, *The Healing Factor: Vitamin C Against Disease,* is the best reference source available on the relationship of the vitamin to medicine and health.

Vitamin C can best be understood by taking a short trip into history. Ascorbic means not having scurvy, the horrible disease which has long plagued mankind.

Scurvy is one of the oldest known human afflictions. Egyptian hieroglyphs dating to 1500 B.C. document the bleeding gums that are typical of the disease. One thousand years later, Hippocrates described conditions that resembled the symptoms of scurvy. Throughout history, armies engaged in long sieges where only dry rations were available suffered from scurvy. And year after year, during the long winters in northern climates, where fresh food was not obtainable, whole populations were afflicted with varying degrees of scurvy and made easy prey for rampant bacterial and viral infections. Millions died.

The disease typically begins with a change in complexion, which becomes sallow or muddy, a relentless and increasing fatigue, breathlessness, and need for sleep. The gums become inflamed and bleed easily. The teeth loosen. Eyelids swell. The breath is foul. The nose bleeds. Hemorrhages erupt all over the body from burst capillaries. The bones become brittle and break at the slightest movement. Pains in the joints render the individual immobile. The downslide from apparent health to a miserable death can take only a few months.

It was Capt. James Lind, an eighteenth-century surgeon in the British Royal Navy, who discovered that citrus fruit could prevent the scurvy that decimated the ranks of men at sea.

It wasn't until this century, however, that scientists found out what it was in citrus fruits that was preventing scurvy. What they discovered was a particularly active and multitalented molecule related to glucose, or blood sugar. Investigating further, they determined the presence of this molecule also in vegetables and the internal organs of most animals. They called it ascorbic acid, or vitamin C, and said it was absolutely essential to the living process.

CATS ARE POOR PRODUCERS

All living creatures either produce ascorbic acid internally or obtain it in their food—or else they die within three months. No other vitamin deficiency acts so fast and so severely.

Besides its classic reputation in preventing scurvy, this substance has a vital role in maintaining biochemical balance in the body. It is highly involved in the immune function, in the growth and maintenance of connective tissue, and in dealing with stress and toxins.

Most animals are able to produce what their bodies need through an enzyme process that uses glucose, the blood sugar, as the raw material for conversion. This process occurs inside individual cells, in tiny cellular particles called microsomes. The system is located in the kidneys of amphibians and reptiles and in the liver of mammals.

Daily production in cold-blooded amphibians and reptiles is limited because of the size of their kidneys. These animals maintain a sluggish metabolism and thus have been able to evolve on relatively small amounts of ascorbic acid.

Not so with mammals and their souped-up, warm-blooded physiologies. They require more ascorbic acid. To do the job, Mother Nature chose the liver, the largest gland in the body. She also equipped mammals with an important accessory, a biochemical feedback mechanism enabling them to produce extra ascorbic acid in times of increased stress. Stress upsets the body's biochemical balance, so more ascorbic acid is required to restore equilibrium. A rat, for example, can boost its output of ascorbic acid tenfold under stress. This protective mechanism has obviously had tremendous survival value.

As they traveled down the evolutionary path, some mammals such as humans, apes, guinea pigs, bats, and a few species of birds lost a key enzyme link in the vital glucose—to—ascorbic acid liver chain. Thus they do not produce their own ascorbic acid. They must get it in their food or die.

The following chart shows the relative ability of some animals to produce their own ascorbic acid, or vitamin C:

DAILY PRODUCTION OF ASCORBIC ACID IN ANIMALS[2]

ANIMAL	MILLIGRAMS PER KILOGRAM OF BODY WEIGHT
Mouse	275
Rabbit	226
Goat	190
Rat	150
Dog	40
Cat	40
Snake	10
Tortoise	7
Ape, Man, Guinea Pig	0

Cats and dogs, as can be seen, are relatively poor producers. They make 40 milligrams per kilogram (2.2 pounds) of body weight per day, less than any other mammals except the totally bereft primates and guinea pigs. A rabbit the same size as a cat manufactures almost six times as much vitamin C.

In nature, cats instinctively seek out food sources containing vitamin C, thus supplementing their own paltry supply. Cats eat the ingested material of the prey, which is abundant in vitamin C. They eat the liver where the ascorbic acid is produced, and the adrenal glands, where vitamin C is stored, and even the muscle tissue, which contains some C. Cats eat their food raw, but man gives it to them cooked. Cooking destroys vitamin C. In the wild, cats also seek out berries and succulent parts of plants, additional sources of vitamin C.

Experts say cats make enough of their own vitamin C and do not need any extra. That's why when cat-food manufacturers fortify their products with vitamins, they leave out the vitamin C. Yet in a natural setting, away from the "wisdom" of humans, the cat behaves as if he needs more.

Against this background, modern domesticated cats are subject to forms of stress entirely new to their species. More cats than ever are flying. "Show business" cats are campaigned vigorously from coast to coast. Breeders ship cats from one end of the country to the other. Cats are often tranquilized and placed into small traveling cages for what must be a journey of horrors to them. Other cats spend lifetimes inside the four walls of apartments, denied the benefits of sunlight, the curiosities of the outdoors, and the natural tendencies of a roaming instinct. Some share living space with humans who smoke. Cats are made to eat food that is unnatural and loaded with chemicals and impurities. They are immunized, spayed and neutered, dewormed, medicated, and sometimes declawed. All that spells S-T-R-E-S-S to a cat.

Along with these man-made burdens, cats have their own natural stresses to contend with: growth, pregnancy and lactation, a kitten's separation from mother and litter mates.

Stress sorely taxes and depletes the already low vitamin C output of a cat. I have found, for instance, that the liver of a cat with a high temperature makes little or no ascorbic acid. Dogs with skin disease have been tested and measured to have low blood levels of vitamin C,[3] and I assume the same situation applies to cats.

The stress situations I have described place a great demand on the cat for ascorbic acid that it seems unable to produce. This inability to meet internal or external challenges suggests a failure of the stress-triggered feedback mechanism or a sluggish liver enzyme system. The reason may be excessive inbreeding or the early domestication of the cat.

When less than optimal levels of ascorbic acid are available to the animal, whether it is derived from inside or outside the body sources, a situation is created that Irwin Stone calls chronic subclinical scurvy. An animal is rendered more vulnerable to viruses, bacteria, disease, and deformities. Chronic means that the condition is constant. Subclinical means that the symptoms are less severe and identifiable than the outright acute signs of terminal scurvy.

Long ago I concluded that chronic subclinical scurvy is rampant among cats and dogs, afflicting most of these animals their entire lives. I believe it lies at the basis of the increasing number of viral leukemia cases and other serious diseases that veterinarians are seeing today.

Among animals there are differences—sometimes great—in their ability to produce ascorbic acid. One cat will produce more or less than the next one. Given the same exposure to stress, one cat will have the genetic advantage over another and better powers of resistance.

The situation is basically the same with humans, except that we have to obtain our vitamin C from food or supplements. Why are some people always coming down with colds and flu? Genetically, they may be less robust than others. But I think that food, nourishment, the vitamin C intake of an individual, and the amount of stress in people's lives also plays a large part. Smoking, aspirins, and medication are common sources of chemical stress on the body. Physical, emotional, and mental strain are also forms of stress. These factors burn up the body's vitamin C stores, and if there isn't much in there to burn up, then you start running into a deficit. The condition of chronic subclinical scurvy is created. The immune system weakens. The body becomes vulnerable to the same kind of germs that it may have successfully repelled if there were enough vitamin C on hand.

VITAMIN C IMPROVES IMMUNITY

Viruses and bacteria abound in places where cats are constantly poking their noses. They are carried in the air, passed on from animal to animal, or person to animal, or picked up from licking fur, eating food, or sniffing contaminated objects.

Viruses are tiny organisms packing a big punch. They are smaller than bacteria, smaller than cells, and to see them you need an electron microscope. They range in size from the 1/1,250,000-inch polio virus up to the full-bodied 1/100,000-inch pox virus, and scientists say there are at least two hundred different types of them around capable of afflicting acute illness on man and beast.

Your average virus appears as a speck or filament of nucleic acid, the chemical essence of all living cells, surrounded by some protein and fatty matter and an outer shell of protective protein. A virus comes equipped with a spike or tail that is used for attaching onto larger bacteria or animal cells. Once attached, the nucleic acid is injected into the host organism and proceeds to reproduce fresh viruses. Scientists have observed how one single virus can invade a cell and in twenty-five minutes reproduce a new generation of two hundred viruses. The attacked cell is destroyed and the new viruses break out looking for new cells to plunder. The cycle is repeated. In this way, whole areas of tissue and eventually normal bodily functions are overwhelmed and destroyed.

Bacteria are one-celled organisms, larger than viruses, and they reproduce by dividing. If conditions are right, one bacterium can become a million in about fifteen hours. While many forms of bacteria serve vital life-supporting functions on this planet, others are harmful and involved in many disease processes, such as pneumonia, typhoid, dysentery, cholera, anthrax, and the diarrhea present in many illnesses.

The body has an elaborate and complicated defense force that guards against harmful proliferation of viruses and bacteria. It is called the immune system. Its major components are interferon, leukocytes, and antibodies. Studies have shown that vitamin C is essential to all of them.

An immune system operating at optimal capacity will keep harmful microorganisms in check. Conversely, a system that is functioning at reduced capacity, weakened because of stress, chronic subclinical scurvy, or poor nutrition, renders the entire cellular community more vulnerable to attack.

Interferon was discovered in 1957 and has been making headlines because of its possible use in treating cancer. It is a hormonelike protein substance produced by individual cells any time they are threatened by viruses. In 1970, Linus Pauling hypothesized that vitamin C was involved in the virucidal (virus killing) activity of interferon. A few years later, experiments at the University of Oregon conducted by Dr. Benjamin V. Siegal confirmed Pauling's expectations. Siegal fed large doses of vitamin C for several months to a selected group of mice. Remember that mice produce their own vitamin C, as do most animals, and are much better producers than cats. Siegal then infected the mice with a virus that causes leukemia. He similarly infected another group of mice that had not been supplemented with vitamin C. These mice had to depend on their own natural production. When blood tests were done, the vitamin C mice were shown to have less cellular damage from leukemia and twice as much interferon than the nonsupplemented mice.[4]

Interferon is believed to work by enveloping the virus and preventing propagation and also by attacking the nucleic acid within the virus and destroying it.

Interferon has been found effective not only against the virus that provokes its production but against other unrelated viruses as well. Interferon seems to be a first line of immune defense.

The immune system deals with bacterial infections in a different manner. It calls into action white blood cells called leukocytes and macrophages. These cells are programmed to engulf and destroy encroaching bacteria. A combined term for them is phagocytes, from the Greek word *phagein*, to eat. The phagocytes contain high concentrations of vitamin C and whenever they charge into a battle zone of infected tissue, they load up with extra vitamin C just as battle-bound soldiers load up with ammunition. One consequence of low vitamin C levels is an increased susceptibility to bacterial infections. The ability to destroy these germs is directly related to the ascorbic acid content in the blood.

Viruses have the nasty habit of stirring up dormant bacteria and thus causing secondary infections. Wherever you find a viral condition, you usually find a bacterial problem as well.

The antibodies are chemical substances secreted by specialized cells in the lymph glands in response to the presence of microorganisms in the body. For the first few months of life, a newborn baby or kitten is protected by antibodies passed through the placenta before birth from the mother. Afterward, the infant has to produce its own antibodies. Immunizations are mild forms of a disease, and if a young animal is healthy, it should produce the antibodies to combat the particular disease microorganisms. Then, if the animal is exposed to the same disease at a later date, the specific antibodies are present in the system and mobilized into action. Specific antibodies are potent only against specific invaders. Antibody A takes on disease A and antibody B takes on disease B. It's a one-on-one situation.

While the interferon and white blood cells are fending off the "enemy," the body's antibody production system goes into high gear. Specialized cells activate, multiply, produce, and then release the antibodies. It takes them up to six days to join battle after hostile microorganisms build up and make their presence felt in the body. Antibodies are somewhat like reserve soldiers.

The foregoing has been an attempt at simplifying what is an extremely complex and not thoroughly understood system. One fact remains clear: An animal that is minimally nourished, that is constantly stressed by dietary toxins and impurities, is not likely to put up as stout a defense as an animal that is supplemented with vitamins and minerals.

The immune system depends on an ample supply of all nutrients. Zinc, for instance, is involved in the role of some white cells to combat viruses and fungi. Any shortages in the B-complex vitamins, particularly pantothenic acid and B_6, retards the production of good antibodies after immunization.

But from my experience, animals that are supplemented with the standard RDAs of vitamins and minerals, without the extra vitamin C, will still not build optimal immune-system strength. Alone, RDA vitamin and mineral supplements on the market will have no effect in countering feline viral leukemia, the deadliest of the cat-killing diseases. But the RDA vitamins and minerals, plus extra vitamin C, do have a positive controlling effect.

The vitamin C must be in mega, or large, doses. This is the key.

In many hundreds of cases since 1965 I have found that the intravenous use of vitamin C (in the form of sodium ascorbate) is highly effective in treating viral diseases. It is dependable and nontoxic.

Depending on the severity of the condition, nearly all viral diseases will respond to vitamin C treatment. This is important to remember in light of the fact that there is no drug in the medical arsenal that will control viruses. The most commonly prescribed medications are antibiotics and steroids. The antibiotic affects only the bacteria that usually accompany a viral infection. A steroid will treat inflammation and stimulate appetite. Neither one lays a restraining finger on the viruses. Vitamin C fills this vacuum.

Successful therapy depends on using it in sufficiently large doses. Much, much higher than the routine levels I recommend for prevention. Vitamin C is not a drug, but if it is administered in large enough doses it acts pharmacologically and deactivates the viral disease process.

Dr. Fred Klenner, the now retired North Carolina physician who first discovered the potency of megadoses of vitamin C against viruses, called the vitamin "more effective than any drug in the pharmacopeia." It was his work years ago with humans that inspired me to try the vitamin C approach on small animals. Klenner insisted that the key to success lay in the large doses. Other medical professionals had reported inconclusive results with small doses.

To give you an example of what Klenner meant by large, he would use as much as 210 grams (210,000 milligrams) per day against viral conditions. Compare that to the NRC's recommended daily allowance for humans of 60 milligrams. Acute viral infection can be a matter of life and death—for people as well as for cats. Klenner found that by saturating the tissues with high levels of vitamin C, by using doses well beyond the limits of therapies tried before, he was getting fast results. With this kind of "heavy firing," he was curing hepatitis (within a week), viral pneumonia, polio, herpes simplex, measles, chicken pox, mononucleosis, influenza, and other viral conditions.[5] He reported success after success in an era before the powerful vaccines had arrived on the medical scene. And each vaccine, keep in mind, can deal with only one type of virus. Vitamin C takes them all on!

Occasionally, Klenner applied his healing touch to small animals, curing a number of dogs suffering from distemper. In doing so, this medical doctor recognized the reality about vitamin C that has eluded so many veterinarians. He commented that veterinarians were misled in disregarding the value of vitamin C in dealing with viral disease.

They would see dogs and cats dying with distemper and knew that the animals could make their own vitamin C, yet "what they did not appreciate was that even the animal could not make enough vitamin C under certain conditions," he said.[6]

Experience has taught me those certain conditions exist continually in a domesticated animal's life—they are stress-related—and that is why supplementing animals with vitamin C promotes optimal health and healing.

Solid scientific support for the megadose principle emerged in a two-part Japanese study published in 1975. Dr. Akira Murata, a microbiologist, tested the effect of ascorbic acid on a wide variety of bacterial viruses—viruses that attach themselves to bacteria inside the body. He found they were all inactivated by the vitamin. Meanwhile, Dr. Fukumi Morishige, a physician in charge of surgical services at a major Japanese hospital, found vitamin C therapy effective in treating patients with infectious and serum hepatitis, measles, mumps, viral pneumonia, herpes zoster (shingles), herpes facialis, encephalitis, and certain types of meningitis.[7]

Medical people familiar with the use of vitamin C believe viruses are incapacitated within minutes after the intravenous administration of a large enough dose of the vitamin. I have personally witnessed the rapid action of vitamin C on dogs with distemper, a highly contagious and deadly virus. I have placed unvaccinated dogs in prolonged close contact with other dogs ill with distemper, but first I gave the diseased animals an initial injection of vitamin C (sodium ascorbate). Never have any of the unvaccinated dogs come down with distemper. That's how quick-acting and effective is vitamin C!

I have not put cats to a similar test, but I feel the results would be similar.

The feline leukemia virus seems to be a much more resistant and virulent virus than the distemper variety. It takes an average of ten to twelve weeks with oral supplementation to turn leukemia-positive cats negative, that is, free of the leukemia virus. That in itself is big news. What is even more amazing is that we have turned it around orally as fast as six days and with injections within twenty-four hours.

Vitamin C is so effective that I have been able to cut my usage of antibiotics in half. I routinely see animals brought in with temperatures and diarrhea, and in many cases the clients are unwilling to spend the money for the blood tests necessary to diagnose the problem. In these cases, I administer vitamin C intravenously, and often the animal is back to normal in short order. Upon discharge, I prescribe oral supplements of vitamin C. Many a cat thus treated recovers quickly. The treatment is inexpensive. The client is happy.

NATURE'S GREAT DETOXIFIER

Vitamin C is one of nature's great detoxifiers. It takes on any hostile substance entering the body and, if in abundant supply, neutralizes the threat to normal biochemical balance. According to Edward J. Calabrese, an environmental health expert at the University of Massachusetts, vitamin C "markedly affects the toxicity of greater than fifty pollutants, many of which are ubiquitous in the air, water and food environments."[8]

Most animals will automatically produce more ascorbic acid than usual when facing a toxic challenge. If toxins overwhelm an animal's ability to detoxify them, the result is sickness or death.

Toxins come in different shapes and enter the system through different doors. They are encountered by simple contact, from breathing, eating, or licking, from poisonous insects and reptiles, through drugs, allergies, bacteria, viruses, fungi, parasites, and infections.

Toxic stress can severely tax the natural supply of ascorbic acid, but when they are supplemented, animals have been consistently found to benefit from the detoxifying powers of extra vitamin C. Dr. I. B. Chatterjee, an Indian biochemist and expert on vitamin C production in animals, found that exposing rats to toxic minerals such as cadmium, lead, or mercury lowered the level of ascorbic acid present in their livers. Remember the liver is where the vitamin is made. Low levels mean low resistance. The C apparently was being depleted or sidetracked to fight the toxicity of the minerals. Chatterjee then fortified the diets of these rats with ascorbic acid, and the liver levels returned to normal.[9] Keep in mind that rats are superior to cats in making ascorbic acid. So if rats benefit from the extra vitamin C, I feel that cats are benefiting at least as much if not more.

Irwin Stone, in his book *The Healing Factor: Vitamin C Against Disease,* cites an interesting Chinese study involving tadpoles and lead. The researchers placed one hundred tadpoles in water containing a high level of lead. In twenty-four hours, eight died. The remaining tadpoles were then divided, with half of them going to a tank containing plain water and the others to a tank with plain water and ascorbic acid. After six days, 88 percent of the tadpoles in the plain water tank were dead, while all the tadpoles in the ascorbic acid–·treated water were still alive. Stone also cites experiments done in the Soviet Union where ascorbic acid and cysteine, an amino acid, were successfully used as an antidote on rabbits suffering from lead poisoning.[10]

Over the years, vitamin C has been found effective in acute and chronic lead poisoning cases involving humans. Many industrial workers have benefited from vitamin C protection since 1939. Dr. Carl C. Pfeiffer at the Brain Bio Center in Princeton, New Jersey, has developed an effective combination of two grams of vitamin C and thirty milligrams of zinc gluconate daily to dramatically improve the health of lead workers.

The vitamin C and zinc approach, says Pfeiffer, is safer, simpler, and cheaper than the current treatments of lead poisoning involving chelation therapy with agents such as EDTA or penicillamine.

Pfeiffer maintains that an abnormal burden of lead and other toxic metals can accelerate aging and shorten life.[11] His opinion is shared by many scientists who have found that even subtoxic amounts of lead can decrease the life-span of laboratory animals. Such scientific opinion builds a strong case for vitamin C supplementation.

Cadmium is another omnipresent by-product of the industrial age. Animals—and humans as well—are exposed to it in their food in small amounts, and in drinking water, the air, from car exhaust fumes, and from cigarettes and even cigarette smoke.

Health officials are concerned about this exposure. In experimental animals, even low dietary concentrations of cadmium impair growth and immune response, cause hypertension and anemia, disturb enzyme function and the utilization of essential mineral nutrients, and interfere with reproductive cycles.

A U.S. Department of Agriculture review on cadmium states that some of the toxic effects may be prevented by supplementary levels of iron, copper, zinc, selenium, and manganese in the diet.[12]

According to the FDA's Department of Nutrition, vitamin C can also offer protection. This was determined in an experiment where a high dose of cadmium was incorporated into an otherwise normal diet for Japanese quail. These birds were selected because they are ultrasensitive to environmental pollution. The feeding of cadmium caused an iron-deficiency anemia and depressed growth rate. Vitamin C supplementation provided a "marked protective effect" against these conditions, the researchers said.[13] If quail can benefit from supplementation, surely our domesticated animals will benefit as well.

In an analysis to ascertain "normal" levels of toxic minerals in commercial pet food, researchers at the Oklahoma Animal Diagnostic Laboratory determined the presence of cadmium and found it at trace levels somewhat higher in cat products than in dog food.

The investigators also found traces of arsenic, another mineral poison. Arsenic can hinder enzyme activity, affect cellular respiration, block metabolism of fats and carbohydrates, and cause reduced vitamin C in tissues.

The Oklahoma study offered no conclusion as to possible affects on health from the levels of cadmium and arsenic found in the commercial pet food. An official of the Pet Food Institute, the manufacturers' trade association, said in an accompanying commentary there were no indications that the reported levels could be dangerous to pets.[14]

My feeling is that our pets are waging a low-grade daily struggle against the lead and other toxins they encounter in their food and environment. While the net result may not be acute poisoning and violent death, I believe the toll is health erosion and weakened, disease-prone animals less able to cope with the otherwise natural stresses in their lives.

In the last chapter I discussed the use of sodium nitrite in pet food to give the products a fresh, reddish appearance. Sodium nitrite is one of many nitrite compounds present in food, food additives, drugs, and pesticides that can enter an animal's digestive tract. Once there, they can react with nitrogen to form so-called nitroso compounds. More than one hundred of such compounds have been found to cause animal tumors. Sodium nitrite alone has been incriminated in over twenty different species of test animals. The long-term effect of routine commercial levels of sodium nitrite in the diet is not known; nevertheless, we are surely dealing with another risk factor for cancer.

Under existing manufacturing procedures, nitrite compounds are known to form in fish meal that is stored over several months in large warehouses. Fish meal is a common ingredient in cat foods.

The compounds develop as a result of a combination of preservatives, drying methods, and the natural nitrites present in the fish.

The use of heat during subsequent processing will decrease the presence of these compounds. However, I understand that some may survive and be present in the fish meal content of the finished product. The risk to health is not known.

Vitamin C's great detoxifying powers can reduce the risk to health here too. Experiments conducted with vitamin C have shown that at high levels it blocks the formation of nitroso compounds in test animals.[15]

Vitamin E has also been found to block these compounds. Dr. Steven R. Tannenbaum, an MIT food scientist, has suggested the routine use of vitamins C and E since exposure to the potentially dangerous nitroso compounds seems unavoidable.[16]

Vitamin C has been used to affect the rapid recovery of dogs from rattlesnake bite and poisonous insects.[17]

Supplements, and particularly vitamin C, can also help animals who have been made ill by pesticides, garden sprays, or undetermined types of poison. I will cover this in the chapter on adult cats.

Vitamin C also helps against one of the body's very own toxins—histamine. This name is familiar to any person who suffers from allergies. Histamine is an irritating chemical released by certain cells in stress situations. It reacts dramatically in capillaries, making them more permeable and permitting excess waste material from the blood to enter the tissues. This results in swelling and discomfort. In animals, a constant itching problem may be due to the effect of histamine from an allergic reaction. Not only allergy but infections, burns, colds, and a wide variety of nonspecific stresses can also trigger the release of histamine into the bloodstream. Ascorbic acid has been shown to inhibit the release of histamine.[18] Thus it is a natural antihistamine.

The manner in which vitamin C detoxifies is a highly complex biochemical affair not clearly understood. The simple fact is that it works.

GOOD COLLAGEN NEEDS C

Collagen is the intercellular protein "cement" that binds connective tissue. It holds together the muscles, the blood vessels, the ligaments, tendons, and cartilage, giving them all strength and structure. Collagen is the honeycomb into which minerals are deposited to form bone. Without collagen, a body would come unglued and collapse.

Vitamin C in ample quantity is necessary for the production, formation, and maintenance of good-quality collagen.

Growing kittens need a solid framework of collagen to build strong teeth, organs, and limbs. Good collagen is really a lifetime necessity. The proper functioning of the body requires it. When animals get older, their ability to produce vitamin C deteriorates. As it does, the quality and strength of collagen deteriorates as well, leading to the physiological breakdowns associated with aging. You very often see older cats losing teeth. I relate this to a vitamin C and in, turn, collagen deficiency. Supplementation of vitamin C slows down the aging process by keeping the collagen strong.

Steroids are commonly used in veterinary medicine to reduce swelling and itching and increase the appetite of ailing animals. Steroid treatment, however, has a harmful effect on collagen formation if it is administered for an extended period of time. The drugs can cause a thinning of bone tissue, skin problems, and growth retardation. It will also suppress the immune system. Adequate supplementation with vitamin C will reverse or prevent the harmful side effects of steroid therapy.[19]

I am not opposed to the use of steroids. I use them routinely in my practice. But I combine them with protective doses of vitamin C and other vitamins and minerals.

In addition to guarding the body against possible harmful side effects, vitamin C also seems to make drugs more effective. Thus, less is needed. I have been able to significantly lower the dosages of drugs when I use vitamin C alongside.

Still another quality of vitamin C—and a comforting one—is its ability to act as an analgesic. When supplemented with vitamin C, small animals with arthritis or other painful joint problems act in a way indicative of reduced pain.

From the human experience, we know that cancer patients given megadoses of vitamin C report a greater sense of well-being. They feel less pain and require fewer pain-killing drugs.[20]

Vitamin C has personally served me well in dealing with pain. Several years ago I developed excruciating pain in my right elbow as a result of the constant lifting of heavy dogs in my practice. It became difficult for me even to lift a glass of water. I treated myself by taking ten grams of vitamin C daily, and in two weeks the pain was gone and has never returned. Since that time I take about six grams every day. If I ever have a headache, I treat it with five grams, and usually the pain is gone in a quarter of an hour.

Don't give your cats aspirin for pain. Cats seem to be extra sensitive to it. Aspirin can cause toxic reactions. Moreover, this is a case of robbing Peter to pay Paul because aspirin is known to deplete the body of vitamin C.

THE KIDNEY STONE MYTH

Clients sometimes will ask me about the levels of vitamin C I am recommending for their cats and dogs. This is a legitimate question since too much of anything, even water, can have adverse effects.

Medical science has determined ascorbic acid to be one of the least toxic substances known. People have swallowed 125 grams (over a quarter of a pound) at one time without harm, and an equal amount has been injected into a human without harm.[21]

I once conducted a toxicity experiment with three small dogs about the size of big adult cats. I used twenty times more vitamin C than the preventive dose I normally recommend for an animal. For five days I administered intravenously two grams daily per pound of body weight. The animals weighed about ten pounds each, so I was injecting some twenty grams into each dog. I should mention that intravenous injections are much more potent than oral administration by powder or tablets. This is due to the fact that injection places the substance directly into the bloodstream while anything taken orally suffers some degree of degradation through chemical reactions in the digestive tract.

At the end of five days of intravenous injections, the dogs were showing no signs of toxicity. There were no apparent side effects. On the contrary, one of the dogs had a prior severe cystitis and was urinating blood, but after the second injection the condition cleared up.

One of the common myths about vitamin C is that large amounts will cause bladder or kidney stones. Linus Pauling has thoroughly researched this controversial point and states unequivocally that "not a single case has been reported in the medical literature."[22] Just the contrary, there is medical evidence that points to a vitamin C deficiency—not excess—as a cause of stones.

In my experience I have never seen or heard of a single case of urinary tract stones in cats or dogs who were maintained on a good preventive dose of vitamin C. As a matter of fact, we indeed find that vitamin C cures the common cystitises and blockages in cats.

In this chapter, I have tried to explain the importance of vitamin C to a cat's health. Cats do not produce as much vitamin C as other animals and they do not receive any in their food. Given the amount of man-made and natural stress modern cats face in a lifetime, I believe the most important thing you can do for the health of your pets is to supplement them with vitamin C.

4

Working Together: The Whole Vitamin and Mineral Team

From the little leagues to the big leagues, every team in the world of sports is made up of players who occupy certain positions and perform well-defined jobs. One pitches. Another catches. Another is a home-run slugger. But along with their primary assignments, athletes also have secondary functions that enhance the performance of their teammates and contribute to the overall success of the team. Players working and pulling together are the basis of any winning team.

So it is with vitamins and minerals too. Each has a celebrated function but also contributes to health in many lesser known—and even unknown—ways. Together they make each other work better. Some minerals join with specific vitamins to get essential physiological tasks done that would not be possible if they were acting alone.

Vitamin D ensures proper utilization of calcium and phosphorus, two major ingredients of bone tissue. Selenium makes vitamin E more efficient. Zinc helps the body use vitamin A and folic acid, one of the B complex vitamins. E protects A, and together they protect the lungs against damage from pollution. Vitamin C helps in the absorption of iron and calcium and, in fact, seems to make all the other nutrients more dynamic.

Vitamins and minerals are said to work synergistically, meaning that together they have a greater total effect than the sum of their individual effects.

The star of my team is obviously vitamin C. Long before I began using other vitamins and minerals, I came to regard vitamin C as a do-it-all. *The Complete Book of Vitamins,* published by *Prevention* magazine, calls C "the most versatile of vitamins with functions so far-reaching that it can actually replace any other vitamin for a limited period of time and keep the body functioning and healthy."[1]

Still, as good and many the benefits of vitamin C, I found that when I brought together the whole range of nutrients into my program, the results were even better.

In the opening chapter, I explained the principle of orthomolecular veterinary medicine: treating and preventing disease by providing the individual animal with extra vitamins and minerals. This is medicine at the cellular level where problems begin, an attempt to deliver an optimal payload of nutrition to all the cells in the body. Relying on commercial pet food alone is not enough.

Down at the level of the cells there may be a condition of imbalance and insufficiency involving any one or more vitamins and minerals that are required by the cells to function well. Any degree of insufficiency can cause any degree of malfunction, and that could mean trouble.

Symptoms show up first in that area of the body where the cells are the weakest and most susceptible to specific nutritional shortages. A prime area is the skin, the largest organ in the body. Skin is ultrasensitive to nutrient deficiencies.

I feel that the great number of skin problems we veterinarians see is testimony to problems in the food supply. And indeed, says Lon D. Lewis, a veterinarian nutritionist at Colorado State University, "the skin is the first organ to exhibit signs of poor nutrition."[2]

The chronic scratching and shedding, the dry and scaly skin, the surface sores—they all represent more than just a problem on a cat's exterior. The symptoms are the likely indications of a general state of unwellness deep down at the basic level of life—the cells.

I often administer vitamin A to cats with skin problems because frequently the trouble stems from not enough A in the diet. Since a general cellular deficiency exists, not only does the skin situation improve but the cat's overall health as well. The appetite perks up. The animal becomes less susceptible to infections. These are other areas where vitamin A helps. The whole body is using the vitamin, not just the skin. Other systems, short on this nutrient, have been bolstered and now show the benefit. You often see unexpected side benefits with supplements. The reason is because you have supplied the whole body rather than treated one specific symptom. Nutrients work this way. Drugs do not. They are targeted to specific symptoms alone and frequently cause harmful side effects.

Finding the precise nutrient needs of an individual or an animal is impossible. Medical science has not yet devised a technique to do so. And besides, these needs change throughout life, even from day to day. Environmental conditions, stress, diet, and age are factors that influence a body's shifting nutrient needs. There are only averages to rely on and they really aren't that meaningful because the requirement for specific nutrients can vary greatly from what is regarded as average. One cat might need ten milligrams of vitamin X. Another cat of the same size, age, and breed might need twenty milligrams, or fifty. And they both will need more, or less, when they are pregnant, old, idle, campaigning in the show circuit, or fighting a disease.

The recommendations of the NRC's Subcommittee on Cat Nutrition are formulated in a sincere and honest effort to provide satisfactory levels of nutrition for cats. By the NRC's own admission, however, these recommendations are based on limited knowledge.

"Very limited research has been conducted on vitamin requirements of the cat," the NRC said in its latest (1978) revision of recommendations.

As for minerals: ". . . there is a scarcity of data on both the qualitative and quantitative requirements for this class of nutrients."[3]

The recommendations, like the RDAs for humans, are obviously not carved in stone. The numbers change as science uncovers more information.

Human nutrition is a groping, embryonic science. Cat nutrition is even more so. Relatively speaking, we have only been at it for a few years, and the work has been largely concerned with determining deficiency levels and minimum requirements. There are many important questions that still remain unanswered in regard to the food we feed our animals day in and day out.

For instance:

• Are there really adequate levels of nutrition available in commercial products after all the heat processing they go through?

• How much do the additives and impurities in the food subtract from the existing nutrient levels?

• Do the heat and the additives render some of the nutrients unusable? In other words, even if you have adequate quantities, what about the quality? Do some or a lot of the nutrients pass through the gut and out into the feces instead of being assimilated?

• What about the many generic products which sell for less than the name brands? Does cheaper price mean inferior ingredients and less nutrient content?

• And getting away from commercial food, if you are an individual who feeds your animals on a homemade diet, how nutritionally sound is the menu?

These are hard questions to answer.

My solution is to supplement an animal with a safe but yet effective daily dose of vitamins and minerals. Such a simple program provides a steady supply of nutrients, making up for possible shortages, flaws, and fluctuations in the diet. It helps create optimally healthy animals.

At this time I want to introduce some of the major players on the vitamin and mineral team and show how they perform on a supplemental basis.

There has been virtually no research done with supplemental levels of nutrition for cats except to determine what levels are toxic. My program of supplementation is based on amounts above the minimums and well below the upper danger zone. To help demonstrate the positive effects of supplementation, I have drawn from work done with laboratory animals such as rats and mice. These creatures are mammals like the cat and essentially react the same to many chemicals and nutrients. Mouse and rat studies are commonly used to evaluate possible health effects in humans.

THE VITAMINS

Vitamin A

Many skin and infection problems are due to inadequate vitamin A in the diet. This is because vitamin A is responsible for the integrity of the epithelium, a tightly knit top layer of cells covering every surface of the body coming in contact with foreign substances. With different shapes and accessories, in dry form or wet, the epithelium covers the teeth and gums, the eyballs, the entire digestive tract, the mucous membrane of the respiratory tract and the air sacs of the lungs, the lining of the bladder, and the living, growing layer of skin. It is both inner and outer armor, protecting against infection.

Even a mild deficiency of vitamin A is enough to manifest somewhere along the epithelium network as a symptom. Most often veterinarians see a dryness, hardening, and itching of the skin or respiratory, gastrointestinal, or urinary tract infections.

Depending on the severity of the problem I will sometimes turn to vitamin A alone for quick relief. Short-term daily doses of 10,000 IUs have been helpful in clearing up many stubborn skin problems. Often it is enough to put the suffering cat on a general preventive program of multiple vitamins and minerals—which contains less vitamin A—and that clears up the problem.

Vitamin A is more than just an epithelium booster. Dr. Erwin DiCyan, a drug and vitamin expert, says vitamin A "can just as well be called the hair vitamin, or eye and sight vitamin, the glandular, or teeth and gums vitamin, since it has a profound effect upon the development and well-being of all these structures."[4]

Vitamin A is also called a growth vitamin. This reputation goes back to the 1920s when experiments first showed that it was a major factor in achieving optimal growth in animals.

Like vitamin C, A offers protection against infections and toxic chemicals. In one experiment, mice that were injected with bacteria and fungus showed more resistance to infection when they were supplemented with vitamin A.[5] Likewise, rats that were supplemented with the vitamin suffered less harm than nonsupplemented animals when highly toxic polychlorobiphenyls (PCBs) were placed in their diet.[6]

Such protection against PCBs is important because these industrial chemicals have thoroughly infiltrated the food chain through seepage into waterways or through industrial accidents. People have suffered health problems ranging from skin eruptions to irregularities at childbirth after eating contaminated food. These chemicals cause cancer in laboratory animals. They have been implicated in the deaths of livestock.

As I mentioned in Chapter Two, the possibility exists that contaminated cattle will be slaughtered for pet foods and the toxins will survive the manufacturing process and wind up in the food you give your animals. Scientists are unable to specify yet what levels of exposure are "safe," but one thing is sure: the levels that do exist in human and pet foods cannot be doing any good. In December of 1979, the FDA organized a meeting of federal and food-animal industry representatives to discuss ways to identify and control chemical contamination of food animals and related food products. The agency called for a "heightened general awareness of PCB and other toxic chemical problems."[7]

It is worth restating the point that supplementation with nutrients such as vitamin A and C offers an animal added protection against these environmental poisons found in the food supply. The investment for this kind of protection is cheap when you consider the risk to the health of your animals.

In addition to increased susceptibility to infections and skin problems, some other signs of vitamin A deficiency in cats are formation of cataracts and retinal degeneration, pneumonia, convulsions, watery diarrhea, emaciation, and weakness in the hind limbs.

Nitrite compounds can deplete the vitamin A stores in the body. Remember that one such compound is sodium nitrite, an additive used in cat foods. Buyer beware!

Vitamin A is a fat-soluble vitamin, and excess amounts are stored in the liver. This is unlike the behavior of the water-soluble vitamins C and B complex. When in excess, they normally trickle out in the urine.

Unlike dogs, cats cannot utilize the form of vitamin A that is present in vegetables—beta carotene. Liver is an excellent source of usable vitamin A for the cat and it appears that cats evolved on an ample supply of it. But beware of too much liver or fish liver oil in the diet. This can lead to an excess of vitamin A and trouble later on. An extraordinarily high vitamin A intake for several months can cause a crippling cervical degeneration with pain, reduced neck movement, and interference of nerve impulses to the forelimbs.[8]

Veterinary nutritionist David Kronfeld of the University of Pennsylvania advises against feeding more than one teaspoonful of liver to a kitten or one ounce per day to fully grown cats.[9]

The B Complex Vitamins

The B complex group is vital to the health of the nervous system and is sometimes referred to as the "nerve vitamins." When deficiencies arise, problems can manifest themselves anywhere. Mouth, eye, skin, and reproductive organs are common trouble spots.

Proper absorption of fats, proteins, and carbohydrates is dependent on a good supply of these vitamins. They provide necessary chemical ingredients for the metabolic process.

Stress is a major enemy of B vitamins. It can quickly burn up the body's supply.

The vitamins in the B family have both names and numbers. The main components I will discuss are B_1 (thiamine), B_2 (riboflavin), B_3 (niacin or niacinamide), B_5 (pantothenic acid), B_6 (pyridoxine), B_9 (folic acid), B_{12} (cobalamin), and biotin (sometimes referred to as vitamin H).

These B factors are a close-knit family, a team within a team. When a deficiency of any one B complex vitamin occurs, there is usually a shortage of another B to some degree as well. This is why supplementation and treatment usually includes several vitamins of the group, if not all.

The B complex requirements of dogs and cats are different. The physiological makeup of the cat is such that it requires roughly twice as much B as dogs. This is another good reason not to feed dog food to your cats. What is adequate for dogs is not adequate for cats.

The B vitamins are extremely sensitive to heat, particularly thiamine. Processing methods can result in critical losses of these vital nutrients.

Vitamin B_1, Thiamine

The history of this vitamin is a lesson on the pitfalls of manufactured food.

Around the turn of the century, a missing dietary ingredient was said to be causing beriberi, a widespread and often fatal Asiatic disease. The symptoms are lesions (damage) to the nerve tissue in various parts of the body with consequent pain and loss of muscular control.

European researchers found that beriberi was the result of eating a diet of white rice, an offspring of mass-production milling methods developed in the nineteenth century. Before milling machinery, rice was hand-milled and retained much of its natural content. This natural, unprocessed whole brown rice was the traditional staple for people in many parts of the world.

The merchandizing problem was that this form of rice became rancid quickly and had a very limited storage and shelf life. So milling machinery was developed to remove the parts subject to rancidity. These parts, unfortunately, contained the most B vitamins and protein. The result was white rice. It could live forever on the shelves, but its nutritional integrity had been raped and plundered.

The early nutritionists found that beriberi could be prevented and even reversed when brown rice was substituted for white rice. Since vitamins had not yet been discovered, these scientists talked in terms of unknown protective substances having been removed from the rice by mechanical milling.

In 1912, a Polish-born chemist named Casimir Funk fed rice polishings, the discards of milling, to diseased pigeons and cured them. His work, and the research of other contemporary investigators, led him to conclude that beriberi and diseases such as rickets, pellagra, and scurvy, were caused by diets deficient in these so-called protective substances. He termed these substances *vitamines*.

The word stems from *vita* — Latin for "life" — and *amines,* a group of chemical compounds to which all such protective substances in food were thought to belong.

Thiamine was the missing protective substance in processed rice, but it was not chemically isolated until 1926. As more sophisticated methods of investigation were developed, other vitamins were discovered in this era as well. Soon, scientists were able to formally define vitamins: natural substances occurring in many foods in small amounts that are necessary for the normal metabolic functioning of the body. Deficiencies of these vitamins in food resulted in varying degrees of disease.

The problem of thiamine deficiency in processed foods was resolved eventually through fortification techniques. Almost resolved, I should say, because commercial pet foods, and particularly cat foods, still give headaches to manufacturers.

The problem is twofold:

1. Cats have an extremely high requirement for B complex vitamins.

2. Thiamine, which is added to many commercial products, is very sensitive to heat and is easily destroyed in heat treatment during processing. Additional loss of potency takes place because of oxidation during storage. Some 50 to 60 percent is destroyed during processing and another half of what is left can be lost during the first six months of storage. Most manufacturers take into account a storage period of six to nine months, so the potential for severe thiamine loss is obvious.

This predicament has prompted manufacturers to fortify their products with levels of thiamine well above the RDAs. Presumably enough will thus survive the rigors of processing and storage to reach the feeding bowl. If, however, the commentary of veterinary nutritionists is any indication, there is some doubt about making any such presumption.

"This is the most readily provoked vitamin deficiency in cats fed on processed diets," said Patricia P. Scott of England's equivalent of the NRC in 1971.[10]

"There may still be problems involving thiamine deficiency in cats fed commercial cat foods," said Harvard's Stanley N. Gershoff in 1974.[11]

Then, in 1978, a number of cats in a large feline research colony were seriously affected by what was determined to be a thiamine deficiency. The cats suffered brain damage, seizures, loss of control of movement, and, in one case, death.

Treatment of the clinically ill cats with vitamin B complex resulted in recovery within twenty-four hours.

For seven months, the cats had been fed a leading commercial cat food, a scientifically formulated canned diet that met all the NRC's nutrient recommendations.

The manufacturer told the researchers this particular lot of food that had been used contained one hundred times the NRC recommendation for thiamine. And even this amount, the manufacturer added, was considered potentially inadequate. As a result the company was increasing its thiamine fortification to one thousand times the NRC recommendation.

The Cornell University scientists involved in the thiamine study commented that "although a reputable manufacturer may make every effort to produce a complete product, he may have little control over conditions or methods of storage or processing."[12]

If top-of-the line products can result in a serious health problem traced to thiamine deficiency, what is the situation with cheaper brands that may be fortified to a lesser degree? What about companies that may try to cut corners and treat vitamin fortification as an area where they can save money? There are several thousand companies producing commercial pet food and some may simply not recognize the critical area of thiamine fortification.

I am not saying that all commercial foods have this deficiency and therefore all cats on commercial diets are deficient. I am saying, though, that here is another one of those uncertain areas in man-made feline nutrition. I am saying to cat owners: supplement your animals. Don't take a chance. Every cat breeder I know uses some form of B complex supplementation.

The potential for thiamine deficiency is not exclusive to commercial food. Any overcooked food will have serious thiamine loss as well.

Also, if you regularly feed your animals raw fish, be alert to a possible thiamine problem. The tissue of some fish, such as carp and herring, contains an ingredient which blocks the absorption of thiamine and can cause a deficiency.

Typical signs of deficiency are loss of appetite, vomiting, loss of muscular coordination, and convulsions.

Another sign that has turned up is hyperactivity. I have been told by some colleagues that hyperactive pets often respond to thiamine supplementation. I will talk more about this in the chapter on adult cats.

Supplementation with the B complex vitamins may help your cat stave off fleas. These pesty parasites seem to have an aversion toward thiamine. The vitamin apparently leaves a particular aroma in an animal's skin that repels the bugs. Brewers' yeast is a rich source of all the B complex group, including B_1, and when some cats are given a good healthy dose routinely they seem to have fewer problems with external parasites. I must admit this does not work consistently on all felines. I have seen cats in the same household fed brewers' yeast for the elimination of fleas and it was beneficial to one or two and had no effect on the others. For this to work at all, the cat must be on an oral dose for at least four weeks.

Studies conducted with thiamine over the years indicate that it has an important role in the learning process and intelligence of animals.

Another beneficial effect is to maintain general well-being and stimulate the appetite. Veterinary nutritionists believe that the B complex, and particularly the thiamine in it, helps stimulate the appetite. The first thing sick cats will do is stop eating. When they aren't eating they need to get their B vitamins all the more.

If you supplement with brewers' yeast and/or a vitamin product, you don't have to worry about your cats receiving too much of the B vitamins. Unused quantities are eliminated through the urine.

Vitamin B₂, Riboflavin

This nutrient is vital to a cat's health in many ways, particularly because of its involvement in protein and fat metabolism. It helps the body transform these foods into energy and cell growth.

B_2 is essential for healthy eyes and may prevent the formation of cataracts. In experiments, cats kept on B_2-deficient diets have developed cataracts.

Not a great deal is known about riboflavin deficiency in the cat or whether there is any particular problem. I have never encountered any difficulties I could trace to riboflavin.

Vitamin B₃

Niacin and niacinamide—both called B_3—are two different compounds having similar properties. The latter is often preferred in treatment because niacin causes an uncomfortable flushing and burning sensation in the skin.

This vitamin is known as the antipellagra vitamin. Pellagra is a disease caused by a deficiency of B_3. It is marked by disturbances to the nervous and digestive systems and in the early part of this century caused the death of thousands of people, particularly poor field hands in the South who were heavy eaters of niacin-deficient foods such as corn and salt pork.

Unlike dogs and even people, cats are unable to convert niacin from the amino acid tryptophane, one of the components of protein. Cats are totally dependent on dietary intake for their niacin. Cooking will destroy much of the niacin in food. Raw meat, in the form of liver, heart, or kidney, is a good cat snack and provides ample niacin. Brewers' yeast is another good source.

In cats, experimentally induced niacin deficiency causes ulcers in the oral cavity, a thick saliva with a foul odor that drools out from the mouth, weight loss, lack of appetite, weakness, and apathy. Death is usually preceded by respiratory disease.

B_3 is important to the cat in converting food to energy and metabolizing fat and protein.

Vitamin B_5, Pantothenic Acid

Dr. Roger J. Williams, the renowned biochemist from the University of Texas, discovered this important vitamin in 1933. He named it for *pantos,* the Greek word meaning "everything." This natural substance, it seems, occurs in all living cells.

One of Williams's experiments some years ago demonstrated pantothenic acid's positive effect on longevity. The scientist took two groups of mice and fed them both a standard diet for their entire lives. The diet was scientifically formulated and had all the necessary nutrients—including pantothenic acid—to sustain an uneventful and normal mouse life.

There was one notable difference in the diet, however. One group received an extra 0.3 milligrams of pantothenic acid in the daily drinking water, an amount several times more than mice are believed to require.

The results: The supplemented group lived longer. The thirty-three mice in that group lived an average of 653 days. The forty-one animals in the nonsupplemented group lived an average of 550 days. There was a 19 percent difference!

Translated to humans this would mean a life-span of eighty-nine years instead of seventy-five. As for cats, it would mean thirteen years instead of eleven.

Williams, as an objective scientist, warned against regarding pantothenic acid as a "miracle food." But he was impressed enough nevertheless to suggest that if people were to take 25 milligrams of extra pantothenic acid daily during their lifetimes, they might add another ten years to their life expectancy.[13]

Williams's interest in the longevity potential of pantothenic acid was inspired by honeybees. He had become intrigued with the possibility that royal jelly, a secretion of the honeybee, vastly prolonged the life of queen bees. The queen bees produce this substance. The short-lived worker bees do not. Royal jelly, it turns out, is the richest known source of pantothenic acid.

Pantothenic acid is sometimes referred to as the antistress vitamin. This is because it is required for the production of good antibodies that are involved in protection against physical stresses, infections, and toxins. This vitamin is one of three B complex members that are known to contribute to antibody production. The others are B_6 and folic acid (B_9).

Pantothenic acid is needed by the adrenal glands in the making of cortisone and other hormones involved in many metabolic functions and in anti-inflammatory roles against disease, infections, and allergies. This vitamin thus bears a similarity to vitamin C: both are important to the adrenal response to stress.

Cats, like dogs, are subject to a wide variety of allergies, the causes of which seem to increase daily as we relentlessly introduce new chemical combinations into the environment.

One of the conditions setting the stage for increased susceptibility to allergens is an inadequate supply of vitamin C and pantothenic acid to the adrenal glands. Cortisone, the adrenal secretion, combats the toxins, or histamines, produced by dying cells in the allergic process.

Adelle Davis, the late nutritionist and author, stated that induced allergies in laboratory animals are invariably more severe when pantothenic acid is deficient. "The lack of no other nutrient has a comparable effect," she said.[14]

An East European physician demonstrated that supplemental pantothenic acid could reduce the histamine output and resultant skin reactions by as much as 50 percent in children exposed to allergy-provoking substances.[15]

Vitamin B₆, Pyridoxine

This nutrient is a biochemical workhorse. It contributes to a vast number of chemical reactions in the body, the most important of which relate to the metabolism of protein.

Since the cat is fed a larger dietary percentage of protein than the dog, it is absolutely vital to ensure that it receives an ample supply of B_6.

This vitamin is easily depleted by modern refining, processing, cooking, sterilization, and storage. If you are feeding your cats a diet with inadequate levels of B_6, there could certainly be some impact on their health.

B_6 plays a role in the functioning of a healthy nervous system. It also works closely with pantothenic acid and folic acid, two other members of the B complex team, in maintaining a strong immune system. The proper utilization by the body of minerals such as potassium, sodium, and iron depends on good availability of this vitamin.

B_6 deficiency is associated with growth failure, convulsions, anemia, and kidney damage.

Vitamin B₉, Folic Acid

Folic acid is essential for the formation of red blood cells in the bone marrow. It also aids in protein metabolism and the maintenance of a healthy immune system.

Experimental deficiencies of folic acid with the laboratory rat have caused a wide range of abnormalities, including headless offspring, underdeveloped kidneys and lungs, and missing glands. Offspring of animals fed even marginal amounts of folic acid have been found less able to cope with bacteria.

Pregnancy is a form of severe biochemical stress and all females seem to have an increased need at this time for more folic acid than normal.

Although it is a rather unsung member of the B complex family, folic acid nevertheless is needed for the development of every part of the body. This is because all nutrients are related and required by cells throughout the entire body. They work as a team. If one member is missing or not playing up to par, the whole team is thrown off balance.

Cats on a flagrantly deficient diet suffer from weight loss and anemia. As far as is known this occurs luckily only in laboratory experiments.

Vitamin B_{12}, Cobalamin

Cats need vitamin B_{12}, but beyond that fact little else is known. The quantitative requirement has not been determined. Deficiency is characterized by anemia, poor growth, and lack of resistance to infections.

In my practice, I have always had good results supplementing animals' diets with B_{12}. I feel that such supplementation contributes to bigger and stronger young. Thus, B_{12} is always an important component in my vitamin and mineral program for pregnant cats and kittens.

An interesting study at MIT conducted with rats demonstrates the role of this vitamin in developing vigorous offspring.

Drs. Paul Newberne and Vernon Young separated pregnant rats into two groups. One group of forty-four received a somewhat better than standard diet and the second group of fifty-seven animals received a similar diet plus a thousand times more B_{12} than what is considered normal. Once born, the offspring from both groups were fed identically standard, nonsupplemented rat chow. The only variable then was the extra B_{12} supplied to the one group of pregnant rats.

The researchers reported that the B_{12} supplementation had both a short- and long-term influence on the young. These baby rats were larger than their counterparts at birth and continued to be so a year later. They were more muscular, with less fat. When challenged with a bacterial infection, they showed better resistance.

The standard diet fed to the one group of pregnant rats was totally adequate for normal birth weight and subsequent growth. However, the researchers were impressed with the long-term benefits of a supplemented maternal diet and particularly the improved ability of the young to withstand harmful microorganisms.[16]

Vitamin B_{12} is known as the "red vitamin" because of its characteristic color and its importance (along with folic acid) to the production and regeneration of red blood cells. It is also vital to the integrity of the nervous system.

Liver is a rich source of B_{12}. More than fifty years ago, scientists found that raw liver could cure pernicious anemia, a dreaded and fatal disease caused by the inability of the body to produce enough red blood cells. In 1948, the precise antianemia factor in liver was isolated and called vitamin B_{12}.

Despite the importance of this vitamin, it actually has the smallest quantitative requirement of any known active nutritional substance, whether vitamin or mineral.

Like folic acid, it is required only in minute amounts in the body, amounts that are measured in micrograms rather than milligrams. One microgram is 1/1000 of a milligram, and a milligram is 1/1000 of a gram.

Biotin

This nutrient, sometimes referred to as vitamin H, is one of the lesser known B vitamins. It is important for its role in maintaining the health of the thyroid and adrenal glands, the nervous system, and in healthy skin and reproduction. It is necessary for the proper metabolism of fat, protein, and carbohydrates.

Precise requirements for animals—cats, dogs, and people—are not really known, because there is considerable evidence that this vitamin is manufactured by intestinal bacteria.

Sulfa drugs and antibiotics can impair the ability of these beneficial bacteria to produce biotin.

Another antibiotin factor is raw egg. Avoid it. Raw egg white contains a protein that ties up the biotin and renders it unavailable to the body.

A biotin deficiency was produced in growing kittens by feeding them a diet containing dried, raw egg white. After twelve weeks on a diet containing 18.5 percent egg white, the young cats began to show skin damage, loss of body weight, excess salivation, and secretions from the eyes, nose, and mouth. These signs increased in severity with time and were accompanied by bloody diarrhea, marked lack of appetite, and emaciation.[17]

If you are going to feed your cats eggs, serve them cooked, please.
Biotin injections have been used to help heal cats with skin problems.

My supplementation program includes some biotin in it and this may be a factor in the healthy skin and hair coats reported by my clients.

Vitamin D

This is the "sunshine vitamin." It has long been recognized as a key element in calcium and phosphorus metabolism. Strong bones and strong teeth depend on it.

Rickets, the crippling crooked-bone disease, is one result of a vitamin D deficiency.

Vitamin D is not found in significant amounts in food other than in fish liver oils. Commercial milk is probably the most common food source of this vitamin, as it is fortified with D. Most animals and humans obtain what they need from the ultraviolet rays of sunlight, which sets off a chain of chemical reactions in the skin. The end result is the production of vitamin D.

I have always wondered if there was any sunlight-deprivation effect on cats kept indoors virtually all their lives. They certainly did not evolve that way.

Since very ancient times, man has known that sunlight has a healing effect on the body. Modern science has paid very little attention to this fact and has been slow to study the benefits of sunlight on animals.

One can only speculate as to whether the indoor cat is being shortchanged or not. I think it is.

Rickets are believed to occur rarely in cats. As far as is known, it has only been produced experimentally with kittens kept in the dark and kittens specifically fed vitamin D-deficient diets. Researchers have made the interesting observation that young cats who survive acute rickets tend to improve markedly the first year of their lives even though they were never given any vitamin D or exposed to ultraviolet light.[18]

Little is really known about the influence of vitamin D in cat nutrition. It seems that the requirements of cats are very low.

Vitamin E

This versatile vitamin is one of the all-stars on my vitamin and mineral team. Here are some of the many things vitamin E does:

- It boosts the efficiency of the heart.
- It promotes the dilation of small blood vessels, thus increasing the supply of blood and nutrients to distant cells and tissues of the body.
- It strengthens the immune system.
- It guards the body against the toxins of cigarette smoke (smokers note!) and air pollution.
- It helps heal nagging skin problems.
- It rejuvenates ailing old cats.
- It promotes fertility.
- It prevents a painful disease called steatitis in cats eating a lot of tuna fish.
- It makes other vitamins and minerals work more efficiently.

Dr. Wilfrid E. Shute, a retired Canadian cardiologist, has been an outspoken champion of vitamin E supplementation for more than forty years. The medical profession at large is just coming around now to endorsing concepts about vitamin E that Shute and his late physician brother Evan put into practice many years ago.

The Shute brothers demonstrated back in the 1940s that vitamin E had the ability to enhance the function of heart and circulation, not only in humans but in animals as well. They found that the addition of vitamin E in the diet could also create an optimal physiology with internal organs working at maximum efficiency.

In addition to his professional career, Wilfrid Shute has long pursued an active interest in the breeding, showing, and judging of dogs. He was personally responsible for the widespread use of vitamin E among dog enthusiasts.

One of the people he inspired was Dr. N. H. Lambert, formerly the president of the Irish Veterinary Association. Lambert used comparatively large doses (100 and 150 IUs) of vitamin E in treating hundreds of dogs and cats, ranging from sluggish racing greyhounds and ailing hunting dogs with heart failure to cats with tumors.

Many animals on a vitamin E program improve rapidly and markedly, he reported to a medical conference. "They regain a feeling of well-being, their youthful behavior is frequently restored, (and) the skin and coat improve . . ."

Lambert found vitamin E therapy effective in curing chronic skin ulcers, especially when applied topically and given orally.

Cats with cardiac disease, in particular a condition called tachycardia, where the heartbeat accelerates rapidly, respond favorably to vitamin E, he noted.

Lambert was similarly successful in treating a number of old females with a cystic mammitis. The condition subsided and in some cases resolved completely, he said.

One of his case histories involved an eleven-year-old female who was in great discomfort with an extensive cystic mammitis.

"The cat was off food, resented handling, and would move around slowly on level ground only," Lambert related. "This condition had been developing over a period of three years and now, as the condition had become so painful, the owner requested sedative therapy, or euthanasia as a last resort."

Vitamin E therapy was prescribed, 100 IUs daily, and there was an immediate improvement.

"A week later the dose was reduced to 50 IUs daily . . . and six months later the glands were normal, with only a few small fibrous thickenings, and the cat behaves like a kitten again."[19]

Scientific work done with vitamin E and animals demonstrates a tremendous rejuvenating and energizing effect of this amazing vitamin.

The U.S. Air Force supplemented the diets of rats and found these animals had more endurance and stamina during grueling physical exercises. Autopsy showed that supplemented rodents suffered less wear and tear to vital organs than did nonsupplemented animals put through the same trials.[20]

A five-year study on the effect of vitamin E on racehorses in Canada concluded that supplemental doses "will bring horses close to their best effort. The vitamin enables the tissues of the body to do the same job on less oxygen. It is as if one strapped an aqua-lung on the horse's back. It opens up huge reserves of capillary circulation, sets of vessels not ordinarily used but waiting there for emergency demands." Older horses were said to be rejuvenated on a supplementation program.[21]

Along with its rejuvenating action on the cardiovascular system, vitamin E has another unique quality that appears to slow down aging. It is a natural antioxidant. Inside the body, vitamin E is the first line of defense against excessive oxidation of fatty substances contained in all cells of the body. The very same oxygen that is required by all the cells for the maintenance of normal functions can also cause harmful reactions, damaging membranes and enzymes and contributing to the general aging of the body. An adequate amount of vitamin E in the system slows down this aging effect of oxygen.

The air we breathe has additional dangers for the fatty components of cells. These are the synthetic oxidants that create air pollution.

There is considerable concern among scientists about ozone, the main oxidant of smog. Even at weak concentrations, ozone can damage the fatty constituents of respiratory tract cells and increase susceptibility to pulmonary infection. This pollutant has been incriminated in bronchitis, emphysema, and lung cancer.

Here is where vitamin E can help if you and your cats live in a polluted urban area. Scientists say vitamin E can strengthen the cellular membranes and thus render the fatty contents less vulnerable to oxidation, virus, and bacteria. Furthermore, vitamin E acts as a guardian of vitamin A, which is vital for the health of the mucous membrane of the respiratory tract.

An interesting experiment conducted by Dr. Mohammad G. Mustafa at the University of California at Davis in 1974 showed how vitamin E can safeguard the health of lungs. He divided sixty healthy rats into two groups and fed them both the same standard diet with the exception of a vitamin E variation. One group received vitamin E in the dose of 11 parts per 1,000,000 daily, an amount equal to "the average concentration in American diets." The other group got 66 parts per 1,000,000, or approximately twice the recommended daily allowance for rats.

After five weeks on the diet, animals from both groups were exposed to levels of ozone for seven days that were half, or less, the normal content of smoggy Los Angeles air.

When the lung tissues were examined, Mustafa found that the rats on the higher level of vitamin E had suffered significantly less injury than the others. An increased supply of this vitamin is likely to reduce harmful cellular reactions caused by the ozone, he concluded.[22]

(Vitamin C has also been scientifically shown to prevent lung tissue damage from ozone).[23]

Smog can do more than harm just the lungs. University of Kentucky food scientist Ching K. Chow and fellow researchers showed that ozone increased susceptibility to biochemical damage in the red blood cells of rats fed a diet deficient in vitamin E. Animals given dietary supplements of 45 parts per 1,000,000 were protected. Vitamin E thus "appears to occupy a unique place in the antioxidant defense of the red cells," the researchers said.[24]

In a subsequent study, Chow showed that vitamin E also protects the health of animals against the harmful effects of cigarette pollution. Two groups of rats were exposed to fumes equivalent to the amount one would be exposed to by spending three days in the presence of a chain smoker. One group was supplemented with vitamin E and the other not.

At the end of the trial, five of the sixteen unsupplemented rats were dead, compared with only one of the thirteen supplemented rats.

Chow said cigarette smoke contains more than three thousand chemicals, some of which may have damaged essential enzymes in the animals.[25]

Pay heed, you pet owners who smoke or live in blighted air conditions!

There is good evidence that extra vitamin E strengthens the immune system against disease-carrying microorganisms as well. Cheryl F. Nockels of Colorado State University fed vitamin E in excess of normal requirements to a variety of animals and said they showed "significantly increased" resistance to such microbial threats. Mice, chicks, guinea pigs, turkeys, and lambs suffered less harm when given more vitamin E, she reported.[26]

About twenty years ago, vitamin E deficiency became a serious problem among cats with the arrival of red tuna meat on the commercial cat-food market. While tuna is an excellent source of protein and nutrition, it contains a high degree of polyunsaturated fatty acid which oxidizes in the absence of adequate vitamin E. Remember I mentioned how vitamin E has antioxidant ability. It protects fatty materials both in food and in the body.

Cats eating a diet mainly of canned tuna fish developed a painful condition known as steatitis. There is a loss of appetite and difficulty in moving. Affected cats tend to sit quietly in one place. If you put your hand on its back where there are a lot of fatty deposits, the cat will howl in pain. On autopsy, the fatty tissue of such cats is very firm and has a yellow-brown discoloration instead of the usual white color and soft consistency.

Commercial cat foods with red tuna meat were subsequently fortified with vitamin E and the problem was contained—but apparently not altogether eliminated.

Patricia Curtis, in her book *The Indoor Cat,* notes that some animals eating even the supplemented canned fish have been known to get steatitis. This raises the question of whether enough vitamin E is added or whether it deteriorates to some degree in the can, she says.

Her advice is to "take it easy in feeding canned fish."[27]

I haven't come across the steatitis problem recently in my practice, but another veterinarian, Robert Goldstein of Yorktown Heights, New York, sees it from time to time in his.

"It is primarily a result of people feeding tuna to their cats all the time," he says. "Cats like the taste, and so people think cats are fish eaters. But by nature they really are not. In the wilds cats don't fish.

"A cat with steatitis can die from the condition. In a serious case I will give a cat 1,200 IUs of vitamin E a day, and in a month the cat will be greatly improved.

"If you insist on feeding fish to your cat on a regular basis, my advice would be to supplement the animal with about 200 IUs of E daily."

THE MINERALS

People tend to forget that minerals are just as important as vitamins. There could be no life without them. Any cell lacking in a single mineral nutrient cannot function up to par. Minerals are involved in nearly every physiological reaction. They combine with vitamins to form enzymes. They participate in the transportation of oxygen in the bloodstream. They are vital to the growth of strong bones, tissue, teeth, claws, and hair coat. Bones, for example, are principally composed of minerals.

By weight, there are ninety-six times more minerals in an animal's body than vitamins. Despite this natural predominance, vitamins have probably received ninety-six times more attention than minerals. This is primarily because nutritional science has only recently developed the instrumentation to properly study minerals.

Vitamins are produced through animal and plant biochemistry. Minerals are inorganic and found in the soil, the sea water and fresh water, and even in the air. In minute amounts they are absorbed from the soil by plants. Animals who are herbivores eat the plants and drink the water and in this way get the bulk of their mineral nutrients. Carnivores get theirs through the mineral content of the flesh they eat, the water they drink, and the sporadic greens they chew.

Calcium, phosphorus, sodium, potassium, magnesium, iron, copper, and iodine have been shown to be indispensable for the cat, according to the NRC. Chlorine, manganese, zinc, sulfur, cobalt, selenium, molybdenum, fluorine, chromium, silicon, and perhaps tin, nickel, and vanadium are assumed to be essential.

The NRC points out that some minerals, while essential to health, may be deterimental if consumed in excess.[28]

At very low levels, several minerals are downright harmful to animals: arsenic, lead, cadmium, and mercury. Studies have shown them to be present in minuscule amounts in food. They have the ability to interfere with the absorption and utilization of required minerals and to suppress the immune system.

Calcium and Phosphorus

These two important minerals are usually discussed together because their utilization in the body depends on a certain similar endocrine glands. They are closely related and interdependent, both nutritionally and metabolically.

Calcium and phosphorus are the major minerals involved in giving bones and teeth their structural hardness. This is why pregnant animals need more calcium and phosphorus than normal. Lactating queens need extra calcium for enhancing the quality of the milk they produce and to overcome the drain on their calcium stores by the nursing kittens.

Calcium and phosphorus are also necessary for the normal functioning of the nervous system.

Calcium also contributes to proper blood clotting and phosphorus to the metabolism of carbohydrates.

Both calcium and phosphorus require the presence of adequate vitamin D for proper utilization by the cat.

The dietary requirements of these two minerals are approximately equal. "Complete and balanced" commercial cat chows should provide an adequate amount and proportion of calcium and phosphorus for the maintenance of the average cat. Many breeders choose to supplement their pregnant and lactating cats with extra calcium, a subject I will discuss in Chapter Six.

Feeding a meat-rich diet to a cat can throw the calcium-phosphorus ratio out of balance and cause problems. This is because meats contain about twenty times more phosphorus than calcium. As British veterinary nutritionist Patricia Scott notes, "In the wild state the cat would consume the whole of its prey, including the bones, which would compensate for the lack of calcium in the meat."[29]

The result of consuming a heavy meat diet is a calcium-deficiency condition that includes nervousness, lameness, a cat that will lie quietly in a dark corner and resent handling, and a generalized decrease in bone density.

When feeding a heavy meat diet, calcium deficiency can be avoided by supplementation with 500 milligrams (half a gram) of calcium for every 100 grams of meat. Cow's milk is another approach. Each three and a half ounces of milk will contain 125 milligrams of calcium, or half the minimal daily requirement. The best source, however, are the bones of small animals such a birds and fish.

Deficiencies of phosphorus are believed to be rare in the cat.

Iodine

Iodine is a vital mineral because of its role in the production of the thyroid hormone that helps regulate the body's metabolism.

The reported incidence of iodine deficiency is rare. I have never encountered an iodine-related nutritional problem in my practice.

Fish is a good source of dietary iodine.

Iron

Unlike dogs and humans, cats appear to readily utilize the iron in meat sources and so they do not suffer from iron-deficiency anemia if there is adequate meat in their diets. However, anemia can occur in cats fed a milk diet with cereals low in iron. Cow's milk contains only a minute amount of iron.

Cats are said to require about five milligrams of iron daily.

My prevention program calls for iron supplementation, in part because iron has been shown to combat the harmful effects of lead. Japanese researchers, working with rats, found that lead-induced growth retardation and anemia and the accumulation of lead in the kidneys were all prevented by the addition of dietary iron. They suggested that supplemental iron reduces lead absorption into the body.[30]

One of the most important functions of iron is its partnership with copper, B_{12}, and protein to form hemoglobin, the red-coloring matter of the red blood cells. The hemoglobin molecules transport oxygen through the blood to the tissues and contain most of the iron in the body.

Magnesium and Manganese

Little is known about these two minerals, which are often confused with each other.

Magnesium is important to the health of the nervous system. It also helps the body absorb calcium and vitamins C, E, and B complex.

This mineral seems to prevent lead toxicity too. A study with lead-fed rats showed that the addition of magnesium to the diet actually draws accumulated lead out of the bone and other tissue, promotes its excretion, and thus reduces the toxic effect.[31]

Manganese is an essential ingredient for various enzymes and is necessary for bone and cartilage growth, normal reproduction, fat metabolism, and the proper utilization of vitamins B_1 and E.

Potassium and Sodium

These minerals are the principal electrolytes in the body. Electrolytes are mineral substances with tiny electrical charges. They appear throughout the fluid content of the body, acting like power generators for cellular activities. In nerve cells, for instance, the electrical charge between potassium inside the cellular fluid and sodium on the outside create the chain reaction of impulses that carry messages to and from the brain.

Natural foodstuffs contain adequate amounts of potassium, and outright deficiencies are believed to be rare.

When a deficiency does occur, a common observation is depressed reflexes.

Sodium is readily taken into the body in the form of dietary salt— sodium with chlorine. When water and salt are lost in excessive amounts, prostration and death can result.

Signs of deficiency include weight loss, dryness of skin, and severe loss of fur.

Selenium

For many years selenium had a notoriously bad reputation. In prairie and Rocky Mountain states where the selenium content of the soil is particularly high, this mineral was incriminated for causing death and disease in herds of cattle and sheep. Twenty years ago selenium was thought to cause cancer.

On the other side of the coin, in New Zealand and Finland, where the selenium content of the soil is the lowest in the world, animals have suffered from a variety of ailments, and the heart disease rate among the human population has been high.

The facts on selenium are clearly paradoxical.

Selenium is extremely toxic for all animals and man. Minute levels of only ten parts per million can kill. As little as two to five parts per million in animal diets are toxic. Selenium is even more toxic than lead at these levels. The difference between lead and selenium, however, is a big one. At much lower levels, something like one-tenth of a part per million, selenium has been determined to be an essential element in the diet of animals and man. Scientists have not been able to find any necessity for lead in the diet—at any level.

For more than twenty years, veterinarians have used selenium supplements—at strengths well below the toxic level—to treat and prevent lameness and muscular weakness and skin, growth, and fertility problems arising among livestock grazing on low-selenium pastures.

In recent years, medical scientists have found that safe supplemental levels of selenium (measured in micrograms) may have an important role in cancer therapy and prevention.

Dr. John A. Milner, professor of food science at the University of Illinois, told a 1980 medical conference that selenium apparently works against a number of tumors.

"In animal experiments, we've seen a significant inhibition of tumor development," he said. Tumors disappear or subside appreciably after animals are injected with selenium.

"Considerable evidence does suggest that selenium is an anticarcinogen," Milner said. Scientific work to date suggests selenium may have a preventive role in lessening susceptibility to tumors, and it should also be considered as a therapeutic agent, he added.[32]

Studies conducted with test animals show that dietary selenium at safe levels above the basic requirement increases the effectiveness of the immune system. One way that selenium works is as an antioxidant, like vitamins C and E. As a matter of fact, selenium and E act as "buddies" to counter the damaging oxidative process at the cellular level.

My supplementation program includes a safe level of selenium that I feel offers another measure of protection against tumors. But do not attempt selenium supplementation beyond that without the guidance of a knowledgeable veterinarian.

There are no known scientific data on the selenium requirements for felines, although a need for this mineral has been shown as a result of studies with other species.

Zinc

Zinc is a key addition to any supplementation program. Every day more and more is being learned about the biological contributions of this mineral and how vital it is in the production of enzymes, the maintenance of healthy hair coat and skin, and just how important it is to the healing process.

More than three thousand years ago, the Egyptians used salves containing zinc to promote the healing of wounds. Now, modern science knows that the stress of wound healing rapidly depletes zinc levels in the body unless supplies are restored through the diet. Zinc, it has been learned, is critical to the growth of new tissue around any wound, be it an injury, scratch, flea bite, ulcer, burn, or surgical incision. Zinc not only is used in the tissue reconstruction, but it also helps to fight infections at the wound site. Damaged tissue is especially vulnerable to microbial attack, but zinc helps keep resistance high by activating certain white blood cells that combat microorganisms.

Researchers have reported that wounded and burned rats fed diets containing extra amounts of zinc healed faster than rats getting a standard diet. I will often suggest to clients that they provide some extra zinc to their animals following surgery or an injury.

A situation exists today that makes routine supplementation of zinc a real necessity. Primarily because of overuse of chemical fertilizers, the soil in over thirty states has been declared zinc-deficient by the U.S. Department of Agriculture. There is a similar zinc insufficiency on a worldwide basis. Of all the minerals in the ground, zinc is said to be the most scarce.[33] This soil deficiency is reflected in the zinc content of crops and continues up the entire food chain—to the food we and our pets eat.

Ongoing research is heaping growing importance on zinc for the health of the immune system. It is necessary for the production of white blood cells. It helps rid the body of toxic lead, which suppresses immunity. It protects against cancer.

Signs of zinc deficiency in cats include emaciation, vomiting, conjunctivitis, inflammation of the cornea, general debility, and retarded growth.

PART 3

The Prevention Plan

5

How to Use the Plan

Your only insurance against tomorrow is what you do today!

— SIR WILLIAM OSLER

My prevention plan is simple and inexpensive insurance for the optimal health of your animals. An uncomplicated vitamin and mineral program is all it takes.

The program effectively covers nutritional shortcomings in the diet and addresses special needs or dependencies on particular nutrients. It strengthens the organs and the immune system and prevents disease. It reduces allergic reactions. It makes your animals better show cats, better breeders, or better companions for yourself and your family.

This is the action part of the book where I spell out the "how to do it" information that will enable you to start an effective prevention program. And the sooner you start the better.

In Chapters Six, Seven, Eight, and Nine, I will be discussing how vitamins and minerals are beneficial in specific stages of feline life: pregnancy and lactation, kittenhood, adulthood, and old age. To use the plan, you simply refer to the stage-of-life chapter applicable to your animals.

In Chapters Ten, Eleven, and Twelve, I will be advising you on how to purchase vitamin and mineral supplements, how much to use, and how to administer them. You will find charts with my recommended dosages for each stage of life.

If you follow my suggestions, and they are essentially what I tell my own clients, you will find the program is quite effortless. Once you have the supplements in hand, the actual administration takes only a few seconds daily.

One question often put to me is how long does it take for the supplements to work. If you are not trying to treat any particular condition but simply want to raise the level of your cats' health, it is a matter of ten days or two weeks before you begin seeing improvement. Sometimes the results can be seen even sooner with the disappearance of minor problems, such as shedding, and with the appearance of youthful vigor. The time factor depends on the individual biochemical status of each animal.

As I mentioned in the last chapter, vitamins and minerals go to work deep down at the cellular level. Unlike powerful drugs that are designed to attack specific problems quickly, nutrients are nature's own compounds. They nourish the whole body, systematically repairing and reinforcing it at the foundation. That's why it takes time to see results on the surface. Their pace is nature's pace.

In the case of sickly animals, I always tell my clients to be patient and not expect results overnight. While wonderful things can and do happen quite rapidly, I usually find problems lessening gradually. Over the long haul, animals just don't get sick anymore as they used to.

The key to success is staying with the program. Don't stop the supplements as soon as your animals perk up and problems vanish. It is a mistake to think they don't need the supplements anymore.

Here is a brief case history to illustrate the importance of sticking with the program: A cat belonging to one of my clients was tested and found to have the leukemia virus. I advised the owner to start the animal on a supplementation program. She did, and a few months later when the cat was retested, it was negative. The cat thrived.

One day the woman gave the cat away because she was moving out of town. The new owners did not keep up the program. Some months later I received a call from the woman. She told me the cat had died from leukemia.

Over the years many a client has returned with a sick cat that I had previously put on a supplement program.

"Are you still giving the vitamins and minerals as I recommended?" I always ask.

The frequent answer is, "No, I ran out," or, "I stopped as soon as little Cuddles improved."

I tell them what I am telling you now. If you stop the program, the chronic problems will come roaring right back. The animals will return to the same condition prior to supplementation. They will be the same old cats again—vulnerable to all the lead, toxins, viruses, and stress that made them sick to start with. A leukemia-positive cat can be turned negative and symptomless and kept that way as long as you maintain the program. Stop the supplements and in two months the animal will test positive again—and be at risk for serious disease. In short order, an animal will slip from optimal to satisfactory or less than satisfactory health, from being hardy to being vulnerable.

To shut the door on common health problems and keep them out you must stay on the program. The body needs those extra vitamins and minerals for lasting protection. Prevention is a lifetime consideration. Once an animal is optimal, you have to keep him that way. There is no reason a cat cannot be healthy throughout an entire lifetime when all it takes is following the simple prevention plan I have designed.

Let's look now at prevention in relation to the pregnant and lactating queen—where life begins.

6

How Supplements Help
Pregnant and Lactating Cats

One day a woman came into my hospital carrying a sick kitten. The two-week-old kitten had runny eyes, was sneezing, and had all the symptoms of an upper respiratory viral disease.

After I examined the animal I asked the woman if the mother was sick.

"No, it seems to be okay," she said.

"What about the other kittens?" I asked.

"They all seem to be okay too," she said.

"That's good," I said. "But it is possible they also will come down with the same disease. They may just have more resistance than this particular kitten."

Sure enough, three days later the woman called and said the other four kittens in the litter were now ill.

There isn't much a veterinarian can do for such tiny animals. I administered some liquid antibiotics and prescribed some vitamin and mineral drops.

"The problem is that all the harm has been done," I told the woman. "It is really too late to do anything. If you had taken the queen and put her on a vitamin and mineral program when she became pregnant, she would have passed on optimal immunity to the fetuses, and you would probably now have a litter of thriving kittens."

Instead, the woman lost all but one of the kittens.

Veterinarians see similar cases all the time—the passing off of deadly viruses to the growing fetuses. For cat owners and breeders this is a most frustrating situation. You have an apparently healthy female showing no symptoms whatsoever, like this particular client's queen. Within the body, however, the cat is carrying a dormant strain of virus. She herself may have the immunity to resist the organisms. But she will pass them on to the growing fetuses who have considerably less resistance.

Hybrid cats seem to be more resistant to this kind of disease process than purebred cats. However, the story I just related involved a hardy "alley cat." The truth is that all cats are susceptible, especially if they are not receiving good nutrition.

The diseases I see being passed along most frequently from queen to fetus are leukemia, feline infectious peritonitis, and rhinotracheitis (upper respiratory virus)—the most serious of the viral conditions that prey on cats.

From my experience, the leukemia virus seems to be involved in a large percentage of pregnancy complications. For this reason I always recommend a lab test for leukemia before a cat is bred. Animals will frequently test positive, that is, prove to be carriers of the virus, even if no signs of disease are present.

The mere presence of the virus in a cat's body is enough to interfere with reproduction. Typical problems are miscarriages, resorptions, stillborns, or an inability to become pregnant altogether.

Most peculiar is the phenomenon of resorbed fetuses. Most cat fanciers and breeders know this problem well. The queen becomes pregnant and sails along nicely for several weeks. Suddenly she becomes temporarily ill. Afterward she shows no further signs of being pregnant.

But where have all the kittens gone?

Were they aborted? Did she eat them? We know that queens will sometimes eat their stillborns.

But there is no sign of abortion. No blood. No fragments. No nothing.

The fetuses have apparently died, undergone a disintegration process, and the disintegrated matter has been absorbed inside the cat—a biochemical reversal of gestation.

Such queens can conceive again, but they may have repeat performances before they actually deliver offspring.

And such animals invariably test positive for leukemia.

Breeders and clients on my supplementation program simply do not have these kinds of problems anymore.

Laneen Firth, who breeds Persians in San Jose, has been on the program since 1975. She says her cats have had no pregnancy problems from that time on.

"I have no resorptions. No abortions. No stillborns. No malformed kittens. No weak kittens. Out of about three hundred kittens there has only been the rare exception that was a breech presentation and died when it aspirated its embryonic fluid. Otherwise, we have had only thriving kittens."

Gerrie Raicevich is a Himalayan breeder in Millbrae, California. Her Jo-Lee Cattery was having serious birthing problems before she initiated a complete vitamin and mineral program.

"Memoirs," a blue creampoint Himalayan, was a typical example of the trouble.

"One year she produced three dead kittens," recalls Raicevich. "The following year only one survived out of a litter of four. But in the third queening we had three live and healthy kittens."

With the program, Jo-Lee has eliminated its queening problems. In fact, the cattery queens are not only producing strong, healthy kittens but also larger kittens and larger litters as well.

Dennis and Laura Dayton of the Blossom Time Cattery in Newbury Park, California, tell me their litters have also substantially increased during the several years they have been using supplements. The Daytons breed Ragdolls.

"Normally Ragdolls produce two or three kittens a litter, and we used to be overjoyed when a queen now and then would get as many as four," they say. "Now it is rather common to have five and six at a time, and we are even seeing occasional litters of seven and eight. This is highly unusual for the breed.

"Other Ragdoll breeders we know who are not on the program report the typical two and three kittens a litter.

"Ragdolls are particularly hardy cats, and what we are finding is that the vitamins and minerals are making them even hardier. Kittens are larger at birth and seemingly much healthier, with a higher resistance to viruses. We don't have kittens coming down with colds. We don't have problems with sudden infant death. We have no litter runts. The kittens all seem to be about equal in size.

"We used to have stillborns. That's a problem with any breed. But now the incidence has dropped way down."

SUPPLEMENTS LESSEN QUEENING STRESS

Pregnancy and lactation is a time of severe biochemical stress as the queen provides for two to six or more kittens. It is absolutely necessary to be nutritionally fit for this added burden.

The point is strongly made by Roger Williams, a biochemist: "It has been amply demonstrated throughout the entire animal kingdom that during the period of pregnancy, nutrition must be at a particularly high level. It has been found repeatedly that specific diets supporting the adult life of rats, mice, dogs, cats, chickens, turkeys, fish, foxes or monkeys will not be adequate to support anything approaching the nutritional requirements for normal reproduction."[1]

Abundant scientific evidence has been compiled from both humans and animals showing that deficiencies in any one single nutrient can lead to reproductive failures and fetus malformations. Fifty years ago a researcher in Texas conducted a dramatic experiment in nutrient cause and effect by feeding pregnant female pigs a diet deficient in vitamin A. One sow delivered eleven piglets all minus their eyeballs! Other pigs produced offspring with extra ears, cleft palates, and irregular kidneys. Later, with adequate vitamin A restored to their diets, the same sows delivered normal young.[2]

In rats, a zinc deficiency has been shown to cause resorption of fetuses and gross abnormalities in 90 percent of the young that survived birthing. A manganese deficiency in rats, mice, guinea pigs, chickens, and hogs causes inner ear defects and equilibrium problems in the offspring.[3]

Deficiencies of B_1, B_2, pantothenic acid, B_6, biotin, folic acid, and B_{12} can cause loss of the fetus. Conversely, no adverse effects have been reported from excessive dosage of any of the B complex vitamins.[4] The B's are very essential for good pregnancies.

Roger Williams declares that if nutrition is good, most animals are vigorous, healthy, and prolific, and if their diet is excellent, they likely will produce healthy offspring. Nutrition can be upgraded in a number of ways, he says, such as by adding more and improved protein, improving the mineral balance, and introducing a "better assortment of vitamins in ample amounts."[5]

Commercial cat chows hardly seem to live up to these standards.

We have seen in an earlier chapter that the quality of protein in many products is suspect.

We have seen that commercial products contain impurities, chemicals, and toxins with the potential for harm. The last thing a cat needs is to be fighting a second front of man-made stress in addition to the natural stresses of pregnancy. This is an important time to read labels and try to keep an animal's food as free from preservatives and additives as possible.

We have also seen that veterinary nutritionists are unsure about adequate levels of many nutrients for cats. "It is probable, but not certain," says the National Research Council, that the recommended levels will support reproduction.[6] What is even less certain is the nutrient level in the finished product you buy in the supermarket or pet shop. And this is what the pregnant cat has to rely on to nourish the fetuses growing inside her.

The fact is that every breeder I know supplements their pregnant cats to one degree or another.

My approach to all pregnant cats is to recommend ample amounts of vitamins and minerals, just as Roger Williams suggests. The kind of vigorous, healthy, and prolific animals he predicts are exactly what my clients are reporting. The queen's diet is being bolstered, and she responds by producing more and better kittens and maintaining a high level of health herself throughout the pregnancy.

The extra nutrition will help the queen resist the dangerous viral conditions that can destroy both her and her kittens. It will help prepare her for the ordeal of queening and nursing and create hardier kittens better able to cope with the dangers of life outside the womb.

I cannot stress the immunity factor enough. Supplementation that includes vitamin C absolutely builds stronger body defenses. If for no other reason, this is why you should supplement. An optimally healthy pregnant cat does not resorb her kittens, does not become ill during pregnancy, and does not produce toxic milk. Through the placenta and milk she delivers potent antibodies and protection to her young.

In addition to the standard contents of pet multivitamins and minerals, I strongly suggest added vitamin C and E. They are marvelous for pregnant and lactating queens. You can find my dosage recommendations in Chapter Eleven.

First, let's look at vitamin C.

Dr. Fred Klenner, the North Carolina physician who pioneered vitamin C therapy in the United States, has repeatedly shown the benefits of large doses of this vitamin in pregnancy. In over one thousand deliveries, he consistently reduced the time and pain of labor. And the babies were so noticeably healthy that they were called "vitamin C babies" by the staff of the local hospital.[7]

Klenner and other doctors who follow his example have been using as much as 10,000 milligrams of vitamin C daily. Compare this to the recommended daily allowance of 60 milligrams suggested by the National Research Council.

As we have seen, cats are comparatively poor producers of vitamin C. The stresses of pregnancy severely strain the internal enzyme system where ascorbic acid is manufactured. I feel that queens often cannot make enough to overcome those stresses and still meet the needs of the multiple lives taking shape inside their bodies. Their vitamin C supply is further taxed by the need to detoxify impurities contained in the diet. Remember, too, the manufacturers are convinced that cats are making all the vitamin C they need and so they do not incorporate any in the food.

Given this background it is not surprising to find similar benefits from supplementation when you compare the human female, who makes no vitamin C, to the feline female, who doesn't make enough.

With cats on vitamin C the mammary glands tuck up nicely into the body about two weeks after lactation ends. There are no lingering and sagging teats, a rather common eyesore. The quick recovery of the teats is related to the power of vitamin C to enhance the elasticity of the connective tissue. With human females on vitamin C, Klenner reported that the area around the womb—the perineum—of his patients always returned quickly to previous firmness. There were few or no stretch marks.

In addition, Klenner sees three- and four-hour labors. My clients, too, consistently report that queening time is reduced, by as much as a half. This means less stress for the queen, less pain, less chance of losing kittens, and less chance of birthing damage to kittens. Again, the elasticity of the perineum in woman and cat facilitates the enormous stretching necessary to make room for the emerging infants or kittens. Vitamin C also has exceptional antifatigue power. The laboring females seem to have more strength and energy.

Klenner's "vitamin C babies" were all noted for their superlative health and appearance. The same can be said for "vitamin C kittens."

From my experience it is particularly the vitamin C in the supplementation program that is giving female cats the ability to overcome or withstand the serious viral challenges and produce healthy litters. Earlier I discussed how vitamin C works against viruses.

Many breeders have come to me with major reproduction problems in their catteries, problems most frequently involving the leukemia virus. They were having complications despite comprehensive diet and supplementation programs. Invariably, there would be one factor missing from their regimen: vitamin C. And I would always tell them it was this missing factor that makes the big difference.

But cats all produce their own vitamin C, the breeders will say.

Yes, but not enough, I always tell them.

I then suggest a vitamin and mineral supplement with megadoses of vitamin C. Without exception, the breeders report back that chronic problems have been eliminated or drastically reduced.

If your cats have reproduction problems associated with a viral condition, vitamin C can resolve them. To my knowledge, there is no vaccine, no medicine, no elixer, nothing whatsoever up a veterinarian's sleeve that can do the same.

Persian breeder Laneen Firth became a believer about the reproduction benefits of a vitamin C—based program with her very first pair of cats.

"'Dutchess' was a sickly six-and-one-half-year-old Persian female who was near death when I got her," says Firth. "She was emaciated, had bad teeth, and was a confirmed leukemic cat. What's more, she had never conceived in her life despite being placed with quite a few fertile males.

"After six months on the supplement program she did what I never thought she would do. She conceived. I mean it just doesn't happen for the first time at this age. She delivered three living, healthy kittens who have grown into fine adults themselves.

"Even more astounding is the fact that the sire was a seven-month-old cat. This just isn't normal for Persians. In this breed, many a two-year-old male will not yet have produced his first litter. My males are all siring by the time they are a year old!"

Vitamin E is well known among animal breeders for enhancing the reproductive process. The scientific name for this vitamin is to-copherol. The word comes from the Greek: *tokos,* for childbirth, *pherein,* for bringing forth, and *ol,* for oil. Thus you have the "oil of fertility." The name was applied after the original research years ago showed vitamin E— deficient rats to have reproductive failures.

Many animals are supposedly getting adequate amounts of vitamin E in their daily feed yet still have difficulty with conception. Some-times it takes amounts over what is regarded as normal to enable an animal to conceive. There is a need for more because of stress or biological individuality. The needs, remember, differ from person to person, animal to animal. In cats, the need for vitamin E is further influenced by the amount of unsaturated fats in the diet. Fish-based diets and particularly red tuna, for instance, call for an increase in vitamin E supplementation.

In a Canadian study with racehorses, researchers analyzed the ef-fect of supplemental vitamin E on a group of thirty-four broodmares, including twenty-one that were either barren, maiden, or difficult to mate. Seven stallions in the experiment were also supplemented.

Tocopherol markedly increased female fertility, the report said. Fully 88 percent of the broodmares conceived when bred to the sup-plemented stallions. Their previous five-year breeding record was 66 percent of foals.

On their part, the stallions showed better breeding behavior, more libido, less nervousness, better sperm, and better condition after the breeding season.[8]

Dr. Wilfrid Shute, the Canadian physician who pioneered the use of vitamin E, says the vitamin simply seems to increase physiological effectiveness in all animals, including their ovum and sperm activity. Shute, a prominent dog breeder, has helped many breeders over the years merely by recommending they use vitamin E to enhance repro-duction.

In Ireland, veterinarian N. H. Lambert found that vitamin E consis-tently restored the normal cycle to queens who hadn't come into sea-son for prolonged periods.

Thea Sutherland, proprietor of the Honey Mist Cattery of Persians in Lynnwood, Washington, automatically turns to vitamin E if a fe-male doesn't come into season.

"I have been doing it for ten years and it always works," she says. "You give 400 IUs of vitamin E a day and within a few days or a week the cat is in heat."

A Persian breeder, Carolyn Bussey of Olympia, Washington, told me an interesting story about how vitamin E helped a breeder friend of hers solve a serious reproduction problem. The friend was a breeder of Manx, a tailless species of cat known for producing weak kittens. A debilitating muscle weakness seems to affect most Manx newborn, and in this breeder's case, the young wouldn't even attempt to crawl out of the breeding box until they were five or six weeks old.

The breeder used no supplements at all. Bussey suggested she try putting the pregnant females on 200 IUs of vitamin E daily.

"Did it ever work," said Bussey. "Those kittens practically walked out of the birth canal. They were up and moving around by the time they were three weeks old. The muscle tone and structure was far and away better in the supplemented kittens."

Vitamin E is a major constituent in the supplementation program for her own Persians and exotic shorthairs. Bussey says all her cats routinely receive vitamin E, but the pregnant ones receive even more.

"For one thing, E decreases the need for oxygen," she says. "If your female has a difficult birth, you are much more likely to get a live kitten if your female has been on vitamin E. The kitten will not suffocate nearly as fast."

BETTER UTERINE CONTRACTIONS, BETTER MILK

Uterine exhaustion and cesarean-section operations are a rarity for breeders using a good supplementation program based on a multivitamin and mineral along with extra C and E.

Breeders who used to assist in removing kittens from exhausted queens no longer have to intervene. The queens easily pop out the kittens.

Here is typical feedback I get from breeders:

Laneen Firth of San Jose—"I breed Persians, and in this breed C-sections occur about 10 percent of the time. That's because you are breeding for a massive head, different from other cats, and you need a big strong female to push those kittens out. I have had only one C-section in seven years on the program and the one case involved a female with a genetic hormonal imbalance. Otherwise, I have had at least a hundred queenings without incident. And these are cats bought from different lines all over the world."

Ann Ransom of the An-Do Cattery of Persians in Virginia Beach, Virginia—"My cats seem to queen very easily on the program. It appears to make them much stronger. I had three C-sections in three years prior to starting the program. And in the three years since, I haven't had a single C-section."

About 75 percent of the C-sections I perform in my practice involve cases of uterine exhaustion. The queen has no energy to push remaining kittens out.

But as more and more of my clients are using the complete vitamin and mineral program, I am having to do fewer and fewer C-sections. A C-section operation can cost you anywhere from a couple hundred dollars to perhaps $375 on a Sunday at the emergency clinic. Supplements are much cheaper.

The minority of C-section cases have nothing really to do with nutrition. These generally occur when kittens enter the narrow birth canal in breech position (buttocks first) or with their head deviated laterally. Another possibility is the extra-large kitten the mother cannot squeeze out. In such cases, a veterinarian has to operate.

If a queen goes through two hours of heavy labor without producing a kitten, this means there are problems and it is advisable to take the animal to a veterinarian as soon as possible. By heavy labor, I mean contractions every five to ten minutes. If this continues much longer than two hours and the cat has not presented a kitten, the animal can become very weak. It will require a veterinarian to make a diagnosis and choose the proper course of action. A word to the wise: The longer the delay in taking the queen to the veterinarian, the weaker the animal will become. If a cesarean is performed on an extremely weak cat, the anesthesia that is used can actually cause the cat's death. So do not delay in such a situation.

Calcium is important for strong uterine contractions, healthy young, and good mother's milk. Yet many breeders and fanciers get into trouble by overdosing their pregnant cats with calcium. Females can produce premature kittens or abort altogether as a result of too much calcium.

Cats are getting calcium in their food and water. If they are receiving a multivitamin and mineral product, there is extra calcium in that. What some people unfortunately do is to supplement the supplement. They will administer additional calcium tablets and sometimes even feed a side dish of cottage cheese just to eliminate any doubt whatsoever.

All this extra calcium may create a biochemical imbalance in the body. It may also create an unnatural dependency on megacalcium for the kittens, a dependency that cannot be satisfied by the normal diet that follows.

Cats need about 200 milligrams daily of calcium for normal maintenance. This requirement may exceed 600 milligrams during lactation when the kittens are making a considerable demand on the queen's calcium stores.

A cat's appetite will increase during the last twenty days or so of pregnancy. For a few days after queening she will show little interest in food, but pretty soon she will eat like a lion. The calcium in her diet, along with the calcium in the one vitamin and mineral supplement, should probably provide her with all she needs. One point to remember is that the vitamin D in the supplement acts as a catalyst to enhance the body's utilization of calcium. Furthermore, the vitamin C helps break down calcium in the cat's gut and promote absorption. So there is really no need to supplement the supplement.

Of course, individual animals have individual needs, and if your cat is not producing enough milk, it is advisable to consult with your veterinarian. The veterinarian will best be able to determine if extra calcium is needed.

In my experience, however, cats following a supplementation program along the lines I recommend do not have problems providing their kittens with milk. There are "no shortages at the pump."

It is not uncommon for a queen to develop an illness during the stress of lactation. She seems to be doing fine and then all of a sudden she runs a temperature. The cause could be viral or bacterial in nature, the result of an overburdened and weakened immune system.

In such a case a cat may either produce toxic milk or stop producing milk altogether. Toxins in the milk are a by-product of the disease process and can have a harmful effect on the nursing kittens. Often they will develop diarrhea.

If a queen becomes ill, the first thing to do is take the kittens away from her and feed them special kitten formulas obtainable at a veterinarian's office or pet shop. The queen should be brought to the veterinarian as soon as possible.

Breeders tell me that cats on a vitamin and mineral program do not have this problem. In my own practice, I rarely see any sick lactating cats. The program really seems to help cats through this difficult period.

"She blew her hair coat!" That's bad news for any pet owner and especially for the owner of a show cat. A blown hair coat is a by-product of the excess stress of pregnancy and lactation. The queen starts losing fur and her coat becomes scruffy and lackluster. Unfortunately, this sorry state is fairly common and it can take months for an animal to regain her previous rich hair coat.

On a vitamin and mineral program, one with plenty of vitamin C and E, this condition never occurs. Both show dogs and show cats are able to return to the campaign soon after the young are weaned.

Ragdoll cats have an exceptionally long nursing time—up to three-and-a-half months. During this time it is difficult to maintain the weight of a queen and keep her hair coat in good shape.

Ragdoll breeders Dennis and Laura Dayton do not have these problems since adopting a good supplement program. "The coats remain healthy and shiny and don't get that ragged-looking appearance," they say. "There is no weight loss. And the cats quickly return to an optimal condition after weaning. Before, it took them a long time to recuperate. The difference is striking."

Another benefit from supplementation is extending breeding life. I used to recommend that once a queen reaches five years of age, she should be retired. After all, at five she is a middle-aged cat. She has had her share of litters. The condition of the uterus is not as youthful and robust as it used to be. She might not be able to produce enough good contractions to push out a full litter, and if there was a need for a C-section, she would more than likely be in a weaker state than a younger animal.

This was the way I used to think before I developed my program. Now, I get reports all the time about geriatric cats producing litters.

Ann Ransom in Virginia Beach told me how her "Seabrook's Lady Love" was still going strong at the age of eleven. Within a year, this Persian matriarch produced a single male, who blossomed into a full-bodied twelve-pounder, and then followed that up with a healthy multiple litter.

According to Ransom, the cat was purchased some years ago from a breeder who was selling only because the animal produced either premature young or sickly kittens.

"Since she has been on vitamins, her kittens have all been healthy," says Ransom.

Carolyn Bussey in Olympia, Washington, told me about a fourteen-year-old Exotic Shorthair who "goes into roaring heat twice a year."

"Taffy," as this hot-blooded grandam is called, had just produced a healthy litter of three kittens.

"She's too old to spay," says Bussey, "so I have to keep a close eye on her. Otherwise, she will tear through any and all barriers to get to the men."

My attitude toward geriatric pregnancies now is this: If you are going to breed an older female, it is imperative she be on a thorough supplement program. This will greatly minimize the risk of losing her or her kittens and maximize the odds for good healthy offspring.

Good supplementation must contain ample amounts of the B complex vitamins. Some breeders like to give their cats brewers' yeast, a popular source of B vitamins. Whether you supplement this way or with a multitablet or powder—which contains the B vitamins—is a matter of your preference or perhaps the cat's. Either way is good. What's important is that the mother receive enough of these critical vitamins. As I noted earlier, the B complex potency in commercial cat food is suspect because water-soluble vitamins are easily destroyed during processing and storage. So do not take a chance. The B vitamins are vital for the development of healthy little nervous systems. Some of the B vitamins are involved in stimulating the production of red blood cells and others in the production of good antibodies that the mother will pass on to the kittens. Pantothenic acid, one of the B complex vitamins, helps the body contend with stress. It will help the queen withstand the two months or more of biochemical tumult.

The B vitamins may also soothe maternal nervous systems that can become frayed during the stress of pregnancy and lactation. You don't see nervous, nasty, aggressive females who are on a program. They are generally very even-tempered and seem more capable of handling the changes in their bodies.

Stress is known to deplete the body's stores of zinc. Studies have shown that pregnant women tend to have low zinc levels. This mineral is far too important to be in deficit at this critical time. Zinc is related to proper collagen formation and body growth and utilization of nutrients. It is also essential in wound healing. Every kitten in the womb is connected through an individual placenta to the uterine wall. When a kitten is queened, the placenta pulls away, leaving behind a raw area that is prone to infection. The sooner it heals the better. Zinc helps the process.

In summing up, let me just mention that supplementation has had so great an impact on some of my breeder-clients that they actually will guarantee the health of the animals they sell as long as the animals remain on the program. One breeder guarantees a cat through spay or neuter if it is a pet. If the animal is used in breeding, she will guarantee its ability to conceive and reproduce.

As yet, she hasn't had to refund any money!

TIPS FOR PREGNANCY

1. If you are planning to breed your cat or if you know she is pregnant, take her to your veterinarian for an examination. The vet will check the cat's general health, look for any possible complications, and test for parasites. If there is to be any treatment for worms or parasites, it should occur at the beginning of pregnancy, if at all, because the stress of chemical toxins in the treatment may be harmful to the animal's strained immune system.

2. Do not breed a cat that is tested positive for leukemia. Even if the cat does not have any outward signs, it is still a carrier. Pregnancies with positive cats often end in miscarriages, resorptions, stillborns, and sometimes in the death of the queen.

When you bring your cat in for the checkup, have your vet perform the test for leukemia. If the cat tests positive, put her on my program. Within two months she should test negative and can then be bred. Make sure you maintain the program!

3. If the queen has not been on a vitamin and mineral program, this is the time to start. (See Chapter Eleven for how much to give your cat.)

4. Commercial cat food is highly processed and laced with chemicals. This is a good time to seek out a product that has the fewest listed additives. Some products have none at all. Your veterinarian may be able to give you guidance.

5. If you have a long-haired cat, cut away the excess hair in the vaginal area prior to queening. A pair of scissors will do the job. Remove as much as possible, especially in the warmer months. The combination of hair, birthing discharge, and blood can make a matted mess that is extremely inviting to flies. No matter how diligent a cat is in cleaning herself, you will be doing your animal a favor. I have seen some animals thoroughly infested with maggots.

6. It is a good idea to take your female to the veterinarian for an examination the day after she delivers. A substantial amount of afterbirth can remain in the uterus. If not removed it can decompose and generate harmful toxins. There is even the possibility of a kitten lodged high up in the uterus that may not have been expelled. An examination at this time is a good precaution.

7

How Supplements Help Kittens

For two months, the period of feline gestation, the kitten has taken
form and wallowed in the comfort, warmth, and security of the womb.
Now the time has come to leave all that behind and enter the real
world.

For the next twelve months, the kitten will streak through infancy
and kittenhood and reach the human young adult equivalent of fifteen
years. The pace is fast. The road is rough. And not every kitten will
make it.

Stress is right there, with guns drawn, to greet the new arrival the
moment it squeezes through the maternal gates. Like an Old West
desperado, stress lurks behind every turn along the route of kittenhood, ready to rob a young animal of its health or life.

Any veterinarian in business a week is familiar with the toll that
stress takes on young kittens. Breeders know it well. And anybody
who has ever experienced the joy of a first litter has a pretty good idea
of the problems that can follow.

Kittens have to compete with jostling brothers and sisters for nipple
time. They are constantly threatened by bacteria, viruses, protozoa,
fungi, worms, and the clumsy handling by humans. They are forced to
eat fabricated food and suffer the jolt of immunization. In a relatively
short period of time, they go from one setting to another, from one
adjustment to the next. As a result of these and other stresses, kittenhood is often measured in terms of pain, diarrhea, runny eyes and
noses, and frequently death.

Those first twelve months, or more specifically, the first few months, represent the best chance you have to develop optimally healthy cats.

Actually I recommend a double kind of health insurance program for cats. You supplement the female during pregnancy and then you supplement the newborn—beginning within a few hours after birth.

Very young kittens receive passive immunity through the mother's milk. However, if the mother isn't healthy or is lacking good nutrition, this maternal immunity will be less than ideal. Soon after kittens are weaned, they have to develop their own immunity, and the high death rate is testimony to the fact that many of them just don't have the immune equipment to cope.

By supplementing their diets from the start, you are bulletproofing kittens against the constant bombardment of stress.

Here is how supplements work for kittens:

- Vitamin C is a powerful kitten booster. It is a well-known antiviral, antibacterial, and antihistamine agent. It spearheads resistance against harmful organisms by strengthening immune response. It makes other vitamins and minerals work better. I do not believe a kitten, under stress, is capable of producing enough vitamin C on its own.

- The B complex family of vitamins contributes to a healthy nervous system. Pantothenic acid, one of the B vitamins, is important along with vitamin C for the proper functioning of the adrenal glands. The adrenals manufacture cortisone, an essential chemical in stimulating the lymph glands, which in turn manufacture antibodies and white blood cells used by the body to fight against organisms. B_6 is also important for good antibody production. Scientists have found that animals deficient in pantothenic acid and B_6 experience a sharp decline in antibody production. Even when animals are vaccinated, their immunity is not stimulated when they are thus deficient.[1] Still other studies have shown that diets lacking in B_2, B_3, folic acid, and biotin also result in a sluggish immune response to vaccinations.[2] So for immunizations to be effective, the B complex vitamins must be amply represented in a kitten's body. As a kitten struggles with stress it is these water-soluble vitamins that are used up rapidly by the body. The B complex in the food is not enough. Young cats need supplementation.

• Vitamin A, in good supply, protects the mucous membrane lining of the respiratory tract. As we will shortly see, respiratory tract ailments are major problems with kittens. If this vitamin is in short supply, millions of cells in the lining of the tract die and serve as fodder for increased bacterial activity. Vitamin A is also a necessary factor in the production of antibodies and white blood cells.

• Vitamin E also plays a vital antistress role. Pituitary hormones are dispatched in the blood to the adrenal glands. The hormones act as messengers, informing the adrenals that the body is under stress and to get cracking and produce some cortisone. There is more vitamin E concentrated in the pituitary gland than in any other part of the body and the vitamin is believed to protect, through its antioxidation power, both the pituitary and adrenal hormones. Vitamin E similarly protects the vitamin A circulating in the body.

SUDDEN INFANT DEATH

By supplementing kittens with these and other nutrients, you are going to prevent or greatly minimize the most serious health problems among kittens. For starters, you are going to protect your cats against sudden infant death, or the fading kitten syndrome, as it is sometimes called.

Sudden infant death is an insidious, mysterious baby-killer that puzzles modern medicine. Among humans, it is the leading cause of mortality from age one week to one year. Babies, kittens, pups, calves—all species—are seemingly vulnerable. Frequently with cats you will have what seem to be strong, healthy kittens, and suddenly they will die for no apparent reason. They look healthy one minute and are dead the next. I have heard of entire litters dying within days.

In the medical world there are many theories about sudden infant death. But there is little agreement. It is an ill-defined entity with multiple causes. It is usually diagnosed only after eliminating other possibilities, and the detective work involved is impaired by the speed of the disease process. The causative agent is rarely determined. In small-animal medicine, our understanding is further hampered by the tendency of most people to dispose of dead kittens and pups rather than bring them to veterinary schools or hospitals for post-mortem examinations.

One of the many theories proposed about sudden infant death concerns vitamin C. In Australia during the sixties, a district physician named Archie Kalokerinos was confronted with a sudden-death problem that was decimating aboriginal babies. When conventional methods failed, he turned to vitamin C and found it was highly effective. He virtually eliminated the problem.

Kalokerinos linked sudden infant death to a vitamin C deficiency. He contended that in a deficiency state any minor infection, or an immunization, could stress the immune system beyond its capabilities and produce a rapid death.

Among the aborigines, he found a widespread state of nutritional impoverishment. Most babies received inferior formulas and those that were nursed were getting poor quality mother's milk. The result was weakened immune systems and, all too often, sudden death.[3]

I vigorously subscribe to the nutritional theory and Kalokerinos's vitamin C connection. I feel the vitamin C status of an animal has a great deal to do with its vulnerability. Low status equals high vulnerability. High status produces low vulnerability.

The natural stresses of a pregnant queen, followed by the susceptibility of the newborn, combine to create the potential for weak immune systems and sudden death. Poor diet increases the potential.

A pregnant queen on a good supplementation program, one that includes plenty of vitamin C, will develop good immunity to pass on to her kittens. And once they are born, if the young get a daily ration of vitamin C as well, the protection is doubled. No more sudden death, or at least much less of it.

Laneen Firth, the San Jose Persian breeder who is a client of mine, conducted a little experiment on her own a number of years ago to test my concept.

"I knew of several female cats in the area who conceived and produced kittens that would never survive," recalls Firth. "The young would always die whether it was a day, a week, or a month after birth. The kittens of these queens never lived beyond a few months' time.

"I called the owners and told them I wanted to try an experiment. I would board the cats for six months in exchange for the rights to the offspring."

"'What offspring? The cats don't produce anything that lives,' the owners said.

"I told them I had heard about some pediatric multivitamin drops containing vitamin C and I wanted to try the preparation.

"They thought I was crazy, but two of the owners agreed to send their cats. The animals were from valuable lines.

"And I bred them.

"And both conceived and both produced kittens, and all the kittens lived. In fact, they are all alive and healthy today, five years later.

"As a result of this experiment, I put all my kittens on the vitamin C– based program. In my cattery, I just do not have a sudden-death or fading-kitten problem."

In 1979, I was contacted by a breeder who had serious kitten losses in one apparently weak line of cats she was trying to upgrade. She was losing 90 percent of the kittens in this line. Most of the young would live several days and then die. Those who survived would often develop a dysentery at around six weeks. The breeder was able to save some of the latter group but not all.

Exhaustive tests of her animals failed to turn up the presence of disease in the cattery. Post-mortems did not reveal any clues. This breeder even had the cat food analyzed thinking there might be something overtly toxic in there. But this was not the case.

I explained my immune concept to her. I told her that with this particularly weak line, even a modest viral challenge might be enough to kill off the tiny kittens. I suggested she add vitamin C to the already wide array of vitamins and minerals she was using. And I recommended she breed her cats again after adding the vitamin C.

She did just that, and in 1980 the kitten mortality rate was down 60 percent. The following year there were no losses at all.

Cats in this one line are still experiencing some health problems, the breeder tells me, but the incidence has been significantly reduced.

She feels that vitamin C has a great deal to do with the vastly improved situation.

I have heard of other catteries beside hers with tremendous mortality rates. Many of these problems are being blamed on the infectious peritonitis or leukemia virus. Any weak feline immune system is a playground for these deadly viruses.

Sudden death in a new kitten can also be the work of bacteria originating from the vagina, the mammary gland, or the environment. The cause of death, if a kitten is autopsied, is often described as septicemia (a systemic disease associated with the presence of microorganisms or their toxins in the blood) or pneumonia.[4] And in either case, death can be very sudden, with little indication to the owner that an illness exists.

In my practice, I am not only seeing purebred cats affected by sudden death. I see the hardier mixed breeds as well, only less frequently. This is probably because owners of mixed breeds and domestics are not as motivated as cattery proprietors who have the health of many cats and a whole business at stake.

Typically, I will receive a call from domestic owners when one or two kittens in a litter have died. Unfortunately, many of these individuals are not attuned to nutrition, so there is not too much I can do for them.

If they are willing to come in and pick up a nutritional preparation I have for kittens, they can often save the remaining cats. That is, if the survivors are not already half-dead.

UPPER RESPIRATORY DISEASE

Kittens are prone to viral infections of the upper respiratory tract which can deteriorate quickly and lead to death. One sneeze from an infected kitten can contaminate a whole litter or cattery.

This disease is a serious threat wherever you have an accumulation of animals: kennels, cat shows, pet shops, even in catteries where hygienic standards are extremely high.

Sick kittens will sneeze constantly, have runny eyes and noses, and nurse or eat very little. The meows are feeble. Such kittens can go downhill rapidly and die of dehydration, starvation, or pneumonia, and there isn't very much veterinarians can do about it.

The sneeze may not bring the average cat owner running into the veterinary hospital, but kittens with runny, pussy eyes will. This sight raises instant fear of blindness, and the owner will panic.

But a kitten with the runny eyes is already pretty sick. The virus has taken firm hold. Medical help may be of no avail. At this point a veterinarian can merely attempt to contain the accompanying bacterial infection and treat any dehydration or diarrhea that may be present. With luck and a strong constitution, a small kitten may be able to weather the viral storm.

Carolyn Bussey, a nutrition-wise breeder in Olympia, Washington, has worked up a combination of food factors she says will knock out upper respiratory sickness. It includes dessicated liver, high-protein powder, brewers' yeast, yogurt, and liberal doses of vitamins A, E, and C. Cats (kittens and adults both) tube-fed the mixture can be healed of this and other illnesses in a week's time, she says.

But Bussey adds, and I surely agree, that the idea is to prevent the upper respiratory problem in the first place. A vitamin and mineral program will prevent or greatly minimize this highly contagious disease.

If you see the signs of this illness and you bring your kittens to a veterinarian for treatment, it may already be too late.

DEHYDRATION AND DIARRHEA

Dehydration and diarrhea are not diseases. They are symptoms of diseases. Usually they are caused by a viral or bacterial condition, an incorrect diet, or toxic milk.

Whatever the cause, the effect can be devastating. A small kitten with diarrhea can lose a fatal amount of body fluids in a few hours.

If the kittens are nursing, the diarrhea problem may be due to the mother's milk. The kittens will have to be taken off the milk and fed a formula.

My best advice in any case of diarrhea with small kittens is to bring all the animals—mother included—to your veterinarian as soon as possible.

I may sound like a broken record by now, but I just cannot emphasize the point enough: You can minimize the time and expense involved with veterinarian visits and treatments by keeping the immunity of your animals high. They will not be an easy prey to viruses and bacteria that can cause diarrhea.

In my practice, I use a pediatric multivitamin preparation containing zinc. On a supplemental basis this mineral has been found to improve diarrhea in human babies.[5] Zinc, too, is an immune booster.

FEEDING

Kittens nurse for three or four weeks, a time of rapid growth. Their little bodies demand good nutrition. The mother's milk is the pillar of the kittens' health—present and future.

After a few weeks of nursing, the kittens begin to develop teeth and start grinding on the queen's teats. Under this constant barrage, the maternal instinct for nursing soon gives way. The queen starts rejecting her kittens, and the period of weaning begins.

Kittens have a great talent for imitating, and as they see their mother eating food they become curious and start nibbling themselves.

The weaning kitten can be introduced to cow's milk, baby cereal, or some kind of commercial kitty chow. For convenience, many people will use a commercial product immediately. If this is what you choose, do watch for preservatives and additives in the product and try to keep them to a minimum. Remember these are very sensitive little creatures. Supplementation during this period will protect the kittens from the sudden onset of impurities and chemicals, but do make an effort to minimize the additives.

I recommend to my clients a combination of oatmeal or baby cereal with milk. Make sure the milk is boiled and then cooled before using it. The boiling deactivates certain factors in the milk that can cause diarrhea. Do not give a young kitten milk without first boiling it. You may cause diarrhea, if you do.

It is important to keep the mixture in a liquid form. Kittens should be able to lap it up. They cannot bite and snatch up mouthfuls of food until about six weeks.

Cottage cheese can be mixed in with the cereal for added protein.

When the kittens are about six or seven weeks old, you can introduce a good quality meaty cat food. Perhaps a canned product. It can be added to the mixture. Around this time the teeth will have developed further and the kittens can handle a more solid menu.

I like to introduce good ground hamburger, slightly browned. I know some people recommend raw meat, but from my experience kittens this young have trouble with it. Some will throw up. My advice is to cook the meat until the red is out of it. Kittens seem to digest it better.

The primary purpose of supplementing the diets of preweaned kittens is to bolster their immune systems, to protect them from microorganisms. The pediatric multivitamin and mineral drops I use in my practice for preweaned cats contains vitamin C and some other key vitamins and minerals, plus protein. I feel this nutrient package delivers an optimum dose of kitten protection. However, I have found that vitamin C alone is very effective in boosting immunity. Pediatric vitamin C drops are available at your nearest drugstore.

As the kitten is weaned from mother's milk, it can also be weaned from the drops and introduced to the full spectrum of vitamins and minerals. Tablets should be crunched up and sprinkled onto the food. Do not administer whole tablets to tiny kittens. They can become lodged in the throat, and a kitten can choke to death. I have heard of people using the Heimlich Maneuver to dislodge foreign objects from the throats of big dogs—but never with wee kittens. So no tablets, please, until they are big enough to handle them. For more details on administering supplements, see Chapters Ten, Eleven, and Twelve.

BUYING KITTENS: PROCEED WITH CAUTION

One day a woman and her young daughter visited my office. The little girl was carrying a black-and-white kitten about seven or eight weeks old. The cat was a pathetic sight. It had tremendous incrustations of the skin. The hair was sparse. The eyes were pussy and running. It had a mild diarrhea.

The girl had seen the kitten in the window of a pet store during a shopping trip with her mother two days before. One look at the kitten and the child was in love. She wanted the animal, so the mother bought it for her.

I told the woman she had bought a sick cat and if possible she should return it.

"No, no," the child cried. "I want to keep it."

The mother looked at the daughter and then looked at me, and we both knew the die was cast.

"Okay," I said. "Your animal is pretty sick and I don't know if we can save him. But we'll try real hard and if you help me maybe we can pull him through."

I explained my vitamin and mineral program and told the mother how and what to administer. I treated the diarrhea, replaced lost minerals, and then gave the cat a vitamin injection to boost the immune system.

We were able to save this lucky cat. The healing process took two months and cost the woman much more than she originally paid for the animal.

There have been many similar cases in my practice over the years—but often without the happy endings.

Buying kittens from a pet shop can be a major headache. Hygienic conditions may be good in some stores, but in many they are not. Veterinarians generally have a poor opinion of pet shops. Animals are often unhealthy, have runny eyes, diarrhea, and symptoms of upper respiratory disease.

The trouble is that some owners want to invest nothing more than bare necessities in these animals. Kittens often arrive sick and remain sick.

Here in California's Santa Clara Valley, members of our local veterinary medical association will give a free examination to all animals purchased from a pet shop or humane society. If the veterinarian says the dog or cat is in poor condition, you have a right within five days to return the animal. Usually, they will give you another animal.

Although some pet shops maintain fine animals, from my experience I hve found people do better when they buy from an individual breeder. You may pay more money but you should receive some kind of guarantee for the health of the cat.

When buying kittens here are some useful tips to guide you:

1. Try to learn where the animal comes from. Kittens bred and sold in the same area tend to be healthier than animals put through the stress of travel.

2. Take a long look at the kitten and its surroundings. Is the setting clean or filthy? Filth breeds disease. Examine the animal's hair coat. Is it full-bodied and shiny? Watch for sneezing, discharges from the eyes and nose, and diarrhea. If the animal does not appear healthy, do not buy it. You want a robust, active, bright-eyed cat, not problems.

3. Make any purchase contingent upon an examination by a veterinarian. This will cost a few dollars, but the modest outlay now may save you big bills later. If the cat gets passing marks, then you can feel safe and conclude the purchase. Horses are examined before purchase, and I see no reason why this practice cannot apply to cats, especially expensive ones.

4. Know whether your new animal is a virus carrier. A veterinarian can perform the leukemia and FIP tests. The money spent is well spent. Keep in mind that a carrier showing no signs of ill health can develop fatal symptoms at any time. It is worth knowing if your animal is at risk.

5. Learn about the family history of the cat you are buying. Does the line have particular health weaknesses? Has there been a history of leukemia or FIP in the line? At least know the status of the mother. Ask to see records.

Many kittens are shipped, sold, or given away shortly after weaning. Separation from mother and litter mates and transit to a new location is a jolting form of stress for young animals.

Any change of address means coping with a change in the bacterial flora. In the pet shop, or breeder's cattery, or the dark corner of somebody's kitchen, where the kitten was born and weaned, there existed a particular population of bacteria. The bacterial environment in the new location is different. For a little animal living very close to its bacterial surroundings, the change is abrupt. This is a point overlooked by most people. We humans are a whole lot bigger than a kitten, but we can get bacterial culture shock quite readily ourselves. A trip from North America or Europe to the tropics can make you painfully aware of bacterial differences in a hurry.

In the new environment, stress is everywhere. Stress is alien bacteria. Stress is new food and new impurities. Stress is a child playing with a new kitten.

Often in this adjustment period, young cats will develop upper respiratory problems or diarrhea simply as a consequence of change.

Every veterinarian sees his share of newly acquired kittens brought in—and ailing. If the case is serious enough, I will keep the animal and treat it in my hospital. But sometimes I can send the animal home after a single treatment and instructions to the owner about using a good vitamin and mineral program. If the owner sticks to the program, I might not see the animal again except for annual immunizations.

Supplementation is the way to protect small animals from the stress of relocation. A simple program is all it takes to assist those little bodies and tiny immune systems that are under constant challenge by microorganisms.

IMMUNIZATION—INJECTED STRESS

Immunization is the next major episode of trauma a kitten faces. Around twelve weeks of age, kittens are usually taken to the veterinarian for vaccination against upper respiratory disease and distemper.

The organisms causing these diseases are injected into the kitten's body in a modified, toned-down form. In essence, the animal is receiving a mild dose of the disease. A healthy body responds by producing antibodies, which then circulate throughout the bloodstream. Should the cat become exposed at a later date to the same disease-causing organism, the antibodies are then present in the system and mobilize to fight off the invader. This is the same way smallpox and polio vaccinations work with humans.

Immunization against feline distemper has been very effective. Distemper is caused by one viral agent, and it has been isolated and modified for use in vaccines. We don't see much distemper anymore in cats.

Upper respiratory immunizations are less successful. Veterinary science has isolated three of the upper respiratory microbes and developed them for use in vaccines. They are the calici and rhinotracheitis viruses and the pneumonitis organism. However, an unknown number and variety of viral strains and microorganisms cause upper respiratory illness, just as the endless array of viruses produce "flu" in humans. It is impossible to vaccinate against all of them. So the respiratory tracts of cats continue to be targets for an "X" number of highly contagious organisms.

There is even some question whether the existing upper respiratory immunizations are effective altogether for cats living in cattery or communal settings. "Communal living" is a form of stress for felines that can undermine the potency of the vaccines. Immunizations are known not to take hold if an animal is sick or stressed. The immune system is in a weakened state and cannot produce antibodies in reaction to the vaccines. There may be yet another problem involved.

Dr. Richard Ott of Washington State University, an authority on animal immunology, has told me that some kittens have crippled immune systems as a result of feline inbreeding. Such impaired immune systems, it seems, are unable to effectively respond to vaccines, or to the actual organisms, and cannot develop the necessary health-protecting antibodies.

Whether young cats or old cats are involved, these factors may help explain why catteries, kennels, and pet shops are commonly riddled with upper respiratory disease despite immunizations. They also help explain why many a breeder or cat fancier returns from a cat show with an ailing animal even after taking all the usual precautions.

There are no vaccines as yet for leukemia or FIP. Conversely, there is some suspicion that routine immunization for upper respiratory disease and distemper may, in fact, stir up dormant leukemia or FIP viruses.

The vaccine manufacturers advise all veterinarians to immunize only healthy animals because an ill animal will not produce the antibodies. For this reason and also for the fear of leukemia and FIP, I am very cautious about immunizing cats.

I will first take the cat's temperature to make sure there is no fever. Then I ask the cat owner if the animal is acting well, eating well, if it is sneezing, if there is any diarrhea. If there are any symptoms whatsoever, even the slightest skin problem, I will not vaccinate. And this happens frequently.

"Come back when the animal is healthy," I will tell the owner. "Right now the vaccine will not do any good and it can possibly do some harm."

A good nutritional maintenance program will build a healthier animal, and when the time comes for immunization, a cat's immune system will respond.

STRONG COLLAGEN FOR GOOD GROWTH

Kittenhood is a period of extreme and concentrated growth. We humans take a leisurely fifteen or so years to do what a cat accomplishes in one.

This pell-mell growth is a constant form of stress to the young kitten who also has to face the many artificial stresses inflicted by man. In this turmoil, the natural output of vitamin C is severely taxed and an animal's normal health and growth can suffer.

Earlier, I introduced you to the biochemical substance called collagen, the intercellular cement that binds the tissues of the body. Collagen provides the framework for muscles, organs, bones, and teeth. It gives form and substance. The production of good collagen is dependent upon the availability of abundant vitamin C.

Laneen Firth tells me her Persian kittens are all heavier, stronger, and more muscled as a result of the supplementation program.

"No fluff," she says. "Only substance."

When her blue Persian male, named "Fajur," won the best kitten award at the 1980 American Shorthair West Show in San Francisco, one of the judges was so impressed with the solid appearance of the cat he asked in jest if Firth was feeding it lead.

Of course, the sick cats I see in my practice are on the opposite end of the health scale.

I remember once a gray domestic, about a year old, brought in for a neuter. This cat had been sick for most of its life. It had had upper respiratory disease and diarrhea and poor appetite. It had very few teeth in its mouth and the fangs were underdeveloped. It was small for its age. Poor collagen production obviously. What if an animal like this had been on a good program?

Thea Sutherland, a Washington State breeder, told me about a kitten who had an apparent collagen problem. One of the hind legs was deformed and actually seemed to be atrophying. The animal was running and playing on three legs.

Sutherland put the kitten on 1000 milligrams of vitamin C (sodium ascorbate) a day. She mixed it into the animal's food.

"I never expected what happened," she told me. "Within a week's time the cat's leg literally had grown back to the size of the other legs. Within two weeks it was walking and running as normally as any other cat. This sounds like a miracle, but I saw it with my own eyes."

I cannot promise that vitamin C will turn your cats into champions. Or, à la Charles Atlas, transform every runt into a he-cat. But it will build better bodies and contribute to optimal size and health. All the vitamins and minerals involved in the formation of collagen benefit by the presence of extra vitamin C. The vitamin C acts as a catalyst. It makes them do their job better in laying down and filling out the matrix of collagen throughout the body.

TIPS FOR KITTENHOOD

1. Maintain the lactating queen on vitamins and minerals. She has a special need for more nutrients. Her own good health and the good health of the kittens are on the line.

2. Supplement as early as possible—from the day the kittens are born or the day of purchase.

3. If purchasing an animal from a pet shop, finalize the deal only after an examination by a veterinarian and confirmation of a healthy cat. This will save you problems later on.

4. No matter from whom you buy your kitten, have the animal tested for leukemia and FIP.

5. It is an old wives' tale about not touching new kittens. Supposedly the human scent makes them *persona non grata* to the queen. You can handle them, but carefully, to help any of the small creatures get their fair share of milk if they are being crowded out. And you can also handle them to administer the pediatric vitamin drops as early as two hours after birth.

6. But do not let others handle the kittens. All the fondling should wait until at least five weeks. People carry organisms that can infect a vulnerable kitten. Furthermore, bacteria vary from person to person. The kittens have a hard enough time as it is adjusting to local bacteria. Do not add to the burden. The kittens may be cuddly, but they are also very vulnerable.

7. Do not allow kittens outside until they have been immunized. Outside your front door are legions of what we call "street viruses" just waiting to attack a young, vulnerable kitten.

8. Do not immunize a kitten if it is sick. A sick kitten will not develop immunity and can become even more weakened from the effects of the vaccines.

9. Keep kittens out of drafts. In wintertime especially, cold drafts can sweep in under closed doors and lead to upper respiratory problems.

8

How Supplements Help
Adult Cats

In my practice I see them all. Mixed breeds. Strays. Street-tough toms. Pampered parlor cats. Bluebloods. National champions.

No matter what the pedigree, or lack of it, and no matter if an animal is in the running for cat of the year or just running around the backyard, each and every one seems to benefit from improved nutrition.

For example, let's take the average domestic tom, the outdoor prowler, the tough guy who goes tooth and claw against any and all territorial intruders.

A woman came into my hospital with such a cat. A big two-year-old tom. The cat had been in a fight four or five months previously and suffered a nasty gash on the right side. The injury had become infected and abscessed.

The woman first brought the cat to another veterinarian, who did all the right things. The veterinarian opened the abscess, drained it, cleaned it out, applied an antibiotic, inserted a latex Penrose tube for further draining, sewed up the cat, and dispensed a liquid antibiotic to be given daily.

A few weeks later the woman and the cat were back in the veterinarian's office. The abscess had returned. The veterinarian reopened and cleaned the wound, applied the antibiotic, and closed the wound with a drain. Again he dispensed a daily dose of antibiotic.

The treatment was totally adequate and it should have worked. But it didn't. Several weeks later the abscess was back in force.

The woman decided to try another veterinarian. Since I was in the neighborhood, she brought the cat to me. I listened to her story and then checked the cat out.

"It seems to me your cat may have an immune-response problem," I told her. "The antibiotic works for the moment and when it is used up the infection returns. Your cat just doesn't have the immune-system strength to knock out this infection once and for all."

I explained to her the importance of nutrition in stimulating optimal immune response and suggested she try a vitamin and mineral program. She said she was willing.

So I repeated the same procedure as the other veterinarian and sent the woman home with some supplements.

The abscess did not return.

The woman has been a client now for six years. She faithfully keeps her tom on the program, and the only time I see the animal is for routine annual vaccinations.

Another client of mine had a black tom who was a regular brawler. This cat was always in a fight. A couple of times a year I would have to treat the animal for infected wounds.

One time the wound abscessed so badly that pus spilled into the bloodstream causing secondary infections elsewhere in the body. We call this condition pyemia. It can be fatal.

The woman who owned this cat believed that animals take care of themselves and do not need any vitamins. It took quite awhile before I could convince her to try my program.

She called one day to say the cat had been in another fight, had suffered a wound, and would I look at it. She said she had squeezed out the pus herself, as she had done in the past, but still wanted medical attention since she feared the wound might abscess. The animal had now been on the program for several months.

I told her to wait a day or two and see how the wound progressed. If the infection grew, she was to come in with the animal.

She called in two days to say the wound was healing nicely and there was no problem. I feel the supplements improved the animal's self-healing capability.

I remember another cat who had a massive abscess on one whole side of his face. He had taken a bad beating in a fight. When everything had been cleaned away there was little or no skin left in that

area. With a standard treatment plus the vitamin and mineral program the cat healed in short order, leaving, I might add, only a very
small scar.

The scratch-and-bite routine of cat fights inevitably results in
hordes of bacteria being deposited into injured tissue. And there, if an
animal's defenses are low, the bacteria can multiply rapidly into a
painful infection and pus-ridden abscess.

The extra vitamins and minerals keep the defenses strong. In addition, zinc and vitamins A, C, and E speed the healing process.

If you want to help your wounded warrior even further, try applying the sticky sap of an aloe vera plant on the injury. Scientists have
found that aloe vera has the ability to hold infection in check while
promoting the growth of new, healthy cells at a wound site. It works
for the superficial wounds, cuts, and burns suffered by humans and it
helps with pet wounds as well. Sometimes called the "first aid plant,"
aloe vera is used to decorate many homes and apartments and can be
bought for a few dollars at most nurseries or health-food stores. They
are very handy to have around the house.

I frequently see the casualties of cat fights in my practice. The
people who maintain their animals on a good nutritional program are
often surprised how fast the wounds heal. There are fewer complications. Unsupplemented cats seem to experience more problems and
take longer to heal.

Now let's look at the glamour pusses, the show cats.

Every breeder knows all too well that shows are extremely stressful
on cats. An animal not in robust health and able to tolerate the stress is
an easy mark for the upper respiratory viruses that habituate the
show circuit. A viral illness can easily sideline a cat for weeks, if not
more. What's worse, an animal can carry the disease back home and
contaminate a whole cattery.

Because of this danger, many breeders take no chances and step up
the vitamin and mineral intake of their cats during the campaign
season. Gerrie Raicevich, whose copper-eyed white Persian "Ice
Angel" was the Cat Fanciers' Association's second-best cat in the
United States in 1982, keeps her campaigners strong with three different kinds of multivitamins and minerals.

"When I bring a cat home from a show, I put it in its cage, give it
food and water, and it will sleep the whole day," she says. "The cat is

exhausted. Shows really stress them and especially now with the multiple format where cats can be judged sometimes six times a day and handled over thirty times. That's a lot of stress.

"For a show cat it is not enough just to be beautiful. The animal has to be strong. It has to have tremendous health."

For any campaigning cat, I routinely recommend 1,000 milligrams of vitamin C daily, along with a regular pet multivitamin and mineral product. This combination will provide solid protection against stress and "show viruses."

I am always pleased when clients tell me how their cats have hurdled through kittenhood without any of the common blowups. The animals have been on a supplement program for a year or so and are strong, alert, and energetic young creatures.

If all goes well and they are not banged up in an accident or a cat fight or fall victim to a parasitic infestation, then I usually do not see them very often. Perhaps once a year for an immunization or whenever a breeder requires a health certificate to ship for breeding purposes.

Let's say you have a cat who has not been on the program. He is apparently healthy, or not so healthy, or downright ailing. The idea now is to jack him up to optimal health. You want to protect him against all the typical dangers that menace adult cats. You want to protect him against leukemia, FIP, and upper respiratory illness, the leading viral killers. You want to prevent the blockages and cystitises that develop in many adult cats. You want to protect him from skin problems, from dental problems, and from the impurities and chemicals in the food he eats and the air he breathes.

You can do all these things by starting an effective prevention program. In Chapters Ten, Eleven, and Twelve, I tell you what to buy and how to gradually build up the nutritional status of your cat. It is simple to do. Start the program and be surprised by the wonderful changes you see!

SPAYS AND NEUTERS

Any surgical procedure, including the common spay and neuter, is a severe form of stress that can open the door to feline leukemia. This fact is well known in veterinary medicine.

One of the cases I experienced involved a pretty white female cat brought in for spaying. The operation had been thoroughly routine. At least I thought so until the owner called a week later and said her cat was sick. She wondered if the spaying had something to do with it.

I told the woman to let me see the cat.

Upon examination there were no signs of surgical complications. The incision was healing in a satisfactory manner.

But I did notice the cat's gums, tongue, and the lining of the ears were colored a very pale pink, almost white. The temperature was subnormal.

What I feared most had indeed happened. The cat had leukemia, and the chances for survival were slim.

I explained to the shocked woman what I thought had occurred. Her animal had probably been a carrier of the leukemia virus. The virus was in a passive state and the cat's natural defenses had held it in check. However, the stress of surgery had been a severe drain on the immune system, and during postoperative weakness, the leukemia organism sprang into life and quickly engulfed the cat. Unfortunately, there was little I could do for the animal, and it eventually died even with treatment.

In my practice this sequence of events has happened at least a half-dozen times, and there likely have been other cases where the owners did not bother to call.

I belong to a local spay and neuter program. Many cat owners bring their animals in to me for the one-time operation. They are not regular clients who follow my nutritional program and, in general, they are not even willing to spend the twenty dollars to have their animals tested for leukemia.

I inform these individuals they are taking a chance if they do not test. I feel they should be aware of the possible consequences.

I firmly believe in this test. I think it should be performed on a cat at least once a year. This way you have a periodic reading on how your animal is resisting the leukemia virus. The test should definitely be done before a spay or neuter operation. If the test shows the presence of the virus, you should not operate.

My regular clients who test before neutering and who maintain their animals on a good supplement program never have deathly sick cats after surgery.

Neutering is a major cause of obesity in cats. The male has been castrated, the testes removed. The female has been spayed, the ovaries removed. The removal of these reproductive glands directly affects fat metabolism. This is because the hormonal secretions— testosterone of the testes, estrogen of the ovaries—are involved in the body's utilization of fat. Without them there is a greater fat deposition in the tissues. In a large percentage of cases, four to six months after the operation you begin to see your cat getting fat.

Some veterinarians feel they can control the weight of these de-sexed animals by limiting the quantity of food intake—cutting down the daily ration. I personally have not had good luck trying to hold down the weight of animals through a restrictive diet. And frankly, I do not feel this approach is good for an animal's health.

When you cut down on the amount of food, you are also cutting down on the amount of vitamins and minerals and other nutrients. As a result of decreased nutrient intake, these animals may be more susceptible to disease. I have seen several cases where animals put on "reducing diets" developed skin, liver, and kidney problems.

Better a cat be chubby than sick.

I suggest to pet owners they simply allow the animal to eat what it needs because most cats will not gorge themselves. The neutered animal will not eat any more than the nonneutered animal.

Any cat embarking on a reducing diet will benefit from extra vitamins and minerals. They compensate for the lost nutrition.

And here is another good reason. The sex hormones have a great influence on the production of adrenal cortisone. And cortisone, you may recall, governs the production of antibodies by the lymph glands. The antibodies, of course, are a vital element in protection against disease. So by taking away a link in this biochemical chain, you create an animal who is potentially more susceptible to illness.

Supplementation can compensate for this as well. Make sure your program includes pantothenic acid, one of the B complex vitamins, and vitamin C. They both have the ability to keep the cortisone machinery humming.

HYPER CATS

Hyperactivity is not the exclusive habit of children. Animals can become hyper and irritable as well, and veterinarians are sometimes asked to treat aggressive, nervous pets.

Just as in humans, hyperactivity in animals can stem from a variety of causes. In cats, the problem could lie in a genetic flaw due to excessive inbreeding or in the indoor confinement of an animal who is by nature an outdoor roamer. Physical discomfort, chronic infections, environmental allergies, and the presence of parasites can also cause a cat to lose his customary cool.

If an animal seems to be in good health, then there is a good possibility that diet may be the problem. More and more veterinarians are turning to nutrition as a common cause of hyperactivity.

There has been little veterinary research into the dietary connection to abnormal behavior in companion animals. However, the human experience has given us much guidance.

"Hyperactive children, for instance, have often been helped by cutting out all foods with various synthetic additives, as well as many processed foods and foods which may aggravate allergies," says *Prevention* magazine's pet columnist, Dr. Richard Pitcairn. "I feel such products may well contribute to animal hyperactivity also.

"I think it is only prudent to feed a behaviorally disturbed animal, at the least, a natural diet free of synthetic additives and excessive processing, supplemented with basic vitamins and minerals."

Pitcairn has suggested a "Diet for Behavior Disturbances," composed of one-half protein sources (meat, fish, dairy, soy, eggs), one-quarter cooked whole grains (oatmeal, barley, rice, buckwheat, millet, etc., with milk and honey added), and one-quarter steamed or grated raw vegetables.

If time does not allow following the total program, he advises using a high-quality dry food free of additives and coloring agents for half of the diet. The remainder can be drawn from the above-mentioned items and especially vegetables, eggs, and oatmeal.[1]

Many of the hyperactive children helped by dietary changes have been following the so-called Feingold Diet. This is the additive-free diet formulated by the late Dr. Benjamin Feingold, who originated the hypothesis that ingestion of preservatives and artificial food colors produces adverse behavioral reactions in some children. Since 1973, the year of Feingold's pronouncement, medical researchers have been testing his theory with variable results, some supportive, some inconclusive.

In one interesting study, researchers found that artificial coloring used in many processed foods triggered behavioral changes in twelve out of fifteen diagnosed hyperactive children. The reactions included restlessness, defiance, boisterousness, irrationality, and physical aggressiveness.[2]

In a 1978 experiment with rat pups, researchers found that a mixture of common commercial food colorings contributed to hyperactivity and impaired the performance of the animals during intelligence tests.

"Our results suggest that the administration of food colorings may affect normal development," they said. The scientists recommended a continued critical investigation of the effects of food colorings in both animals and children.[3]

Could the dyes in processed pet food contribute to hyperactivity and other problems in sensitive cats and dogs? I think so. It would be foolish in my opinion to think that the dyes and all the other chemical additives are perfectly harmless. Veterinarian Carvel Tiekert of Bel Air, Maryland, feels the same way.

"Getting off of commercial diets and their chemicals has proven in some cases to tone down cats quite nicely," he has told me. "If that does not work we will suggest the owner use a high-potency B complex vitamin.

"Some of the animals respond by the dietary change alone, some respond to the high B complex given with commercial diets, and some have required both removal of chemicals and the high dose of B.

"Of course, there are some animals that simply do not respond at all, but our results have been rather successful."

Veterinarians Robert and Marty Goldstein of Yorktown Heights, New York, report helping aggressive and hyperactive animals with an approach similar to Tiekert's.

In addition to the B complex, which has a calming effect on the nervous system, Tiekert, Pitcairn, and the Goldsteins also recommend the other essential vitamins and minerals.

Vitamin C and zinc, for instance, can help the body get rid of unwanted lead. This toxic mineral tends to accumulate in kidney, liver, and bone tissue and also has a harmful effect on the normal operation of nerve cells. Lead has thus been linked to nervous disorders, emotional disturbances, and irritability.

Lead, of course, is ubiquitous. It's in the air, in the ground, and in the food. Canned food products, especially those containing liver and kidney, can be particularly high in lead content. Another source for the cat may be household or street dust which acts as a catchall for airborne particles of lead. The dust settles on a cat's fur, and spiffy creature that he is, he licks himself clean and absorbs the lead. Old, peeling, or chalking lead-based paint can be picked up the same way. For this reason it's a good idea to remove the cat from the area if you are remodeling or sanding painted surfaces in the house.

Over the years medical researchers have discovered that nutritional deficiencies can cause both major and minor mental disturbances in humans. They have also found that certain people are genetically in need of extra special nutrient needs. Human patients have been helped through individually designed nutritional therapies including large doses of vitamin C and some of the B vitamins. It stands to reason that nutrient deficiencies or special needs in pets could also result in behavior problems. Thus you have another good reason to follow a thorough supplement program.

Los Angeles veterinarian Alfred Plechner specializes in small-animal allergy problems and he feels that beef and tuna are major feline allergens that contribute, among other things, to bizarre behavior and epilepsy. Many commercial kibbles can also be offensive to cats, he says.

If you have a hyperactive animal, consider switching to a homemade diet or to products that do not contain chemical additives. Read the labels. Some of the products I can personally recommend are Cornucopia, made by Veterinary Nutritional Associates in Huntington, New York; Nature's Recipe, distributed by Earth Elements, Inc., of Orange, California; and Tyrrell's of Seattle, Washington.

In addition to dietary changes, keep your animal on a solid vitamin and mineral program.

POISONED CATS

A good nutrition program, and particularly one that includes vitamin C, helps a cat survive in this modern age of chemistry. A supplemented cat is better able to withstand the harmful effects of the many poisons present in his environment and the poisons foisted upon him by well-meaning owners.

According to Dr. William B. Buck, a veterinary toxicologist at the University of Illinois, companion animals in both rural and urban settings are frequently poisoned by organic insecticides.

Buck told a 1978 gathering of the American Veterinary Medical Association that compared with livestock, "dogs and especially cats are relatively susceptible to poisoning.

"Their fastidious grooming habits predispose them to toxicoses (poisoning). Cats often walk through lawns or flower gardens that have been recently sprayed, and then promptly lick the insecticide from their feet and fur. They also tend to lick themselves after they have been sprayed or dipped in insecticides."[4]

Flea and tick collars are actually insecticide strips. This means an animal is wearing a dose of poison twenty-four hours a day around his neck, an extremely sensitive area of the body. I have seen many felines with angry bands of irritated, red skin around the neck.

The use of collars can actually lower the resistance of animals to more acute exposures of insecticides, such as the administration of organophosphate and carbamate compounds for worming. Furthermore, the simultaneous use of a collar and application of a worming treatment or flea dip can overload a cat's system and result in poisoning.

According to Buck, chlorine compounds including organochlorine insecticides such as DDT and chlordane are extremely toxic to a cat. Poisoning from these chemicals have primarily resulted from bathing or dipping in excessive concentrations.

Clinical signs of organochlorine poisoning are hyperexcitability, exaggerated responses to touch, light, and sound, tremors, whole-body spasms, and violent seizures. These symptoms can last twenty-four to forty-eight hours from time of exposure until death or recovery.

Organochlorine compounds have largely been banned or restricted from the market because of their ability to remain potent for long periods of time in the environment or body tissue.

The phasing out of organochlorines has been accompanied by the phasing in of organophosphate and carbamate insecticide compounds. They are actually more toxic than organochlorines but have a shorter active life and thus are regarded more acceptable for general use. However, because of their wider use, they are responsible for most of the present poisoning incidences. Some of the common compounds belonging to this group are carbaryl, Sevin, methyl carbamate, Vapona, dichlorvos, ronnel, diazinon, parathion, and the famous malathion that was sprayed in many parts of California to rid us of fruit fly infestation. These compounds are used in dips, collars, powders, sprays, and mange and worming preparations.

Symptoms of poisoning include profuse salivation, vomiting, diarrhea, hyperactivity, twitching of the muscles of the face, eyelids, tongue, and the general musculature, labored breathing, and a systemic rigidity.[5]

Happily, there are some nontoxic alternatives available to deal with parasites. I will talk more about them in separate chapters on skin problems (fleas) and worms. As far as environmental poisons are concerned, you can help your animal protect itself by making sure your supplementation program includes extra vitamin C. Earlier in the book, in the vitamin C chapter, I explained how this vitamin has the ability to neutralize many toxins that enter the body. It markedly affects the toxicity of more than fifty different pollutants, insecticides among them.

Chlordane, one of the organochlorines, acts primarily on the nervous system, causing hyperexcitability, tremors, and convulsions. It also produces degenerative changes in the liver, kidney, spleen, and heart. Vitamin C has been shown to counteract the effects of this poison, which is extremely toxic to cats.

In an experiment with rats, one group of animals given chlordane suffered a 43 percent mortality rate. A second group was given the chlordane and vitamin C. Mortality was zero, growth retardation was considerably minimized, and while the vitamin could not protect all the damaged organs, it was observed to have reversed some of the degenerative changes in kidney tissues.[6]

Vitamin C obviously will not resolve every case of poisoning. But it is my opinion that if the treatment of poisoned animals includes vitamin C, the chances for survival are increased.

Two cases may demonstrate the restorative powers of vitamin C for poisoned cats.

One involved a local cat fancier who contacted me one evening. She desperately wanted help for her severely ill Siamese. The cat had been seen by two veterinarians, and both felt it had been exposed to a poison, which they could not identify. The cat was unable to walk, was subnormal in temperature, had no appetite, and showed general weakness.

The woman followed a nutritional program herself and had heard about my interest in nutrition and vitamins. She asked if I thought vitamin C could be of help.

I told her I could not ethically recommend a therapy without discussing the case with her veterinarian. She understood and asked her veterinarian to call me. He gave me the case history and admitted he did not know how to treat this perplexing situation. I suggested a specific vitamin C approach, and he said he would try it. A few days later the cat fancier called to say her cat had recovered.

The other case involved Virginia breeder Ann Ransom's "Party Girl," a white copper-eyed Persian judged the sixth best cat in the United States in 1978–79.

According to Ransom, there was a spate of mysterious poisonings at major cat shows on the East Coast during that year and the year before. Leading campaigners for the top awards were being poisoned without the perpetrator or the type of poison used ever being uncovered.

The day after a show, a prostrate "Party Girl" was found throwing up blood, bleeding from the rectum, with eyes widely dilated, and unable to stand. The cat was rushed to the veterinarian, who said the animal had been poisoned.

"This cat was in very serious shape, and I didn't think we would be able to save her," recalls Ransom. "The veterinarian treated her and advised me to give her a great deal of attention and keep the lights on at night, because a cat in this condition will crawl into a dark corner and give up.

"We did manage to save 'Party Girl,' but I never thought we would have any kittens from her, for two reasons. One is that I had campaigned her heavily, two or more shows a month for over a year. This puts a tremendous amount of stress on cats. Females campaigned so vigorously and for so long generally do not conceive.

"The second reason was the poisoning. Other cats poisoned at these shows were unable to sire or conceive afterward.

"My cat was poisoned in January, and in March I placed her on a vitamin and mineral product containing a substantial amount of vitamin C. In April we tried to breed her, but she didn't conceive. But the next time she came into season she conceived and has now produced two litters of fine, healthy kittens. One of her offspring is a top campaigner with whom we have reached fifteen finals out of sixteen shows.

"Frankly, I think it is remarkable we were able to build up 'Party Girl' so that she could conceive."

I have not discussed dosages in this section because I do not believe anyone besides a veterinarian should treat an animal for acute poisoning. If any veterinarian is interested enough to contact me, I will be glad to share the details of my therapeutic approach.

If your animal shows signs of poisoning, bring it immediately to a veterinarian. If possible, take along any evidence of the source of poisoning, such as a container or package.

TRANSPORTATION

Conditions for shipping animals over long distances by air have improved in recent years; however, travel is still a form of intense stress. The health certificate signed by a veterinarian and required by the airlines guarantees that animals leave in good shape. How they arrive is another matter.

A cat or dog may spend eight or more frightening hours confined inside a dark shipping kennel, exposed to fluctuating and even extreme temperatures and a variety of strange sights, sounds, and handling. The trauma of shipment often creates woeful, nervous arrivees suffering from diarrhea, vomiting, sneezing, dehydration, and loss of appetite.

Clients who administer a supplement program are not beset with the transportation blues. One such client is Laneen Firth of San Jose, who does a great deal of shipping and receiving of cats in connection with her breeding business. Her experience is that supplemented cats fly through the air with the greatest of ease.

"The stress factor in shipping is astronomical," she says. "It can kill a cat, especially a highly bred animal who tends to be more sensitive in the first place.

"Cats not on a good program often arrive with a cold or an upper respiratory virus of some degree. Sometimes it takes days before some cats will calm down enough so they can be handled. Generally I have to keep such cats two or three months before I can breed them. Regardless of whether they cycle or not, I will not breed them until they are fit.

"Cats on a good program arrive healthy and happy and glad to see a human being. They adjust easily to the new surroundings."

No matter how a cat travels, whether air, rail, or car, a good supplement program will minimize the apprehension and stress involved. It's good travel insurance.

I personally do not believe in tranquilizers for traveling animals. I have seen where they work in reverse, actually causing animals to thrash around and become exhausted. Tranquilizers can also make breathing more difficult.

WEATHERPROOFING

Cats can tolerate hotter temperatures better than dogs and people. In fact, cats usually look for the warmest spot to settle into. This characteristic probably has something to do with their desert origin. It doesn't mean, however, that a cat enjoys being left in a closed car on a hot day. Even if you open the window a little, the temperature can rise rapidly and make life miserable for an animal. A cat left in a carrier inside a hot car can easily suffocate. So beware when traveling with cats in hot weather. It's advisable to take the cat with you, in its carrier if need be, rather than leaving it to roast in the car.

The feline affinity for warmth can sometimes cause problems. During the colder time of the year, outdoor cats will sometimes climb up under the hood of parked cars and snuggle into the still warm area between the radiator and engine block. Over the years I have treated more than a hundred cats cut up to one degree or another when an unsuspecting motorist turned the key.

Vitamins and minerals obviously won't help a cat in this predicament but they can help to weatherproof an animal from the cold. Cats are not able to withstand cold weather as well as a dog. A cat put out in the cold will have a lowered resistance and be more prone to street viruses. Every fall and winter I see a parade of cats suffering from pneumonia and pleurisy and upper respiratory ailments as a result of exposure. And I live in northern California where the winters are much milder than back east.

Cats exposed to cold weather benefit greatly from a supplement program. In scientific experiments, extra vitamin C and pantothenic acid have been shown to be highly protective for both humans and animals exposed to cold. The chances of coming down with viruses and pneumonias are lessened.

I advise clients not to let cats stay out overnight or for hours at a time during the cold months. A few minutes is okay, but bring them back in as soon as possible. Letting them out to roam in the cold is invitation to trouble.

BOARDED CATS

In the early days of my practice I used to board animals in order to earn extra income. I stopped doing that after one particular incident involving several boarded cats. These cats were doing fine until a new cat came onto the scene. This animal had a mild illness and was sneezing. In a couple of days all the other cats were sneezing, and I wound up having to treat them all. That's all it takes—one cat with one sneeze.

When you go away on vacation or business and have to board your cat in a kennel, you are leaving behind one very unhappy animal. The cat is going to be very disenchanted about removal from routine and familiar surroundings. This will be a stressful situation for him.

Stress, as we have seen, depletes the water-soluble vitamins—B complex and C. When these are in low supply in the body, the stage is set for illness.

Kennels are parade grounds for upper respiratory viruses and other health-threatening organisms, no matter how hygienic the premises are kept.

Cats in a stressed condition, in a setting with other cats, are suscep-tible to these contagious organisms.

Remember what I said earlier about the limitations of immuniza-tion. Many people will immunize their cats before they board them. That is no guarantee of immunity. There are any number of viruses producing upper respiratory problems. Only three of them have been isolated and modified for use as vaccines. Furthermore, the vaccines may not produce the desired results in a stressed animal. So it is virtually impossible to get full protection against this common kennel problem by immunizing.

Your best bet is to immunize and follow a supplement program. This will give an animal maximum coverage against the threat of kennel disease.

TIPS FOR ADULTHOOD

1. Obviously, supplement your animals' diets. Do not forget the vitamin C. It's the key to maximum protection and optimal health.

2. When the weather is cold or rainy, bring your outdoor cat inside, where it is warm and dry. This will minimize the risk of upper respiratory illness.

3. In very hot climates, make sure your cat has enough fresh water.

4. Have your cats tested annually for viral leukemia and feline infectious peritonitis (FIP).

9

How Supplements Help
Aging Cats

One of the most unforgettable cats I ever treated was "Jake," an orange tabby with big jowls à la television's celebrated "Morris."

"Jake" was about ten going on fifty when I first saw him. He was fat, lethargic, had a thin, rough hair coat, and an ugly abscess on his jaw.

The woman who brought him in said she was taking care of the old cat after neighbors had abandoned him. She described "Jake" as a timid weakling who was always being bullied by neighborhood cats, particularly two younger, more virile toms. They harassed him even to the point of chasing him away from the food she put out for him.

"When he sees either of the other cats coming, he takes off and jumps up on a fence, a safe distance away," she said. "A couple of times the other cats have pushed him away from the feeding bowl and old 'Jake' just slunk away. It was pathetic."

As far as the abscess was concerned, the woman said that "Jake" apparently had fought back recently and had suffered a wound which was now badly infected.

While I was treating him, I decided he was a prime candidate for vitamin E.

The time was around 1970, before I had become deeply involved with supplements other than vitamin C. I was already familiar, however, with the ability of vitamin E to promote youthful vigor in older people and animals.

My practice at this time primarily involved canines, and one thing I had observed for several years was an apparent drop in the vitality of dogs after they reached three years or so of age. When the animals reached five or six, they seemed to be much older than their years—in appearance and energy. They acted ten or eleven. This was a general impression I had. I felt something was wrong. Something had to be wrong. It did not seem normal to me.

I began looking around for ways to rejuvenate these "old-young" dogs. I had read about the work done by the Shute brothers in Canada with mice and people and vitamin E, and I was particularly interested in how they could seemingly reverse the aging process or at least slow it down. I thought I would try vitamin E with dogs and see what happened. I did try it and I observed a tremendous change in animals. Shute, as a dog breeder, noticed the same thing with his dogs. So did Dr. N. H. Lambert, the Irish veterinarian, who put old, ailing hunting dogs back into the field with vitamin E.

The good results I was having with dogs prompted me to eventually try vitamin E on old cats as well. If it worked for dogs why not for cats? So whenever I had a geriatric cat to treat, I would suggest vitamin E to the owner. "Jake" was one of the first cat cases in which I used vitamin E.

I asked his owner if she would be willing to try a little experiment with vitamin E. I said the vitamin might give the cat more strength to defend himself against the other toms.

She said okay, so we put the old boy on something like 100 IUs of vitamin E a day.

A few weeks later the woman called to report that her decrepit cat was turning into a tiger.

"He fights back now and wins," she said, obviously pleased with the transformation. "What's more, he is showing interest in females which he never did before. He's on the constant prowl, whereas before all he did was just lie around."

Months later, the woman called again to say she believed that "Jake" had impregnated a neighbor's cat who had duly produced a litter.

"How do you know it was 'Jake'?" I wanted to know.

"Well, the kittens were orange and look like him," she said.

"If that's the truth, then it seems like the vitamin E really rejuvenated that old cat of yours," I said.

I then suggested we put the vitamin E to a test.

"Take the cat off the vitamin for a while and let's see what happens," I said.

In two or three weeks the woman called and said "Jake" was going in reverse and slipping back to his old decrepit self.

"It seems pretty clear the vitamin was really helping him," I said. "Start it again now and see if he perks up once more."

Ten days or so later she called and reported that he had reversed field again. His vitality was back.

Since the days of "Jake" I have become a staunch advocate of supplementation for old cats. Not only vitamin E but the whole team of vitamins and minerals. All the nutrients on the team are needed to promote youthful vigor and give aging organs the nutritional boost they need to keep operating at the best possible level.

In my experience, vitamins E and C are the keys. They seem to stand out the most in helping older animals, both cats and dogs.

In my prevention program I step up the amount of vitamin E for cats five years and older to 50 International Units a day. The vitamin C level remains the same as the regular adult dose: 500–750 milligrams daily.

C AND E—THE AGE FIGHTERS

Let's see how these two particular vitamins work to slow down the aging process.

First, vitamin E.

Down at the microscopic level of the cells, life is a battlefield. Enemies abound: viruses, bacteria, toxic chemical molecules. If nutrition is good, the cells are strong. If nutrition is poor, the cells are weak.

The challenge is constant. Strong cells can fight off the bad guys but the weaker ones are often mowed down. Over the years the toll of dead and wounded cells mounts.

Scientists have known for some time that one of the primary factors in this aging battle is the oxidation process. Oxygen is vital for life, and yet when oxygen molecules react with vital fatty membranes and components that are present in each cell, these parts are said to undergo "peroxidation" and become damaged. In essence, the fatty parts become rancid and atrophy. The function of enzymes and proteins and other minuscule mechanisms inside the living and working cell is impaired. Eventually the cell can stop functioning altogether.

The process multiplies. More and more cells are knocked out. Tissues deteriorate, become more susceptible to microorganisms and toxins, or become hardened and lifeless. Systems go awry and fail. Death follows.

Scientists have measured the tempo of this degenerative process. They have observed it in the tissue of the heart, blood vessels, brain, muscle, liver, adrenal glands, and reproductive organs. The scientists have also seen how vitamin E, a fat-soluble substance, mixes right into the fatty cellular parts and protects them from peroxidation. What happens is that vitamin E actually sacrifices itself to the oxygen molecule to form a harmless compound.

(In the biochemical scheme of things, vitamin E is the first line of defense against the peroxidation of fatty cellular structures. Scientists say, however, that even with adequate vitamin E some peroxidation takes place. The mineral selenium has been found to act as an intimate backup to E. It helps form an enzyme that stops this destructive process before any damage can be done.[1])

A number of animal studies have demonstrated the life-protecting ability of vitamin E. Dr. L. H. Chen of the University of Kentucky has shown the effect of vitamin E on the age-related increase of oxidative damage to liver cells.

Vitamin E was added to the diet of laboratory mice of all ages and it indeed reduced peroxidation of the cells. But the amount of vitamin E sufficient to protect the liver in young and adult mice was not enough to protect the liver from peroxidation in very old mice, Chen noted. This was because the rate of peroxidation increases with age. A higher level of supplementation was thus necessary to provide protection against the ravages of accelerated geriatric peroxidation.

"There is an increased requirement of vitamin E as aging progresses in order to protect tissue from peroxidation," Chen suggested. "It is possible that in animals of older ages, vitamin E or another antioxidant is required in relatively larger quantity in order to slow down the oxidative deterioration of tissues and thus prolong the life span."[2]

Chen said this might easily apply to aging humans. I certainly feel it applies to aging cats and dogs.

In another study with laboratory animals, the vitamin E requirement of rats 49 weeks of age was calculated to be 67 times greater than rats 9 to 11 weeks old.[3]

The nutrient requirements as formulated by the NRC do not take into consideration whether an animal is adult or aged. The recommendation is the same for both. What is in my mind a questionable standard for the adult may be a downright deficiency level for the aged animal.

In addition to the antioxidant power of vitamin E, here are other reasons why vitamin E benefits old animals:

1. Vitamin E, above basic levels, enhances transportation of nutrients to the far reaches of the body. In effect, it is like using a semitrailer truck to deliver the goods instead of a small pickup truck. The result of this improved transportation is better circulation and a heart that doesn't have to work so hard to pump blood and all the nutrient constituents in blood to the extremities.

2. The efficiency of the immune system declines with age. Studies with mice have shown that old animals have only a quarter or even less the immune response of younger animals. In one experiment, the addition of vitamin E to the diet of mice was found to invigorate the failing immune system.[4]

3. Vitamin E can help protect cats against steatitis, the painful disease of fatty tissue that can result from diets high in the unsaturated fats of fish oil.

4. Vitamin E has been found to help old dogs with heart conditions[5] and I am confident it does the same for cats.

5. Older cats put on a vitamin E regimen seem to regain a sense of well being and have healthier hair and skin.[6]

6. Vitamin E is also said to improve the bowel tone in old cats.[7]

Vitamin C, like vitamin E, is an antioxidant. It has the ability to trap and deactivate tiny molecular fragments caused by peroxidation. These fragments, called free radicals, disrupt and damage cellular structures and set off chain reactions of destruction. Vitamin C and vitamin E work together—along with selenium—as an antioxidant team to stop the sabotage of peroxidation. Each nutrient increases the effectiveness of the other.

Since C is produced naturally in a cat's liver, you might think it could rush to the rescue in any case of vitamin E or selenium deficiency. Unfortunately there's a hitch. The very liver enzyme system where ascorbic acid is manufactured is highly sensitive to the peroxidation process I have just described.

In order to find out if peroxidation in the liver could slow down an aging cat's ability to make C, I turned to one of the world's leading authorities on ascorbic acid synthesis—Dr. I. B. Chatterjee of the Department of Biochemistry at Calcutta's University College of Science.

There probably is an impairment due to peroxidation, he told me. He has found that animals of other species produce less C as they age. For instance, an old goat has about one-fourth to one-third the production of a young goat.[8]

Chatterjee has discovered in experiments that a vitamin E deficiency sharply decreases the vitamin C output in animals. This deficiency, we have seen, probably exists in all aging animals unless they are supplemented. Chatterjee also found a similar drop in C production when laboratory animals were deficient in vitamins A, B_1, and B_2.[9]

Whatever the biochemical dynamics, it is a good bet your old cat is producing less C now than in the past. And less C means more trouble. It means a weakened immune system, a diminished ability to detoxify the impurities in the food and toxins in the environment, and a deterioration of collagen.

Collagen, remember, depends on vitamin C. Collagen is the cement of the body that keeps cells and tissue components in place, much as concrete keeps the bricks of a wall in place. Strong collagen is vital in early life. It is essential to growth. In later life, the collagen content of the body must be adequately nourished and maintained or else the cement starts to come unglued. The tissues deteriorate just as a wall crumbles. The tissues become less resistant to disease and less able to carry out their specialized functions. Vital organs begin failing.

Aging has been associated with deteriorating collagen and a vitamin C deficiency in both humans and animals. The strength of collagen, for example, is a key factor in the ability of body tissue to resist proliferating tumor cells. Weak collagen means weak resistance.[10] Perhaps this helps account for the incidence of tumors which are more frequent in the older cat.

TOTAL SUPPLEMENTATION

Aging cats stand to benefit most from supplementation with the whole team of vitamins and minerals. My prevention program calls for geriatric animals to receive a supplementary daily dose of the RDAs of most vitamins and minerals along with extra C and E. Of course, some animals will require higher levels of specific nutrients because of individual needs or conditions. These needs are best determined through an examination by a nutritionally oriented veterinarian. To find the name and address of the one nearest you, refer to my concluding comments in Chapter One.

A strong case for supplementation of older animals has been made by Dr. Jacob E. Mosier, president of the American Veterinary Medical Association. In a report distributed to veterinarians on nutritional supplementation of geriatric dogs and cats, Mosier says, "We should not take for granted that a balanced commercial dog or cat food will fulfill the nutrient requirements of every individual, especially every geriatric animal."

Mosier goes on to say that "the special effect of diet on the condition of elderly individuals is not sufficiently understood, but nutrition has been shown to be the only environmental factor that increases the life span of animal models . . .

"Proper supplementation of the geriatric animal's diet will significantly enhance the relative longevity of the individual's (the animal's) health."[11]

Many of the scientific facts contained in Mosier's paper relate to studies done with humans and laboratory animals. He feels—and I would agree—that these examples may serve as insight for understanding the nutritional status of older cats and dogs. Following is a selection of key points from his paper:

- Administration of B complex and vitamin C improve general vitality and vigor among the aged and alleviate symptoms attributed to senility and cardiovascular disease.
- Aging has been associated with lower levels of B_1 (thiamine). A definite relationship with cardiac dysfunction and B_1 deficiency has been long recognized.

● Aging disturbs the biochemical processing of B_1 in an animal's body. Older animals with lack of appetite, weight loss, rough coat, poor muscle coordination, paralysis, or convulsions are candidates for supplemental B_1.

● Some of the symptoms of B_3 (niacin) deficiency observed in humans resemble signs often seen in older cats and dogs: poor appetite, reddening of the gums, ulceration, thick, foul-smelling saliva, sluggishness, and rough, scaly hair coat. B_3 given along with other B complex vitamins seems to improve the health of gum tissue in both dogs and cats. (I will speak more about unhealthy gums shortly).

● Increased levels of pantothenic acid (B_5) may improve antibody production.

● Leukopenia, a condition marked by a decrease in the number of white blood cells in the body, occurs frequently in old cats. White blood cells are important in combating microorganisms. This condition may respond to treatment with folic acid, one of the B complex vitamins.

● The use of B_6 and other B complex vitamins may improve some cases of itching in dogs that have no visible skin conditions.

● Aging is associated with lowered levels of vitamin B_6 in the blood, despite an apparently good diet. A chronic deficit of this vitamin weakens the immune response in the aged.

● Studies with elderly people and old dogs have revealed lowered zinc levels in the blood. Supplementation of zinc is useful in enhancing protein metabolism, immune response, the growth and repair of wounds or incisions, and in the treatment of horny growths, scaly skin, coarseness of hair, brittle hair, and skin infections.[12]

Breeders and nutritionally minded veterinarians are well acquainted with the effect of vitamin and mineral supplements on older animals. Taking a few seconds a day to administer them to your animals can do wonders.

The following comments are typical:

Susan Ironside, a breeder of American Shorthairs and Scottish Folds in Alameda, California—"After I began using vitamins and minerals I found I had healthier animals. The activity was much improved. Hair coats were improved. There was a noticeable difference in brightness and general condition."

Dennis and Laura Dayton, breeders of Ragdolls in Newbury Park, California—"None of our old cats lose body fat and get bony. We have several eleven-year-olds who are just as active and healthy-looking as much younger cats. We have one fifteen-year-old who still looks like he did ten years ago. He's very active and playful. We don't see older cats slowing down as much."

Robert and Marty Goldstein, veterinarians in Yorktown Heights, New York—"When you put older animals on good healthy food, along with supplements, you are dramatically increasing the quality of their lives. After several months on the program they are moving around like young cats. Clients tell us they have old cats chasing after birds for the first time in years."

Frequently people ask me if vitamins and minerals can help very old and decrepit animals, creatures who are barely alive. This is a tough question to answer. I have seen some pretty feeble old animals come alive with the program, but I have also seen others for whom the program was too late. Obviously the sooner you can put your animal on supplements the better.

By now I have restored enough hopeless cases so that word has filtered out about the veterinarian in San Jose who saves old animals with vitamins. As a result, I will see many a castoff from other veterinarians, cats brought in to me as a last resort after more "conventional" treatments have failed.

If an individual carries in an animal near death and I feel it has any kind of a chance to live with less pain, then I will attempt vitamin therapy. The owner has to recognize the effort may not work, however. I will not make any claim for life extension. I only say that the possibility to live longer may be increased. The ultimate decision in cases like this lies with the owner of the animal.

If you have such an animal, my suggestion is to consult with your veterinarian about the potential usefulness of supplements. There is nothing to lose and perhaps something to gain—added time with an old cherished animal.

Vitamins and minerals will not interfere with the action of drugs when a cat is on medication. Instead they will actually correct nutrient deficiencies created by many drugs. So adding the supplements can help the therapeutic process.

DIGESTIVE PROBLEMS

One of the common problems in older cats is a chronic pancreatitis. You will have a skinny cat on your hands, one who cannot gain weight despite a vigorous appetite. You may also notice a rough hair coat and a somewhat soft stool, usually lighter in color than normal. Sometimes the animal vomits an hour or less after eating. The vomiting may be due to hairballs, in which case you will see hair mixed in with the expelled food. But if there is no hair present, then you are dealing with a digestive problem.

The cause of these symptoms is a degenerating pancreas. This vital organ is not producing sufficient enzymes to break down the food.

When a client presents an old cat with any of the typical symptoms, I will routinely run a test to determine the level of pancreatic enzymes. In old cats, the test usually confirms my suspicions.

This condition can be helped by supplementing the animal with pancreatic enzymes. I use a veterinary product called Gastrizyme in my practice. In about two weeks you begin to see improvement. After two or three months a cat should put on a noticeable amount of weight, and generally there is no more difficulty holding down food.

A cat on a good vitamin and mineral program all his life is unlikely to develop this condition. The pancreas remains healthy.

FAILING KIDNEYS

Vitamin and mineral supplements also keep the kidneys healthy. These vital organs filter the blood. They collect useful substances and recirculate them, and excrete the undesirable material, the toxins and nitrogen waste products from protein breakdown.

Kidney failure is common in old cats and dogs. Over the years there is a gradual deterioration of kidney function, caused in large part by the constant and excess burden of impurities, chemicals, and poor-quality protein in the diet. The kidneys also have had to cope with toxic lead and other heavy metals and all the chemical toxins that reach the bloodstream via flea collars, sprays, deworming compounds, insecticides, and other environmental contaminants.

All this takes a toll. Nature never intended kidneys to bear such persecution. Constant overwork results in irritation, scar tissue, and reduced capacity to do the job of eliminating. Eventually, excess waste products are retained by the body. These poisons often collect in skin tissue, causing poor coats and scratching. If unattended, the internal buildup of toxins can lead to vomiting, loss of appetite, and uremic poisoning and death.

Cats with failing kidneys become lethargic, urinate frequently, and drink a good deal of water. Sometimes the situation becomes so bad you can actually smell the urine on the cat's breath.

When an animal possesses these signs, a veterinarian will usually perform a BUN test. This test determines the level of urea and nitrogen in the blood, indicators of kidney function. High levels mean the kidneys are no longer adequately doing their filtering job and the cat's life is in dire peril.

If the condition is not hopeless, I can often arrest the kidney degeneration with 500 milligrams of vitamin C twice a day along with a general vitamin and mineral program. I also make some dietary recommendations. Often, in about two months, the animal is greatly improved and showing more activity.

You can get a headstart on this problem by having a veterinarian perform a BUN test on your cats. Animals five years old and up should have the test every year.

TEETH AND GUMS

Many an old cat is "down in the mouth" and one of the most common problems is gingivitis, an inflammatory condition of the gums. They appear reddish in color, bleed easily and may swell, leading to a loosening and then even a loss of teeth. The problem is usually related to poor dental hygiene and poor nutrition.

Teeth need to be kept clean in order to prevent the buildup of dental plaque (tartar). Accumulation of tartar irritates the gum tissue or creates a fertile bed for bacteria. I have actually seen animals with such a collection of tartar, bacterial infection, and pus in the oral cavity that they were systemically toxic and in mortal danger. By cleaning their teeth we were able to restore their health.

Animals should have their teeth and gums checked by a veterinarian at least once a year and then cleaned if necessary.

The nutrition connection is obvious to me. Cats eating a good diet and maintained on a vitamin and mineral program do not seem to have gingivitis as often or as severely as nonsupplemented cats. When they do have it, usually it is associated with tartar formation. I see the chronic gingivitis most often in cats not on a good program.

Veterinarians Robert and Marty Goldstein tell me they have observed a relationship between semi-moist cat food and mouth problems. "One of the signs of years on a semi-moist diet is a mouth full of gingivitis and tartar," they say. "Many of these cats have bad teeth."

The B complex vitamins can help a case of chronic gingivitis. When such a case comes along, I will put that animal on a high-potency human B complex tablet. The tablet I use contains 55 milligrams of B_1. If the cat owner cannot pop it down the animal's throat, then I suggest crunching it and mixing the pieces right into the food.

This powerful dose of B complex really seems to stimulate the gums. You will see tremendous improvement in a matter of four or five days. After that time you can stop the high dosage and maintain the animal on a regular vitamin and mineral program, such as the one I recommend in the following chapters.

You can speed the healing process along by packing vitamin and mineral powder—if you use a powder product—onto the gums. Vitamin E oil from a capsule can also be rubbed onto the gums once a day.

Don't forget vitamin C in your dental program. This vitamin plays a role in healthy gums and strong teeth by maintaining the integrity of collagen, the cement that binds the tissues. One of the typical signs of scurvy is inflamed and bleeding gums. Scurvy, of course, is the result of a vitamin C deficiency. Remember that older cats do not manufacture as much vitamin C in their livers as do younger cats. This situation may underlie the appearance of gingivitis.

Breeder Susan Ironside works in a veterinary hospital in Alameda, California, and she tells me she sees a parade of older cats with tooth and gum problems.

"I never have this problem with my cats," she says, "and I equate this good dental health to a vitamin and mineral program, one that includes vitamin C.

"Once I obtained a seven-year-old cat who had a history of severe dental problems. He lost one tooth just after I got him. But as the vitamin and mineral program began to take effect, the condition of his oral cavity improved and he has had no trouble since then."

TIPS FOR OLDER CATS

1. Diet. Supplement! A must.

2. Water. Make sure an older cat has plenty of water at all times. Aging kidneys are generally not functioning well and an animal needs more water to assist in elimination.

3. Dental care. Older cats have a tendency to collect dental tartar. Yearly cleanup is advisable. Also it is not a bad idea to periodically brush the teeth of your cat. Use a soft toothbrush and baking soda.

4. The yearly checkup. I strongly recommend annual veterinary checkup including tests for kidney and pancreas function as well as tests for feline leukemia and infectious peritonitis. The money spent on these tests can prevent a lot of heartache later on.

10

What Supplements to Buy

By now you should be sold on the need for extra vitamins and minerals. But which vitamins and minerals and where to buy them? you ask. There is a confusing array of products on the market; however, if you follow my suggestions carefully, you shouldn't have any trouble making the right choices.

The best places to buy your supplements are at health-food stores, pet shops, or through a veterinarian.

At any of these places you can purchase a good multiple vitamin and mineral product for pets, which is what you will be giving your weaned kittens and adult cats. There are a number of good supplements on the market, and your veterinarian or the owner of your favorite pet shop or health-food store may be able to help you choose one.

These items are sold either in tablet, powder, or liquid form. It doesn't really matter which form you choose. I personally prefer the powder. I think it's easier to administer. You simply mix it right into the cat's food. Tablets can be crunched up and similarly mixed right in with the food. Some of the tablet products feature a meat flavor, and animals often will eat them right out of your hand.

If you choose powder, make sure the label on the product tells you how much to administer to an animal. Stay away from bulk products which only give you a minimum vitamin guarantee per pound of powder. You want to know how much is in a teaspoon or tablespoon and how much of a spoonful you should dole out daily to your cats.

The tablet products will tell you the nutrient strength of each tablet and how many you should administer to your animals.

Next, I want you to buy vitamin C powder and, if you have a pregnant or aged cat, some vitamin E capsules. The C and E can best be purchased in a health-food store.

There are two kinds of vitamin E: natural and synthetic. The natural E is probably more effective. But in my practice, I have had as good results with the synthetic as with the natural. Both types are often on sale at health-food stores. Natural is more expensive, usually double or more the synthetic price. You can tell the two apart by the price and by their scientific names written in small print on the label. The natural vitamin is called d-alpha tocopherol. The synthetic has an extra letter "l". It is called dl-alpha tocopherol.

Both forms of E work. Which one you buy depends on whether you want to pay more or pay less.

Vitamin E is measured in dosages called International Units, or IU for short. The dosage is clearly marked on the label. You'll be buying the 100 IU strength.

Vitamin C is the key to the success of my program, but none of the multivitamin and mineral products designed for pets contain enough vitamin C—if they contain any at all. That's why you'll have to buy a separate supply.

I recommend the slightly alkaline form of vitamin C—sodium ascorbate. The reason is because ascorbic acid, the best-known and more common type of vitamin C, is on the acidic side and may possibly cause some initial minor gastrointestinal upset. Ascorbic acid has a pH rating of 3.0. Sodium ascorbate is 7.4. I know of many people who use ascorbic acid without any problems, but I like to suggest the alkaline form just to be on the safe side. It is the form of vitamin C that I have primarily used in my practice.

You may find it difficult to purchase sodium ascorbate in the powder form. Not all health-food stores stock it. They may carry only the ascorbic acid powder. If that's the case, then buy the ascorbic acid and order the sodium ascorbate for the next time. The powder is half the price of tablets and easy to administer.

If the store has no powder at all but only tablets, then go ahead and buy the tablets and use them until you can obtain powder.

(If you have difficulty purchasing powder, you can order it through the mail from Bronson Pharmaceuticals, 4526 Rinetti Lane, La Canada, CA 91011. Bronson's prices are very competitive and they ship via UPS to your door).

Tablets of ascorbic acid are available in a large variety of sizes. You can buy them in 100-milligram, 200-milligram, 250-milligram, 300-milligram, 500-milligram, and 1,000-milligram (1 gram) sizes. See the charts in the next chapter for the size most appropriate for your cats.

Sodium ascorbate tablets usually come in the 1,000-milligram (1 gram) size only.

Ascorbic acid can be purchased as tablets with many different "accessories." Some are manufactured with rose hips, which means that a very small and insignificant amount of rose hips, a natural source of vitamin C, is contained in the tablet. Other products feature bioflavonoids. The bioflavonoids are the pulpy part of citrus fruit, right beneath the outer skin, and are actually a separate vitamin: vitamin P. They help in absorption of vitamin C and are particularly beneficial for the health of the small blood vessels—the capillaries. Products with these extra features tend to cost more, and I have not found them to be necessary. If you buy a vitamin C product with rose hips, you are definitely spending extra money unnecessarily. If you buy a product with bioflavonoids, you are getting a more potent supplement. But ascorbic acid alone is totally adequate, and this is what I recommend when sodium ascorbate is not available.

There are no varieties of sodium ascorbate as there are of ascorbic acid.

Do try to get the powder. It's cheaper.

Don't become confused if you see vitamin C being offered in the crystal form. Crystals and powder are one and the same. The bottle will tell you how much vitamin C is contained in a teaspoonful. Usually there are 4,000 milligrams (4 grams) to a full teaspoon. If you are administering 500 milligrams to a cat, you measure out approximately one-eighth of a teaspoon.

Any vitamin C product you buy should be kept in a dark, cool, and dry place with the lid tightly closed. Do not refrigerate, because moisture can accumulate inside the jar and destroy the vitamin. Vitamin C potency—and B vitamins too—can deteriorate quickly from heat, light, moisture, or air. All supplements should be stored in a cool place.

For preweaned kittens, I recommend vitamin C pediatric drops for human babies. You can find them at your favorite pharmacy. Vitamin C will stimulate the immune system and greatly reduce the risk of sudden death and viral and bacterial infections. When kittens reach the weaning stage, they can then be introduced to the full range of vitamins and minerals.

In my practice I have developed special multiple vitamin and mineral formulas for dogs and cats that contain vitamin C. One is in powder form for weaned and adult cats and the other comes as liquid drops for preweaned kittens. Any reader wishing more information about these supplements can write to Orthomolecular Specialties, P.O. Box 32232, San Jose, CA 95152.

11

How Much to Use

The charts on the following pages represent my recommendations for safe, effective, and manageable daily vitamin and mineral dosages. These are levels I use in my practice.

Do not worry about having to deal with many different bottles of vitamins and minerals. That won't be the case. My prevention program calls for one, two, or three supplements for an animal and that's it. Just follow the instructions and you will see how simple it is.

As I said in the previous chapter, I want you to purchase a good veterinary multivitamin and mineral product. Read the dosage instructions on the label and administer to your animals accordingly.

Ingredients will, of course, vary from product to product and probably will differ from the dosages I use in my practice. One supplement product will have things that another one will not have. But do not be confused or concerned. The only differences I am concerned with for this prevention plan are the vitamin C and E levels. Commercial veterinary multivitamin and mineral products do not have enough vitamin C. Most don't have any at all. This is why I am asking you to purchase a separate supply of vitamin C. For pregnant and lactating queens and for aged cats, I want you to buy extra E as well.

Breeders! If you are already supplementing, is vitamin C in your program? If not, it should be. Add the doses as I recommend and watch the health of your cats improve.

The nutrient levels in multiple vitamin and mineral supplements for pets are largely based on the nutrient requirements for food as determined by the National Resarch Council. In other words, the cat receives supplementally what he should be getting in his food. As I mentioned earlier, the NRC requirements for food are essentially minimum nutrient guidelines for adequate health and maintenance. I regard these guidelines as insufficient alone to provide optimal protection against the multitude of stress and disease conditions encountered in a cat's lifetime. I have my doubts that even these minimum levels are contained in commercial cat food.

What the multiple vitamin and mineral does then is to guarantee that your cats will be receiving at least the NRC requirements. The supplement gives you this assurance, because you have no idea what your animals are getting in their food, no matter what the label says, but you know what they are getting in the supplement. And when you add the extra C and E, which enhance utilization and transportation of the other nutrients as well as doing so many other vital jobs in the body, you are boosting the nutritional input and creating the basis for optimal health.

At a glance, the blueprint for better health calls for these items:

1. Weaned and adult cats receive a multivitamin and mineral. Follow the dosage instructions on the label of the product. These cats also receive extra vitamin C. Follow my dosage recommendation in the appropriate chart.

2. Pregnant and lactating cats and aged cats receive a multivitamin and mineral plus extra vitamin C and E. Consult the charts for the recommended dosages of C and E.

3. Preweaned kittens receive vitamin C pediatric drops. See the preweaned chart for how much to administer.

For individuals who want to use human multivitamin and mineral products, please remember that cats are much smaller than people. Choose a low-potency human multi.

Dosages for the charts are expressed in micrograms (mcg.) and milligrams (mg.) and International Units (IUs). One thousand micrograms equal one milligram and one thousand milligrams equal one gram.

A large cat or a campaigning show cat should receive 1,000 milligrams of vitamin C. This larger amount is best divided into two doses over the day.

The dosages listed here represent what I use in my practice with

DOSAGE CHARTS

Adult Cats

VITAMINS		MINERALS	
C	500–750 mg.	Sodium	87.5 mg.
A	750 IU	Potassium	15 mg.
B-1	4 mg.	Calcium	7.5 mg.
B-2	.4 mg.	Magnesium	5 mg.
B-3	7.5 mg.	Phosphorus	6 mg.
Pantothenic acid	1.5 mg.	Zinc	1 mg.
B-6	.4 mg.	Iron	5 mg.
Folic acid	16.5 mcg.	Copper	.5 mg.
B-12	1.5 mcg.	Iodine	.1 mg.
Biotin	6 mcg.	Selenium	6 mg.
Inositol	11 mcg.	Manganese	.4 mg.
D	15 IU		
E	7.5 IU		

great success. Dosages of individual nutrients will vary from product to product. For your adult animals, follow the dosage instructions on the label of the multiproduct you purchase. Then add the extra vitamin C to conform with my recommendation.

Pregnant and Lactating Cats

Watch for unusual weight gain, a swelling abdomen and rib cage, a filling out of the breasts, and increased appetite. These are the usual signs of pregnancy. If you observe these signs, or if your female has been bred, then start her on the program immediately.

There are only two differences between this and the regular adult prevention program:

1. All pregnant cats receive the big cat daily dosage of 1,000 milligrams of vitamin C, best doled out in two equal helpings over the day.

2. All pregnant cats receive 100 IUs of vitamin E.

Maintain the multivitamin and mineral level according to the instructions on the product label.

Aged Cats

Older cats will receive more vitamin E than the younger adult cat but not quite as much as the pregnant or lactating queen. Give your cats, five years and older, 50 IUs a day. Vitamin C and the multivitamin and mineral level remain the same as an adult cat.

Preweaned Kittens

Supplementation is in the form of vitamin C pediatric drops. Dosages are figured in milligrams according to the age of the animal. The label of the bottle will tell you how many milligrams per drop. The amount administered is increased after the first five days and then again after ten days. Maintain the last dosage until weaning, at which time the kitten will gradually be introduced to a tablet or powder form of supplementation.

VITAMIN C

1 – 5 days	5 – 10 days	To weaning
20 mg.	35 mg.	65 mg.

Weaned Kittens

Follow the instructions on the label of the multiple vitamin and mineral product you buy. Dosages are determined according to the weight of the animal. If you use tablets, make sure they are finely crunched up with no sizable chunks that could get caught in a tiny throat.

The vitamin C should start at about 250 milligrams and be increased by six months to 500 milligrams.

12

How to Administer
Supplements

Vitamin and mineral supplements are concentrated forms of food. They should be given to your animals at mealtime. The supplements will thus be metabolized by the same wave of digestive juices that the cat is producing to handle his food. It's more efficient to do it this way than give the supplements separately. This same principle holds true for humans.

There should be no problem with administering the supplements. Some veterinary multiple vitamin and mineral tablets are meat flavored, and cats will gobble them right out of your palm or out of the feeding bowl with the rest of the food.

Some cats are turned off by the acidic taste of ascorbic acid vitamin C tablets. Maryland veterinarian Carvel Tiekert has a solution for this. He recommends dipping the tablet in corn oil or rubbing it in butter before giving it to the cat. This disguises the taste, and cats then accept the tablet more readily.

Powdered supplements can be sprinkled onto the food and then mixed into it.

Vitamin E comes in a capsule. Simply prick the end of a capsule with a pin or sharp object and squeeze the oily contents onto the food. Cats five years and over will be receiving 50 IUs a day, which is half of the contents of the 100 IU capsule you will be buying. After you prick the capsule and squeeze out half, return the capsule to the bottle and use the remainder the next day.

The one no-no is pill popping—unless you are a full-fledged expert. I know of too many clients who have been bitten in the act of cramming tablets and pills down the throats of resentful animals. And I have heard of many a cat who after having been pilled once will turn tail and hide when you attempt it a second time. Cats are pretty smart, in any case, in getting a pill or tablet out of their mouths.

If your cat won't take the tablet out of your hand or out of the bowl, then crunch it up and sprinkle the pieces onto the food. Then mix the pieces in with the food.

Many cats may resent tampered food. They are naturally suspicious of a different smell. The strong aroma of the B complex vitamins may be one reason why cats reject the addition of vitamins and minerals. In a situation such as this, I use the "sneak attack" method. What you do is start with a minute amount of the supplement, well below the recommended quantity. This way the animal isn't likely to detect a change. Every two days you up the ante—increase the dosage. It may take a week or ten days for a finicky cat to be brought up to his appropriate level, but I have found this method helps to trick even the most resistant of cats. One breeder, Laneen Firth, uses Gerber's Baby Beef to camouflage supplements when she has a real persnickety cat.

"You envelope the supplement with a teaspoonful or however much you need of the beef, and the cat will eat it," she says.

"After you do this a few times, you put the supplement and the baby beef together on top of the regular food. The cat will keep eating it.

"Pretty soon you can eliminate the beef and just mix the supplement in with the regular food, and the cat will no longer reject the supplement.

"Cats get so accustomed after awhile that they will quickly notice if you forget to put the supplement in their food. I remember one time I had a bunch of cats on my hands that weren't touching their food. They just sat around the full bowls looking at me as if I had filled the bowls with poison instead of food. I finally realized I had forgotten the vitamins. When I corrected the oversight, they dug into the food with their usual gusto. Cats are smart. They know what they're getting and what they're not."

VITAMIN C BOWEL TOLERANCE

I want to take a few moments to discuss vitamin C, because it is so important to my program.

The slightly alkaline form of vitamin C—sodium ascorbate—will usually be more gentle on a cat's gastrointestinal tract than the more acidic type, straight ascorbic acid. Many people I know use ascorbic acid and have no problems. From experience, I prefer sodium ascorbate. They both have the same beneficial effects, however.

Large doses of vitamin C, whichever type, and if administered at once, can cause temporary diarrhea in the beginning when an animal is not used to it. This is the only side effect of this extremely nontoxic vitamin.

Diarrhea can be avoided by gradually raising the dosage up to the recommended level instead of starting with the full load. If you do encounter soft stool or diarrhea while you are thus increasing the amounts, then simply cut back the next day to the previous lower level you used, and stay with it. That will be your cat's optimal dose.

If you can fit it into your schedule, another way to avoid the possibility of diarrhea is to administer the vitamin C in two doses. One in the morning and another in the evening.

Dr. Robert Cathcart of San Mateo, California, is a physician who uses megadoses of vitamin C in his practice. He discovered that in a situation of stress or illness, an individual can ingest much more vitamin C than usual without experiencing diarrhea. He determined that more C is needed by the body in these conditions and thus more is tolerated. The reason is because large amounts are being used by the body to fight off the toxins of disease and to maintain biochemical balance. Cathcart calls this the vitamin C bowel-tolerance effect.

The principle applies to animals as well as humans. The sicker the animal, the more vitamin C it needs—and will tolerate. Cats ill with a serious viral problem, for instance, will take considerably more C than if they are healthy. There will be no diarrhea. Their bodies absorb more because they need more.

In my practice, I will use the bowel-tolerance concept in post-surgery or on extremely ill or stressed animals. I have found this a good way to get them back in shape in a hurry.

If you are concerned about the sodium (salt) content of sodium ascorbate, let me put your mind at rest. Dr. Fred Klenner has used massive doses of sodium ascorbate for years, and even his cardiac patients benefited from it. He told me he never encountered any problems. In working with large doses of sodium ascorbate with animals, I have never observed any harmful effects either. I have only seen the animals benefiting. The sodium content of sodium ascorbate is only 10 percent. Thus if you are administering 500 milligrams to your cat, one-tenth of that, or 50 milligrams, is sodium. The rest is vitamin C—ascorbic acid. The added sodium salt buffers the acid, making it slightly alkaline.

If you have a cat with a heart problem, you should be more concerned about the sodium (salt) content in the commercial cat food the animal is eating. Pet foods, like human food, contain excessive amounts of salt, and this is hardly in the interest of good health.

KITTY DROPS

Preweaned kittens will be receiving vitamin C pediatric drops made for human babies. These products come with a handy dropper that enables you to drip the liquid directly into the kittens' mouths. The label will tell you how much vitamin C is contained in the drops, and you can check with the preweaned chart in the previous chapter to determine the amount to administer.

You can start giving the drops several hours after birth. Lift each kitten gently, cradling it in the palm of one hand, and with the other hand slide the dropper inside the mouth and squirt in the appropriate amount of the preparation.

If the kittens are walking, all you have to do is hold their heads back gently with one hand and insert the dropper with the other.

You can take care of each kitten in a few seconds. Insert the dropper, squeeze off a round of drops, and move on to the next animal.

As the kittens start weaning, you can apply the drops to their food and then gradually introduce the powdered or crunched-up tablets. Never give tablets to a preweaned or newly weaned kitten. A whole tablet or even a half of one can become stuck in a tiny animal's throat. I have heard of cases of very young animals choking to death on deworming capsules. Always crunch up tablets and mix them into the food.

PART 4

Controlling the Viral Killers:
Feline Leukemia,
Feline Infectious Peritonitis (FIP),
and Upper Respiratory Disease

13

See Your Veterinarian First

Before discussing the viral diseases and other common cat ailments, I want to make one thing clear. Unless you went to veterinary school as I did, I do not think it is wise for you to play doctor when your animal becomes sick. At the first sign of illness the best course of action is always to bring the animal to a veterinary hospital for diagnosis and treatment. Early treatment improves the chances for recovery.

Once you have a diagnosis, you will find that the treatment prescribed by the veterinarian can be enhanced with supplements. Many drugs given to animals and humans for illness actually interfere with biochemical and nutritional values and create secondary problems. I have always found vitamins and minerals supportive of medication. The better the cells are nourished, the more readily the body can respond to medication and the better the chance of recovery.

If you are considering this kind of nutritional support for a therapeutic program, it is best to consult with your veterinarian. Perhaps you may be lucky enough to have a veterinarian who is attuned to nutritional medicine and can give you a positive guidance. If not, there should be such an individual in your area, and it may be worthwhile to seek that person out. By writing to the address I have provided at the end of Chapter One, you can obtain the name of the nearest nutritionally oriented veterinarian.

The purpose of this book is to prevent disease by developing a strong immune system through nutritional supplements. On the following pages, I will discuss how the viral diseases can be controlled, that is, prevented or minimized, with vitamins and minerals.

You *can* have a cat or a cattery free of viral infections. However, feline viruses are extremely contagious and deadly organisms, especially the leukemia and FIP viruses. You will have to follow and maintain the kind of vitamin and mineral program I have just detailed. And you should also test your animals periodically for leukemia and FIP. That is part of a good prevention plan.

If any of your animals should display any signs of disease, make haste to a veterinarian. Early treatment is a must.

And remember this point, too, when an animal does become ill: a cat needs to be loved, needs to feel wanted, needs to have a reason for living. Tender loving care is a must. Your affection is as important— or maybe more so—than any medicine.

14

Feline Leukemia

Feline leukemia is the number one cat killer in the United States. The disease is caused by a highly contagious organism transmitted from an infected cat to other cats primarily through the saliva but also via contact with contaminated urine and feces. Additionally, a fetus can pick up the virus from an infected mother.

There is no known effective treatment for leukemia and up until the time this book was written there was no vaccine either. For some years researchers have been striving to develop a workable vaccine against leukemia. At Ohio State University, veterinary pathobiologist Richard Olsen has developed a promising formula based on a viral protein. In June of 1982, the Olsen vaccine was still pending approval by the U.S. Department of Agriculture. Once approved, only time and experience will tell how effective it is.

Meanwhile, you can still keep your cats free of the disease. You do not have to shudder in horror any longer at the mere mention of the word *leukemia*. I have a simple and proven method that prevents it.

First, let's cover some of the basic facts about this killer disease:

- The virus is contagious only among cats.
- Animals in multicat settings are more prone to infection than cats living alone. Exposure to a single infected animal can spread infection to an entire household of cats. The infection persists in about 30 percent of affected cats, who then become the most susceptible to disease.[1]

● Young cats have less immune capacity and are more vulnerable to leukemia infection. However, older cats become persistently infected after prolonged exposure to contaminated animals. In one study, 42 kittens and 28 adult cats—all determined to be leukemia-free—were placed in multicat environments where about 30 percent of the resident animals were leukemia carriers. Within seven months of exposure, 12 of the kittens had died and a total of 71 percent had developed signs of viral disease. Of the adults, 11 percent became infected, but in two years' time some 43 percent were affected.[2]

● The feline leukemia virus is an insidious organism with an ability to attack on different fronts:

1. First and foremost, it acts as an immunosuppressive agent. This means that it impairs the immune system and renders an animal vulnerable to other infectious and degenerative diseases. In a study of 466 cats with various chronic infectious conditions, 223 (48 percent) were found to be carriers of the leukemia organism.[3]

The leukemia virus appears to be a potent enhancer of FIP, another viral killer disease. Approximately 40 to 50 percent of cats with FIP are infected with leukemia. The virus has been determined to play an immunosuppressive role in many cases of upper respiratory tract infections, chronic cystitis, and recurrent abscesses, tooth-rot abscesses, severe inflammation of the ears, inflammation of the intestines, arthritis of multiple joints, and some neurologic, bone, kidney, and skin disorders.[4]

Thus, the leukemia virus is responsible for a big share of serious health problems in cats—and often without being directly incriminated. An animal may die of upper respiratory disease after the leukemia virus first undermines the strength of the immune system. The upper respiratory virus takes hold and spreads as the immune system is preoccupied with the leukemia virus. Any animal who is a leukemia carrier has an immune system working overtime to combat the leukemia virus present in the body. Such a taxed immune system does not have the soldiers to fight off other organisms which appear on the scene—that is, unless the animal is on a super nutritional program.

2. Lymphosarcoma is another major manifestation of the leukemia virus. This means tumors of the lymph tissue. The cat has the highest incidence of lymph malignancies among mammals. All breeds and all ages are affected. I will discuss this further in the chapter on tumors.

3. The leukemia virus directly causes anemia. The organism somehow blocks the biochemical assembly line in bone marrow, where red blood cells are produced. Common signs of this condition are lethargy, weight loss, pale gums, and difficult breathing.

4. The virus also creates a condition resembling distemper. It is called panleukopenia-like syndrome, panleukopenia being the medial term for distemper. Symptoms are bloody diarrhea, vomiting, lack of appetite, and weight loss. This disease is difficult to distinguish from distemper, however, it occurs in animals known to be immune to the distemper virus.

5. The virus can also cause an abnormal proliferation of white blood cells. This condition, known as myelogenous leukemia, is associated with anemia, lethargy, and depression.

6. Thymic atrophy is a variation of the immunosuppressive action of the leukemia virus. The virus attacks the thymus gland in kittens born to leukemia-infected queens. The thymus is an important lymph organ that regulates the potency and activity of certain disease-killing white blood cells. The virus causes a degeneration of the gland, resulting in a defective immune system. Kittens thus affected often die of secondary infections soon after birth.

7. The virus has a severe effect on pregnancy. Dr. William D. Hardy, one of the leading researchers of feline leukemia, has found that nearly 70 percent of queens who abort or resorb their fetuses are infected with the virus.[5]

When a cat is exposed to the leukemia organism—perhaps through contact with the saliva of a contaminated animal—the viruses usually set up a beachhead in the epithelial cells lining the mouth and tonsil areas. Once established, they begin reproducing furiously and attack lymphatic tissue (see page 43 for a description of the viral-proliferation process). Viruses and infected white blood cells spread through the bloodstream of the lymphatic system, carrying the potential for disease to other regions of the body. Depending on the strength of the immune system, a cat will then develop one of the leukemia diseases or become a carrier.

During the primary stage of infection, lasting for a few weeks, symptoms are usually subtle. Once they become more apparent, this means the cat has not been able to fight off the organism and will probably develop clinical symptoms.

According to Dr. Niels Pedersen of the University of California–Davis School of Veterinary Medicine, there is a 95 percent recovery rate among the general population of cats following the primary state. The other 5 percent become carriers and have the potential for becoming fatally ill.

These figures change dramatically for animals in a multicat setting or cattery. There, 70 percent recover and 30 percent become chronically infected, says Pedersen.

Initial clinical signs of disease include fever, lethargy, loss of appetite, lymph-node enlargements, and reduction in the number of red and white blood cells and blood platelets.

These signs are often followed by what appears to be a recovery. However, this promising interlude for many cats may be nothing more than a lull before the storm, a progression into the secondary stage of disease. This is the danger point, says Pedersen.

Without proper care, one-half of the animals thus affected will die each year. But with proper care and if an animal is not subjected to stress, this mortality rate can be lowered, he adds.[6]

In my practice I have experienced a very high death rate associated with leukemia despite the best possible care we can give animals.

I see a variety of symptoms when a leukemia cat is brought into my hospital. This reflects the many faces of the disease. Most commonly I see the paleness, the loss of appetite, loss of weight, and lethargy.

People often present a cat who has not been eating for two or three days. This lack of appetite appears due to a painful throat. Remember the oral cavity is the area first attacked by the virus. It is inflamed. The animal has difficulty swallowing. Often a cat will hang his head over a water dish. He wants to drink but won't because of the pain in swallowing.

In the early stages the animal may nibble a little food, but this will tail off and stop as the infection progresses.

Often a cat seems to be unaware of his surroundings. He appears reluctant or unable to move.

Another common sign is a ghostlike pallor of the mucous membrane of the oral cavity. The gums and tongue are very pale. Similarly, the healthy pinkish hue of the lining of the ears has faded and turned almost white. The pads are also pale.

This anemic pallor is caused by the leukemia virus shutting down red blood cell production in the bone marrow. Anemia appears to be common to feline leukemia diseases.[7]

An animal's temperature can vary. During the early stages it can soar to 106 degrees and over. Other times an animal can be virtually comatose and the temperature is subnormal.

STALKING THE KILLER

In 1967, the virus causing feline leukemia was isolated and identified. Recommended treatment was similar to other viral conditions: antibiotics, high levels of steroid drugs, and administration of fluids to restore electrolyte (essential minerals) balance in case of dehydration.

Over the years, we veterinarians have used a parade of new and improved antibiotics, starting with penicillin. But they do not attack the virus. They are only effective in reducing the secondary bacterial infection that accompanies a viral condition. Unfortunately, there is no drug that neutralizes viruses. The role of the steroid drugs in virus therapy is to stimulate appetite.

Antibiotics, steroids, and fluids are still the accepted method of treating feline leukemia and then, as now, they are essentially ineffective.

Because this treatment was not working, I also tried blood transfusions in the early days. This was symptomatic therapy in response to the anemia. The cat would receive a transfusion, and soon afterward the pale gums and ears would become pink again. But this was like pouring water into a bucket with a hole in it. The organism apparently devoured the red blood cells about as fast as you could replace them. The next day the cat would be pale again.

None of these methods worked. The animals would either die or I would be requested by the owner to euthanize.

In the mid-sixties I began having success using megadoses of vitamin C to treat dogs and cats ill with distemper, another viral disease.[8] Vitamin C, as I explained earlier in the book, can knock out viruses when used in large doses. Cats with distemper would receive 2,000 milligrams or more of sodium ascorbate (the nonacid form of vitamin C) twice daily, and they often recovered in several days. In recent years I have seldom treated a distemper case. Immunization seems to be keeping this viral condition in check.

Since conventional methods were proving worthless in dealing with leukemia, I attempted vitamin C therapy on patently sick leukemic cats. What I discovered is that the leukemia virus is a much tougher and elusive organism than the distemper virus.

I was indeed able to make cats more comfortable and keep them alive longer with vitamin therapy. They would begin to pick at their food and drink a little water. But it was not enough to bring them completely out of it, and sooner or later they regressed.

In some instances, I administered more vitamin C. But this was problematic because of the difficulty to get the needle into cats' veins. Feline blood vessels are very small and can collapse if abused.

I would estimate that out of a hundred symptomatic cats, I was able to save perhaps a half-dozen.

Leukemia became an extremely frustrating challenge. I spent many a weekend and holiday at my hospital trying to save sick animals. The results were disheartening.

I virtually gave up trying to treat leukemic cats. There was nothing conventional or unconventional that seemed to work consistently once animals developed symptoms.

With no effective treatment against so contagious a virus, many cats who are tested and found to have the leukemia virus are put to sleep. Even animals who show no symptoms—who are merely carriers—are often euthanized.

Breeders especially fear the risk of contamination of a whole cattery. They are also afraid about news leaking out that leukemia has appeared among their cats. It's bad for business.

"You might just as well announce you have leprosy," one breeder told me. "People stay clear of you."

It was around 1976 that "Dutchess" and "Sassy," two Persian females, changed my luck with leukemia. Both cats had been acquired by Laneen Firth, a nutrition-minded new breeder in the San Jose area. Both animals had been found to be leukemia carriers.

"Dutchess" was over six years old and had never conceived. "Sassy" was a young adult who had produced two previous litters of two kittens each. Both animals were rather thin and sickly when I first saw them. Firth admitted she had fallen in love with them and hoped her tender, loving care would improve their health. Both cats were of valuable breeding lines.

During one particular visit to my hospital, Firth spotted a bottle containing a multivitamin and mineral powder I was using primarily for preventing hip dysplasia in large-breed dogs. The powder contained sodium ascorbate (vitamin C) along with the standard spectrum of NRC-recommended nutrients for domestic pets.

Firth wanted to know if cats could use it, I explained the action of vitamin C in boosting the effectiveness of other vitamins and minerals and how it stimulated the immune system. None of my other cat-owning clients had used the formula until this point, but I felt sure it would boost feline health in a general way just as it did for dogs.

Firth said she wanted to try a bottle.

A few weeks later she called to say that "Dutchess" and "Sassy" had improved greatly in health and appearance and because of this improvement she was interested in the possibility of breeding the animals. Even though it was commonly accepted that once a cat tested positive for leukemia it would always test positive, Firth suggested retesting the animals.

We drew blood and sent the samples off to the San Jose laboratory that does most of my blood work.

Two days later I received a phone call from the laboratory pathologist.

"These two cats tested positive for leukemia before and now they have tested negative," he informed me. "What are you up to?"

Somewhat shocked, I told him about the vitamin C and other vitamins and minerals.

I then called Firth and told her the startling news. She was overjoyed and said she would go ahead and attempt breeding the cats. And please, she added, send her a supply of supplements for the whole cattery.

It wasn't long before "Sassy" became pregnant and produced a whopping litter of five kittens, all of them healthy. One of the males became a grand champion before he was a year old.

As for "Dutchess," who had never conceived, she went into heat several months after starting on the program and delivered three healthy kittens. She was subsequently sold as a pet.

Firth became so confident of the vitamin C– based program that she shipped "Sassy" across country to breed with an East Coast "aristocat." The animal handled the stress of flying without trouble and became duly pregnant. Three kittens emerged from this mating, two of them females who made their championships and went on to become excellent breeders. In subsequent queenings, "Sassy" produced three or four thriving kittens each time. The program apparently enhanced this animal's fertility as well as protecting her from leukemia. Today, "Sassy" is the pampered matron of the Firth cattery.

About the time of the "Sassy" and "Dutchess" episode, I was contacted by a cattery owner from Southern California who desperately needed help for a serious leukemia problem. Some of her females were not conceiving. Others had aborted. A few adults and a number of kittens had died.

The owner contacted me after reading an article about my success with vitamin C in treating canine viral conditions. I frankly informed her I had not had much luck treating symptomatic cats with leukemia. She wanted me to try nevertheless.

She drove up with one of her sick cats, and I treated the animal as best as I could. But the cat was beyond my help and I had to put it to sleep.

The experience with Firth's two cats prompted me to suggest she try the vitamin C– based supplement on the animals in her cattery who were determined to be positive carriers of leukemia. I also suggested an experiment to test the validity of the concept.

We divided six leukemia-positive cats into two groups. One group received an oral multiple vitamin and mineral (the RDA recommendations) and the other group received the same multiple vitamin plus 500 milligrams of sodium ascorbate.

This cattery was being tested twice yearly for leukemia by a team of medical students as part of a clinical pathology exercise. Several months after our experiment began, the students returned to test the cats.

The three animals on the straight RDA multiple vitamins and minerals were still positive for leukemia. The three on the RDAs plus vitamin C were negative.

The vitamin C group consisted of one male and two barren females, ages two and three. Several months later both females were bred and both conceived. The two-year-old had four healthy kittens, all of which lived. The three-year-old produced three kittens that all thrived as well.

The non–vitamin C cats were then placed on the full program and when tested six months later were all negative for leukemia. These three eventually became very active in the cattery's breeding program.

Back at Laneen Firth's cattery, there were five cases of positive cats introduced to the cattery over the following three years. The animals were placed on the program and eventually became negative. At the time of this writing, the cattery is in the fourth generation of offspring, and all the animals have been negative for leukemia.

Over time Firth became aware that she was experiencing no blockage problems in her males, no respiratory problems, no C-sections, no sudden death, and her cats were traveling far and wide without incidence. She began passing the word to other cat owners. Soon I started receiving calls and letters from all over the country about how cats who routinely tested positive for leukemia were now testing negative and how many health problems were gradually disappearing.

C IS THE KEY

Not every cat tested positive for leukemia is going to die from the disease. Yet many breeders with such cats cannot take any chances for the virus to spread. They usually remove such animals or put them to sleep.

The discovery that vitamin C can turn around positive cats and render them highly immune to leukemia has been big news to cattery people around the country.

The program enables cat owners—breeders, fanciers, and one-cat owners alike—to show, ship, board, breed, or simply enjoy their animals without the doomsday fear of leukemia hanging over their heads.

I do not want to sound like a medicine-show pitchman hawking vitamin C as a panacea, yet experience has shown that when C is added to the team of routinely administered vitamins and minerals, we are able to prevent and control leukemia.

For years, breeders and cat fanciers have been using all sorts of supplements. But not vitamin C. And why? It has long been known that vitamin C is naturally produced in the liver of cats. Veterinary scientists feel that the 40 milligrams per kilogram of body weight of C produced daily is adequate to meet all an animal's needs. I have explained why this concept is wrong. So even though Vitamin C is known to have a powerful killer effect on viral diseases, nobody bothered to use it or research its effect on leukemia.

My clinical experience has taught me a number of lessons about dealing with leukemia:

1. The vitamins and minerals used to fortify commercial cat foods do not have a positive effect against leukemia.

2. The standard RDA vitamin and mineral supplements for pets presently on the commercial market have no effect against leukemia. They do not have vitamin C.

3. The RDA vitamins and minerals plus a mega amount of vitamin C *do* have a positive controlling effect against leukemia. Together, they eliminate the virus from a cat's body. The doses for vitamin C are spelled out in Chapter Eleven.

4. Vitamin C detoxifies the dietary and environmental lead ingested by a cat. It is my opinion that the anemia associated with feline leukemia may be lead-induced or lead-abetted. Furthermore, I believe that the predisposition to leukemia altogether may be the effect of an accumulative lead buildup. We have seen how lead is accumulated in the body—the bone marrow is one favored target—and how scientists have demonstrated that lead impairs the immune system. Along with vitamin C, we know that zinc, calcium, iron, magnesium, and vitamin E are helpful in preventing lead absorption.[9]

5. It appears that increased antibody production is not the ultimate protection for the feline, but rather, the stimulation of the primary immune components—interferon and the white blood cells. Vitamin C along with the other essential nutrients puts muscle into this total network of defense.

6. Your animal must remain on the program. If you lapse in providing the supplements, an animal will return back to its previous susceptibility and test positive once again.

Most of my clients—both breeders and one-cat owners—are using the vitamin C–based program and I can happily say I do not get many leukemic cats to treat in my practice anymore. The only time I will see a leukemia cat is when a new client brings one in.

Cats on the program are thriving. Queens who were positive before for leukemia become negative and produce healthy offspring without resorptions, abortions, and sudden infant death. One cattery that lost 90 percent of its kittens in 1978 has had hardly any losses at all since adding vitamin C to its supplementation program.

I am sure that around the country veterinarians are pulling the odd leukemic cat through. But you want more than a now-and-then success. You want to be able to control a disease, and even better, to prevent it. That's what good medicine is all about.

I hope this book, and the news being spread from breeder to breeder, may stimulate veterinary research to look into the effects of vitamin C on the immune system of cats. I hope it will also encourage other veterinarians to start controlling and preventing leukemia with this very simple and effective method.

The beautiful thing about this program is that you are not dealing with some drug that may have an adverse effect. You are dealing with super nutrition that is not only going to protect the animal from leukemia but also from a whole host of problems.

TESTING

An out-of-town woman brought a very sick feline into my hospital. She said the cat had been diagnosed as having leukemia. I examined the animal and found no symptoms I could relate to the disease. However, during the examination, I did palpate a mass in the abdomen of the kind I had found many times before in constipated or impacted bowels of cats.

I queried the woman as to why she felt the cat had leukemia. She told me her regular veterinarian had reached this conclusion after a positive laboratory test. The other veterinarian had recommended the pet be put to sleep.

I said the cat may indeed have the organism, but this was not the cause of its immediate problem.

An X ray was taken and there it was in all its splendor—a seven-inch bowel impaction.

After medicating the animal for two days with a bowel lubricant and stool softener, the mass passed through and the cat was its normal self again.

This pet was almost put to death because of a test with no supporting symptoms. One of the mistakes in veterinary medicine is that laboratory tests are being used to make diagnoses instead of confirming them.

There are basically three tests for feline leukemia. The most widely used are the immunofluorescent (IFA) test and the Pitman-Moore test (Leukassay test). Through examination of blood samples, these two procedures determine whether an animal is carrying the organism. A positive result means the virus is present in some degree. A positive cat may be healthy or it may have any one of the leukemia-related diseases I have described. Whether healthy or not, such a cat is a source of infection for susceptible uninfected animals.

I am aware of many cases where individuals have put their animals to sleep on the basis of a positive result, even when their animals appeared healthy. A positive finding means the organism is present but not necessarily the disease. This is where the great misinterpretation lies. If a cat is positive and already has some of the symptoms, then there may be justification for euthanization. But surely not if the cat is running, eating, playing, and appears healthy.

Do not put such a cat to sleep!

This animal can be rendered immune to acute infection and disease by starting it on a vitamin and mineral program, one including vitamin C. When retested six months to a year later, this cat will have a negative result.

The third test, and the one I use in my practice, is the Feline Leukemia Antibody Test. I prefer this procedure because it not only tells you if an organism is present but it also measures antibody production.

In this particular test, a negative result means no measurable antibody protection against the virus and resultant disease. The exception to this interpretation is the animal who has been supplemented with vitamin C regularly for at least six months to a year. This animal may also test negative. The reason for this is that the primary forces of the immune system—interferon and the white blood cells—are efficiently countering any leukemia virus that may be present. Antibodies do not come into play until some six to ten days after infection by the virus and their presence is a sign that interferon and the white blood cells have failed to hold the line. A negative reading for a supplemented animal means its immune system is doing the job.

Tests for leukemia and the other viral killer, FIP, are very important and should be done annually. This is part of good prevention.

Furthermore, any time a new cat is introduced to a cattery or a multicat household, it should first be tested for leukemia and FIP. It should also be isolated from the other animals for about two months, regardless of whether it tests positive or negative. This protects all animals from possible infection. The new cat should immediately be placed on a vitamin C− based program, and the regulars, if they have not already been on one, should start at once as well.

If the new cat originally tested positive, he can be retested again after about three months. By this time, the vitamin C should have boosted the immune system to the point where the virus is being effectively controlled. I have found it usually takes ten to twelve weeks to turn a leukemia-positive cat negative with oral supplementation. It can work even faster in some cats, within a week in fact.

BEWARE OF STEROIDS

Synthetic corticosteroid drugs—called steroids for short—are widely used in veterinary medicine as an antiinflammatory agent, to stimulate appetite, and to prevent animals from scratching and biting themselves because of skin irritation. Some animals remain on such drugs for weeks and even months.

Large doses of steroids are used consistently to stimulate appetite in animals with serious diseases such as leukemia and FIP.

The liberal use of steroids is a mistake in my opinion.

A 1979 study conducted by Ohio State University veterinary researchers found that steroid drugs actually can enhance susceptibility to leukemia and serious disease by impairing early viral containment in the immune system.[10]

When I use steroids in my practice, it is always for a very short period and always at doses much lower than recommended by the drug companies. The last thing I will do is give a steroid to a leukemic cat. That is like trying to douse a fire with gasoline. It is introducing a synthetic immune-suppressing agent to a cat already infected with a viral immune-suppressing agent. Furthermore, why try to stimulate the appetite in an animal whose body is in no condition to utilize the food?

I believe a more efficacious approach is attempting to nourish a sick cat with intravenous feedings of amino acids, dextrose, electrolytes, vitamin C, and the B complex factors. If a cat is salvageable, this will improve the chances for recovery.

15

Feline Infectious
Peritonitis (FIP)

FIP is a deadly viral disease first diagnosed in 1963. Most clinically ill cats die from the disease, and attempts at treatment are generally futile.

The disease manifests in two severe forms—wet and dry FIP—and in a third and less serious type.

The wet form (effusive) is the most easily recognizable due to the accumulation of fluid in the abdominal or chest cavities. Such a cat will display a potbelly or distended chest. There is also a lack of appetite, high temperature, and loss of weight. When the fluid builds up in the chest, a cat will experience labored breathing and be reluctant to lie down.

The dry form (noneffusive) is harder to recognize. There is no fluid accumulation. Here, a variety of organs can be attacked by the organism, resulting in death of tissue and eventually the death of the animal. The organs most frequently affected are the kidneys, spleen, liver, lymph nodes, the eyes, and the central nervous system. Weight loss, fever, and lethargy are common signs, along with symptoms related to the specific organ affected.

Both the wet and dry FIPs may be accompanied by an anemia, diarrhea, and vomiting.

Finally, there is a subclinical form of the disease that shows up as a minor upper respiratory ailment.

FIP is a common disease that strikes primarily young cats. Ninety percent of the reported cases are cats less than three years old.[1]

FIP occurs with no particular preference for breed or sex. Feline viral authority Niels Pedersen at the University of California–Davis says the disease does not occur more frequently in purebred cats, as has been sometimes reported.[2]

The disease is highly contagious among cats, although the exact vehicle of transmission is not known. Bloodsucking insects such as the flea are suspected carriers. Transmission of the virus in utero is another likely method.

Once infected, a cat may become a carrier showing no signs of disease or only minor symptoms. A stressful episode, however, such as a spay can activate the virus and trigger severe symptoms.

According to Pedersen, most cats apparently recover from the initial mild infection and only about one in fifteen develop classical FIP.

The major problem is in densely populated catteries, where mortality rates can run from 5 to 25 percent following the introduction of the virus into the environment.[3]

As we noted in the last chapter, the feline leukemia virus impairs the immune system, and this permits activation of other organisms and diseases. Leukemia is said to be a potent enhancer of FIP, and thus death due to FIP is often greater in catteries that also have a concurrent leukemia problem.

Approximately 40 to 50 percent of cats exhibiting FIP will test positive for leukemia, and "elimination of the leukemia infection would decrease the overall incidence of FIP by about one-half," says Pedersen.[4]

THE ANSWER TO FIP: PREVENTION

Prevention in both FIP and leukemia is clearly the only way to go. Treatment of both diseases, once classical signs have developed, is usually ineffective. My experience in trying to treat FIP animals has been largely disappointing.

I will never forget the first animal I saw with classical FIP symptoms. He was a big, black cat named "Zorro." This was back in the sixties when we didn't even have a name for the disease. My wife Marlene was assisting me at the time, and while she was holding the cat for me to examine, "Zorro" lashed out and raked her arm. We referred to the resultant wound as "the mark of 'Zorro'."

This animal was extremely ill and soon died. With the owner's permission, I performed an autopsy because I had never seen this condition before. When the chest cavity was opened, there was a considerable amount of fluid and fibrous tissue that obviously had impaired the action of the heart and lungs.

Over the years I have seen quite a few cases of FIP, particularly the wet type. In would come a client carrying a thin, noneating cat with a distended belly or chest. The temperature would be high. We would immediately draw blood and send it to the lab for confirmation of the FIP diagnosis.

Whenever I would see such a cat I knew I was in for an ordeal. It meant weekends and holidays. The animal had to receive continual care. None of the conventional methods worked, so I would try intravenous injections of vitamin C over several days.

But I was not having predictable results. I lost more patients than I saved.

As a result of my positive experience preventing leukemia, I applied the same vitamin and mineral approach to FIP. With a continual maintenance program of supplements, including vitamin C, animals are rendered more immune. You can prevent infection of cats to a large degree and in cattery situations where a chronic FIP infection exists, you can gradually bring the organism under control.

I have found, however, that FIP seems to be a more virulent organism than the leukemia virus and is more difficult to bring under control. Actually, FIP is believed to be caused by a mutant strain of the leukemia virus, and this may account for its extraordinary persistence.

In a contaminated cattery it may take as long as two years to eliminate the FIP virus from the premises. This timetable for clearance can be unraveled if a new animal is introduced into the cattery who is not on a vitamin C– based program. This animal is likely to have less resistance to the organism that is still being carried by the other cats—even though they themselves have it under control. Any new cat should be isolated from the others and placed on the supplement program for at least sixty days before being allowed to socialize with the cattery regulars. It is also a smart idea to have the new cat tested for FIP to know the immune status. A new animal can either spread or contract this highly contagious virus and increase the chance for a cattery-wide reinfection. FIP is an extremely virulent organism.

There is no vaccine on the horizon, so prevention is going to require a considerable amount of caution and diligence.

Dale Armon of Bloomingdale, Illinois, operates an orphanage and adoption agency for several hundred stray animals and she tells me that vitamin C has been a major factor in helping to control the FIP problem.

"We use large doses of vitamin C and find it extremely encouraging for FIP," she says. "In my experience if we can catch the disease before the bloating becomes extreme, we have an excellent opportunity of not only controlling the disease but curing it entirely."

As in preventing leukemia, vitamin C is the key to the supplement program. C stimulates the immune system to the maximum ability of an individual animal.

There is an antibody test that can determine whether your cat is infected with the FIP organism and to what degree. This test should be performed periodically for the sake of good prevention. It is also performed to confirm a diagnosis on a sick cat.

It is important to remember that a cat with no apparent symptoms can test positive. This means the animal has been infected and is a carrier and has the potential for disease in the future.

There is no need to panic, however. By initiating a vitamin and mineral supplement program—and *keeping* an animal on the program—you are providing the best possible protection against the eventuality of serious disease.

It will take about four months for a positive-testing cat to return to a normal status. There will be a dramatic drop in the antibody level when the cat is retested. This is a sign that the primary forces of immune response—the interferon and white blood cells—have been bolstered to the extent that the virus has either been eliminated altogether or significantly reduced. In this situation the antibodies—as the backup forces—have a diminished presence.

Besides maintaining your animal on a good supplement program, it is important to have an FIP antibody test performed annually. Also, check out your cat's gums frequently. They should be pink and not white. Pale gums are a sign your animal may have the FIP or leukemia virus, or both.

Remember, the earlier you catch these diseases, the better the chance of saving your cat.

SURGICAL SUCCESSES

Veterinarians may be interested to know about two cases of FIP that I successfully treated with surgical removal of the spleen combined with vitamin C supportive therapy.

A one-year-old mixed-breed male was presented with the classical symptoms of FIP. The cat had a temperature of 104 degrees, no appetite, pale mucous membranes, and a greatly distended abdomen.

With a hypodermic needle and syringe, I removed 400 cc of a straw-colored fluid from the abdomen. After removal of the fluid, I was able to palpate an enlarged spleen.

Blood was drawn and sent to the laboratory for FIP confirmation.

Because of the rapid deterioration of the cat, I decided to perform a splenectomy. An enlarged spleen is known to impair immune response. I felt that by removing this organ we might have a better chance at stimulating immune activity.

In order to rebuild the immune system as quickly as possible, vitamin C was incorporated into the surgical IV drip, and this was followed by intravenous injections of 2,000 milligrams of sodium ascorbate twice daily for two days postoperatively.

The morning following surgery, the cat's condition had improved considerably. He began eating and his temperature returned gradually to normal.

The second day we were able to release the animal to the care of the client, who was given a vitamin and mineral supplement—high in vitamin C—to be mixed into the food.

The cat made an uneventful recovery and lived for eighteen months until he was run over by a car.

The second case was a huge, yellow tom who was owned by a San Jose policeman. In this instance the FIP was the dry form. However, there was a similar enlarged spleen.

Without delay, I removed the organ and administered the same levels of vitamin C. The following morning a great improvement was noticed. The animal healed nicely and has been feeling fine ever since, even to the point of taking on dogs, I am told.

In the cat world, word gets around fast. Sometime after the second case, I received a phone call from a veterinarian in Illinois who had heard about the success of the splenectomy and vitamin C treatment.

He was treating a cat for FIP, and the animal displayed an enlarged spleen. He wanted to try the procedure. I gave him the details, and a few weeks later he called back to say the treatment worked. The cat had recovered.

Any veterinarian who would like to have more information on this combined treatment can feel free to contact me.

16

Upper Respiratory Disease

Feline upper respiratory disease is one of the most common sicknesses seen by veterinarians. It is sometimes called "rhino," short for feline viral rhinotracheitis, one of the viral agents that cause the disease. This and other microorganisms produce a typical set of dramatic symptoms, notably sneezing, coughing, and runny, pussy eyes and noses.

The disease is extremely contagious and presents a particular threat wherever cats congregate, such as in shows, kennels, pet shops, spay clinics, and catteries. A single infected cat can pass on the disease to other animals with a mere sneeze.

Cats of all ages are affected. While the disease is generally regarded to be self-limiting, the infection can be severe enough to cause death. Early treatment is important. Young kittens are particularly vulnerable, and the death rate among them can run as high as 75 percent.[1]

A large number of cats who recover may carry the viral organism in a latent state for more than a year. Such cats are at risk for relapse when subjected to stress.[2]

Immunization for upper respiratory disease has been effective to a significant degree. Nevertheless, boarded cats, show cats, and animals in catteries are frequently reported to become seriously infected despite having had inoculations. There are several reasons for the failure of immunization. I will deal with them here only briefly, since I covered this ground in detail in Chapter Seven:

1. Vaccines have been developed for three organisms causing upper respiratory illness. Other disease-causing organisms exist, and there are no vaccines for them.

2. Healthy animals produce antibodies in reaction to immunization. Antibody potency diminishes with time, however. That's why annual booster shots are recommended. But owners often forget or fail to revaccinate on schedule.

3. A weak, stressed, or unhealthy cat may not produce adequate antibodies following inoculation. If the body is not up to par, then the antibody production will be low and the animal will have less than ideal protection. Such a weak animal is unlikely as well to have robust primary immune strength at the level of interferon and the white blood cells.

4. An animal may be harboring the leukemia virus. If so, the production of antibodies following inoculation can be impaired because of the immunosuppressive action of the leukemia virus.

My method of preventing or minimizing respiratory disease is to utilize routine immunization along with the vitamin and mineral program. Supplementation should include, of course, extra vitamin C which is so vital to building a strong immune system.

I have heard from various cattery people around the country that upper respiratory disease still presents a serious problem. Among my clients, I am happy to say there is very little of it, and I attribute this to the combined effect of immunization and supplementation. Young kittens, the most susceptible to upper respiratory disease, receive a double degree of protection from my program. Firstly, their mother is supplemented throughout pregnancy and lactation and passes on optimal immunity through the placenta and milk. Secondly, soon after birth they themselves begin receiving extra vitamins. By the time they are immunized at twelve weeks of age, they are strong and healthy creatures able to develop maximum antibodies.

Many years ago I found vitamin C to be highly effective in treating upper respiratory disease. My routine was to administer 500 milligrams of sodium ascorbate intravenously per pound of body weight twice a day. After the initial injection, the temperature drops, the sneezing greatly diminishes, the appetite begins to return, and there is increased activity. After two or three injections, cats are usually in good enough shape to send home. The owners are given a supply of sodium ascorbate powder with instructions to add 2,000 to 4,000 milligrams to the food each day until all symptoms subside. In this manner, scores of cats have been successfully treated and the duration of the disease process significantly reduced.

The effectiveness of vitamin C therapy against upper respiratory disease was confirmed in 1967 by Dr. W. C. Edwards of Iowa State University. Over the course of several months, Edwards treated some sixty-four cats using either vitamin C (1,000-milligrams IV daily) or tylosin, an antibiotic, or a combination of both. The average recovery time was 4.9 days for the cats treated with vitamin C, 5.3 days for those treated with vitamin C and tylosin, 8.9 for those given tylosin only, and 13 days for those animals who received no treatment at all.[3]

In more recent years, I have improved the effectiveness of the vitamin C therapy by adding vitamin B complex and amino acids to the intravenous injections, along with oral vitamin A. This combination works even faster. I am getting dramatic recoveries in two days.

Both the B complex and vitamin A help to stimulate the immune system. Vitamin B_{12} aids in stimulating the appetite as well.

PART 5

*Preventing and Minimizing
Other Common Cat Disorders*

17

Digestive Disorders

PANCREATIC DYSFUNCTION

Does your cat eat well, even voraciously, and yet is all skin and bones? Does he have frequent bowel movements and produce a soft stool, lighter in color than normal? Is he lethargic and does he have a rough hair coat?

If the answer is yes to these questions, you probably have a cat with a malfunctioning pancreas. As an animal ages, there is a general slowing down of vital functions, and the pancreas is often affected. This is the organ that produces, among other things, some of the important digestive enzymes.

When the enzymes are inadequately supplied, food is not properly broken down for nutrient absorption in the intestines. Much of the nutrient value of food is thus unavailable to the cat and passes out in the stool. A cat will eat more in an attempt to compensate for lost nutrition. However, despite the excess eating, he is unable to utilize the food and becomes thinner and thinner.

In my practice I have found this condition not only in old cats but in young ones as well. I have treated animals with pancreatic dysfunction who are just a year old. I feel this premature occurrence may have something to do with poor diets. It is very possible chemical additives impair pancreatic function or possibly slow down the digestive process in the gut itself. However, in the young, this pancreatic impairment is short-lived.

If you have a cat showing these symptoms, best bring the animal to your veterinarian to have a pancreatic function test. If the diagnosis is indeed pancreatic dysfunction, the condition can be readily resolved in a majority of cases by administering a supplement of multiple enzymes.

Several weeks on this supplement and your animal should be well on its way to normal appearance and vigor.

A good vitamin and mineral program can help prevent this condition.

CONSTIPATION

Just like people, cats can have constipation problems, particularly older animals. The colon has degenerated and is not able to move the fecal matter out of the body as well as it used to.

I remember years ago having to periodically treat a senile tom with chronic constipation. Twice I had to go up his rectum with a forceps and pull out impacted fecal matter.

Eventually, I took this cat off his commercial chow, which contained bone and fish meal, and put him on a softer food such as canned liver, kidney, heart, or ground beef. Additionally, I asked the owner to cook some oatmeal and mix it in with the food. Oatmeal is a good source of roughage and protein and will help keep the bowels moving.

I also prescribed vitamins C and E for the old boy. I gradually increased him to a maintenance dose of 750 milligrams daily of sodium ascorbate, mixed into the food. The vitamin E dose was 100 units daily.

The combination worked fine. The cat was seen defecating with regularity.

Any animal with this problem can usually benefit from some dietary oatmeal. And of course, following my prevention program will prolong the efficiency of all vital functions, including elimination.

Susan Ironside, a breeder in Alameda, California, suggests adding bran to an aging cat's diet.

"I have been doing this for more than five years and found it effective in eliminating constipation in older cats. All my older animals have well-formed stools."

Ironside says the bran may also be helpful in reducing the diarrhea that some older cats experience as a result of bacterial imbalances in the intestine.

"Cats don't mind the bran at all," she says. "It has no aroma, so even finicky eaters are not turned off. I find that new cats take to it just as readily as all my regulars."

Ironside recommends one serving spoon of bran per pound of canned food. If raw meat is fed, she uses two serving spoons per pound of food. For the single cat, she suggests one teaspoon per serving. Mix thoroughly in the food.

Ironside uses a natural bran that she buys in health-food stores.

18

Eye Problems

PARALYTIC NICTITATING MEMBRANES

That's a fancy term for a rather common condition among cats and dogs where the third eyelid rises and covers a quarter or more of the eyeball.

This can happen to both sick or healthy animals. The rather bizarre sight brings pet owners rushing to the veterinarian, some worried that maybe their animals' eyes are sinking into the back of their heads. That, of course, is not the case.

I have come to regard this condition as an expression of subclinical scurvy—not enough vitamin C in the system. In well over a hundred cases now I have successfully used vitamin C to correct the condition.

I inject an animal with 500 milligrams of sodium ascorbate per pound of body weight, and several hours to a day later the eyes are normal.

I also advise owners to maintain their animals on vitamin C—along with other nutrients—because I have not found this condition to occur in any animal who is supplemented.

ULCERS

Vitamin A and C are being used by some breeders around the country to treat eye inflammations and ulcers. I personally have not used this approach, although from what I hear it can be successful.

One of my clients reported clearing up a condition called keratitis—inflamed corneas—among several Siamese kittens with vitamin A. This breeder said she used vitamin A fish-oil capsules in the strength of 10,000 International Units. She pricked the end of a capsule and applied one drop a day to the kittens' eyes. In three weeks the cloudiness disappeared, she said.

Two breeders have told me of curing ulcers, possibly of viral origin, with vitamins A and C.

One used vitamin A drops from capsules in the strength of 25,000 International Units three times daily in the affected eyes, along with 500 milligrams of vitamin C orally twice a day. She thus healed two Persian cats within two months, she said.

The other breeder cured a young American Shorthair in one month's time by orally administering 2,500 milligrams of vitamin C daily. She said she had been using a steroid eye medication for more than a half-year without resolving the problem. The steroid was merely keeping down the inflammation in the tissue around the eyeball. When she added the C, the condition quickly began to show signs of healing, she said.

I do not recommend to pet owners that they treat eye conditions with vitamins. It is always best to first bring a cat to a veterinarian for a professional diagnosis. If the veterinarian cannot handle the problem, he may be able to recommend a specialist. Today there are more than fifty veterinary ophthalmologists in the country. Once treatment is prescribed, a supplementation program can accelerate the healing.

TAURINE

The increasing cost of commercial pet food has prompted many cat owners to feed their animals with less expensive dog food. This can have grave consequences, however.

Dog food has little or no taurine, an amino acid that cats require in their diet. Without it, cats experience a degeneration of the retina and can become blind.

Dr. Gustavo Aguirre, a veterinary ophthalmologist at the University of Pennsylvania, has thoroughly investigated this problem and made veterinarians and cat owners aware of the danger. In a 1978 report in the *Journal of the American Veterinary Medical Association,* he noted that while cat foods generally have a higher taurine content than dog foods, some cat products "contained marginal or low concentrations."[1] He urged cat-food manufacturers to pay special attention to the taurine content of their products, and indeed, in the ensuing years, the labels or some items of cat food reflect the addition of taurine.

Aguirre has also advised vegetarians not to convert their cats into nonmeat eaters.

"There is not enough taurine in these diets to supply their needs," he says. "Vegetarian cats go blind."[2]

Taurine is found in high concentrations in meat, fish, liver, and, to a lesser degree, in milk.

Lack of taurine is not the only cause of retinal degeneration. Heredity and environment are other likely factors. However, by purchasing foods listing the addition of taurine on the label, you can essentially eliminate one of the major causes.

19

Feline Urologic Syndrome (FUS)

As of mid-1982, when this book was written, the veterinary jury was still out on FUS. There was no consensus regarding the causes of this common ailment, and in the words of the University of Minnesota's Dr. Carl A. Osborne, a leading authority, there was a lack of understanding as well. The issue continued to stir considerable disagreement, speculation, and research.

In recent years, suspicion has been narrowing in on viral or diet-related factors as the cause of FUS.

Osborne, for one, questions the commonly held idea "that FUS has to be initiated by one mechanism or the other." In a 1981 article he raises the possibility of a variety of entities being involved.[1]

What we do know for sure about FUS is that it affects a great number of animals—nearly one percent of the feline population in the United States—and represents some 5 to 10 percent of cat admissions to some vetrinary hospitals.[2]

The common forms of FUS are inflammations of the bladder and urethra, formation of bladder stones, and particularly in male cats, development of potentially fatal blockages in the narrow urethra. Unless the obstruction is removed, the poisonous wastes of the urine can back up into the body and cause uremic poisoning.

The telltale signs of an FUS problem are difficult urination— squatting, straining, and voiding of tiny amounts of urine—and traces of blood in the urine. There may also be excess licking of the genitalia, especially by males.

Without treatment, the condition can worsen: vomiting, depression, dehydration, coma, convulsions, and finally death.

FUS has a tendency to recur. According to Osborne, this may be related to a persistence of the underlying causes or failure to surgically remove all formations from the urinary tract.

"The two most common choices of management of urolithiasis (FUS) in cats have been surgical removal or euthanasia," he notes.[3]

Much of the debate on FUS has centered around the influence of high dietary levels of ash—minerals—that are contained in dry cat foods. The composition of the urinary tract stones and plugs is primarily mineral.

The ash argument has been boiling for twenty years. In my opinion the ash in the dry food definitely has an effect. However, I have seen no end of cats on high ash diets, on dry cat food all their lives, who did not develop FUS.

The question I have to ask is Why do some cats eating high ash develop FUS and others do not?

Here are some possible answers:

- **Water consumption.**

  If a cat does not drink enough water, this can lead to concentrated urine and perhaps create the conditions for stone formation. Maybe. Ralston Purina research has found that reduction of 20 percent of normal water intake has "no apparent detrimental effects to the urinary tract regardless of type diet being fed."[4] Nonetheless, a cat should always have available a supply of fresh water.

- **Stress.**

  This can cause trouble in any part of the body. I know of one female cat who started straining and passed bloody urine on four occasions when she came into season.

- **Poor diet.**

  Many diets simply do not provide enough good-quality nutrition to maintain the degree of health that may be necessary to prevent urinary tract infections and stones.

- **Vitamin C production.**

  Some cats have more biochemical assets than others. Cat A will produce more vitamin C in the liver than Cat B and, therefore, may be more resistant to FUS.

Let me tell you why I think this may be a clue to FUS. Back in 1946, Dr. W. J. McCormick, a Toronto physician, published a medical paper in which he stated that urinary tract stone formations may very well be due to a deficiency in vitamin C. His conclusion was based on a worldwide survey and his own long clinical experience. He found that stones could be cleared up when patients received corrective doses of vitamin C.[5]

In my practice I have been able to prevent FUS in cats simply by maintaining animals on a regular regimen of vitamin C. My prevention program of vitamins and minerals includes vitamin C, even though veterinary gospel says cats do not need extra C. I think they do. Cats are poor producers of this essential vitamin, the key to health—and some animals do not produce as well as others. When we supplement their own natural output with extra vitamin C, they just do not develop FUS.

Other veterinarians and breeders have been discovering this as well.

One veterinarian from Chicago has told me that since he began using a vitamin C– based supplement in his practice, the incidence of FUS has been "greatly reduced."

Carolyn Bussey, a veteran breeder in Washington State, informs me she has not had a single case of FUS in the fifteen years since she initiated vitamin C into the nutritional program of her cattery.

"At first my veterinarian laughed at me," she says. "But not any more."

If stress is somehow involved in FUS, vitamin C is kown to provide protection. The female cat who developed FUS four times when she came into heat did not do so again after being supplemented.

If a virus is involved in FUS, as some authorities say, vitamin C is known to be a potent antiviral agent. It boosts the immune system against any viral influences in the body.

If ash is involved, and I believe it is, then vitamin C appears to enhance the solubility of minerals and particulate matter, and prevent crystalization.

My treatment for cats with acute FUS includes a catheter douche of 25 percent solution of sodium ascorbate. Cat owners are advised to remove such animals from a dry-food diet and feed good quality low-ash products that can be purchased commercially.

I prescribe a multivitamin and mineral powder to be administered at the regular adult maintenance level. This includes some 500 to 750 milligrams of vitamin C, usually in the form of sodium ascorbate (but it can be ascorbic acid as well). In addition to this, I prescribe another 500 milligrams of vitamin C (ascorbic acid). The multi with C is administered in the morning, the extra dose of vitamin C alone in the evening.

Cats are not healed overnight. I often have to prescribe a muscle relaxant to aid cats in eliminating until the supplements effect a change in the body chemistry and keep the crystals in solution. An animal may plug again in six weeks or so, but crystal formations become smaller and smaller and fewer and fewer.

In serious cases I find it takes about six months to thoroughly resolve the problem—the elimination of all stones and subsequent blockage. If an animal is maintained on this program, I never have to treat it again for FUS.

Veterinarians Robert Goldstein and Geoff Broderick in New York State and Carvel Tiekert in Maryland use variations of this vitamin C therapy to successfully treat their FUS cases.

20

Skin Problems
(*Including Fleas and Allergies*)

Cats scratching nonstop. Cats with their skin licked raw in places. Cats with shabby hair coats. Cats constantly shedding. Baffling bumps and sores of unknown origin. Poor suffering cats who are victims of flea and parasite molestation.

Traffic is always heavy in skin cases at the veterinary hospital. In my practice I see more skin problems than any other ailment.

Together, skin and hair coat provide a darn good window into an animal's inner health—or lack of it. Some experts believe that fully 90 percent of domestic animal skin disorders stem from internal physiological disturbances.[1] Chronic low-grade ailments or major troubles brewing inside an animal's body often show up on the skin, the largest organ in the body.

A good example of this is the common abscess veterinarians often treat after animals become scratched or bitten in cat fights. Dr. Danny Scott of the Cornell University School of Veterinary Medicine warns that "when you get a cat with recurring abscesses, or a cat with abscesses that just won't heal, you'd better start thinking about feline leukemia virus." Remember the leukemia virus has an immunosuppressive action and impairs a cat's ability to fight off infection.

The presence of the leukemia organism, even if the cat appears otherwise healthy, can be indicated by chronic skin infections. "One of the most common underlying causes for chronic abscessation and not healing well is concurrent leukemia infection," says Scott.[2]

In veterinary medicine, diagnosis of parasitic skin conditions is relatively easy. The nonparasitic problems, however, require real detective work. There can be any number of internal factors involved.

Most pet owners do not have the time or the finances for elaborate testing to find out exactly what is causing the excess scratching, licking, biting, and resultant sores. They just want a medicine to cure the problem.

But it's not so easy.

While you can clean up a sore or administer a steroid drug to stop the scratching, you still have not touched the cause. You cannot maintain an animal forever on a drug or else you invite side effects. Anyway, when the drug wears off, the problem often comes galloping right back.

When talking about skin and hair coat, I feel you have to return to basics and consider nutrition. Skin is very sensitive to any deficiency of essential nutrients and is the very first organ to exhibit signs of poor nutrition. The fact that we veterinarians have such a large case load of skin problems is pretty convincing evidence to me that our domestic animals do not get the best possible food.

Can you confidently say your cat is getting a harmless diet? What about the impurities I mentioned earlier? What about the chemicals that color, preserve, stabilize, and flavor! Some of them have indeed caused skin disorders in animal experiments. Your cat's unhealthy or itching skin might be an allergic reaction to one or more of the chemicals or ingredients.

What about kidneys required to filter a lifetime of impurities and excess protein? Overworked or malfunctioning kidneys do not filter out impurities effectively, nor do they properly handle the waste products of protein metabolism. The impurities and wastes recirculate throughout the bloodstream and provoke problems such as itchy or dry, scaly skin. Failing kidneys is a fairly common condition in older cats.

And what about deficiencies of essential vitamins and minerals? It is unlikely your animals are receiving the total nutrition they need from a diet based solely on commercial cat food.

Let's take a look at some of the nutrient factors closely related to skin health:

- **Vitamin A.**

The skin reacts very quickly to even a mild deficiency. An animal becomes more susceptible to skin infections.

Deficiencies can be prevented by feeding liver (see the vitamin A section in Chapter Four) and maintaining a cat on a good supplementation program.

- **The B complex vitamins.**

These vitamins are decimated during processing and storage. Skin problems have been directly linked to deficiencies of some of the B vitamins.

One of them is biotin. Dr. Joan O. Joshua, a British veterinarian, has cleared up many nonparasitic skin conditions with injections of biotin. This vitamin suppresses irritation, reduces scratching, makes hair coats bloom, and improves appetite, she reports.[3]

In human medicine, biotin has been reported to improve skin conditions too.

Keep in mind, however, that all of the B complex vitamins and not just biotin alone are required for good skin health.

- **Vitamin C.**

In my practice I have been successful using vitamin C for numerous skin conditions and for maintaining healthy skin. Like dogs, cats with chronic skin problems may be short of vitamin C. In a 1942 study, a group of 104 dogs were tested for vitamin C blood levels. Among the animals there were 13 dogs with nonparasitic skin inflammations, and all were found to have below normal levels of the vitamin. The researchers treated the dogs with C and the conditions healed satisfactorily.[4]

A chronic skin condition can be the sign of an immune system overloaded by toxins, dietary impurities, environmental allergies, or an immunosuppressive agent such as the leukemia virus. Vitamin C beefs up the body to fight against these harmful influences.

- **Vitamin E.**

Food deficient in vitamin E can lead to a mild skin rash and marked hair loss, says Dr. Lon Lewis of Colorado State University, a specialist in veterinary nutrition. Although vitamin E is an antioxidant, it can still undergo oxidation, and this occurs in food products under extreme temperature and storage conditions. Two or three months of feeding this deficient food will bring out symptoms, which also include appetite loss, convulsions, and gastrointestinal problems, adds Lewis.[5]

Dr. N. H. Lambert, formerly the president of the Irish Veterinary Association, found that supplementation of vitamin E healed many chronic skin ulcers in both cats and dogs. He used E both orally (100–150 units daily) and topically. Lambert also noted that E improved general skin and coat conditions.[6]

• Zinc.

Researchers working with other species of animals have found zinc deficiencies involved in a number of skin problems. Cattle and sheep, for instance, exhibit loss of coat with scratching and thickening of the skin. Dogs show poor growth and rough hair coat.[7]

The major reason for zinc deficiency in food is the depleted state of our agricultural soil. If the soil is short of zinc, the food that grows in it will be short as well.

According to Lon Lewis, a cause of zinc deficiency may be excessive calcium in the diet, which interferes with zinc absorption in the intestine.[8] This is another good reason to go slow on calcium supplementation for your cats.

Zinc, taken on a supplemental basis, has been shown to speed healing of wounds, inflammations, and a variety of skin conditions in both humans and pets.

The moral of this short lesson in skin nutrition is that deficiencies, impurities, or specific allergenic ingredients in the diet can cause skin disease. A veterinarian sees many nonparasitic skin conditions that fail to respond to usual methods of treatment. Often not until a nutritional approach is tried does the problem clear up. Unfortunately, veterinary medicine is not nutritionally oriented, and a good deal of money can be spent by a client on useless therapies before nutrition is tried as a last resort.

To prevent getting "skinned" by skin bills, switch your animals to a good food product, one with few or no chemical additives. Remember, the more ingredients and chemicals on the label, the greater the chance for trouble. At the same time start my preventive vitamin and mineral program. The supplements will fill nutritional gaps, neutralize toxic substances bothering animals, and boost lagging immune systems. Improved nutrition results in increased resistance to parasites and improved skin health in every animal.

This opinion is shared by Robert and Marty Goldstein, holistic veterinarians who practice in Yorktown Heights, New York.

"When we put an animal on supplements and health food or home-made diets, we find the whole image of the cat changes for the best," they say.

"There are fewer fleas and fewer flea bites, less scratching, no more constant shedding, and an obvious improvement in the health and appearance of skin and hair coat.

"Cats are finicky eaters, so we make the diet change gradually over a two-month period."

In my practice I always trot out the story of a cat named "Woodstock" to help convince clients how nutrition can resolve skin problems.

"Woodstock" was the favorite cat of Nina Hendrix, a local animal savior who gave shelter to many stray cats and dogs right up until her death in 1982. This kindhearted lady was always bringing in strays for immunization and treatments, and she was always going out of her way to find good homes for animals.

"Woodstock" was a black, long-haired female about four years old who began losing her fur. In a matter of time, nothing was left but an ebony tuft at the end of a pinkish-gray tail.

Until her cat went bald, Hendrix was a stubborn nonbeliever in vitamins and minerals. She felt cats and dogs got all they needed in their food.

It took some doing, but I was finally able to convince her that supplements might help her denuded darling.

Two months after starting, she called to say there was a general regrowth of fur. In subsequent months more and more fur returned. Finally, Hendrix brought the cat in for me to see. "Woodstock" was the proud owner of a healthy, full-bodied coat of rich, black fur.

And what's more, said Hendrix, "Woodstock" no longer had the runny noses that were symptomatic of a chronic minor respiratory infection.

FLEAS AND FLEA ALLERGY DERMATITIS

Any cat owner is well aware of the havoc insects play with a cat's skin, particularly during the warmer months when insects are more active and plentiful. The cat acquires a flea, the flea bites the cat, the flea saliva irritates the cat's skin, and the cat responds by clawing or biting at the flea and constantly licking the bitten surface. The results: loss of hair, inflamed bumps, raw skin and scabs, infection, and a very uncomfortable animal.

A single flea can bite twenty times an hour, so the potential for misery is great indeed.

We veterinarians usually treat such abused skin with steroid drugs to keep the itching down and reduce the inflammation. But that doesn't get to the problem.

There are two things you can do to help protect cats against fleas and other insects. One is improving an animal's nutrition and the other is treating the immediate environment.

Cats on a good nutritional regimen are better able to resist parasites. They have stronger immune systems which can react more efficiently to flea bites. They seem to have fewer allergic reactions.

An effective antiflea nutritional campaign can include brewers' yeast, a rich source of B complex vitamins. This powdery substance seems to be able to reduce the effect of flea bites in many animals. It also is believed to develop an unusual aroma in the skin that fleas find distasteful. You will not notice the odor, but insects do, and they go looking elsewhere.

In many cases, a teaspoon of brewers' yeast mixed in each day to the daily ration can eliminate a flea problem in about thirty days, possibly even sooner. You might have to start with a lesser amount and gradually work up if your cats object to their tampered menu.

I often suggest to clients they start adding brewers' yeast in the spring and continue right through the hot weather. Many use brewers' yeast the whole year around. The extra B complex and good protein content of this foodstuff serves cats well. Brewers' yeast can be purchased in any health-food store.

Some veterinarians say brewers' yeast is useless against fleas. I can only say in my experience it works for many cats—not all, but many—and that's why I recommend it.

If you have an infestation, you will have to treat the source of it—the environment. Keep in mind an important fact of flea life: these parasites spend only 10 percent of their time poking around an animal's hide and sucking blood. The other 90 percent they are off the cat—though not very far away. They are living and multiplying in and under carpets, furniture, animal bedding, sand, and grass. It's not enough to make your cats more resistant. You must eliminate the fleas as well.

If you have an outdoor cat, the best you can do is spray the yard monthly. You will need to do it this often because the spray does not kill flea eggs. You eliminate the newly hatched fleas the second time around.

If your cats are the indoor type, you may have to use a chemical bomb to eliminate the infestation somewhere in your house. Bombs can be bought in a pet shop. Follow directions on the can. Daily vacuuming is also helpful.

An indoor-outdoor cat probably will require action on both fronts.

By now you may be asking where does the flea collar fit into all this. It doesn't. Not in my practice.

I do not recommend flea collars. They contain an insecticide that can be absorbed directly into an animal's bloodstream and cause trouble. If there is sensitivity or systemic weakness or if the animal is ill or stressed, an increased risk of reaction exists. I have treated a number of animals who became ill after their owners fitted them with collars.

Other than a miniature buckle and loop, the flea collar is much like the insecticide strip you hang in your house or garden. "Flea-collar dermatitis" is an angry-looking band of skin around the neck of dogs and cats and is a common consequence of wearing an insecticide.

People with sensitive skin have experienced skin irritation after handling the collar or fondling an animal wearing one. Indeed, the wrappings carry warnings that children should not handle the devices. People are advised to wash the chemical off after any contact. Despite these risks to humans, many individuals go right ahead anyway and use the contraptions on their pets.

Besides the possible harmful effect flea collars can have, I feel they are absolutely worthless for what they are promoted to do. The flea collar may kill a couple of insects a day, but others, by the numbers, are thriving nearby in the carpet or yard.

You are better off rubbing ground cloves or eucalyptus oil into a cat's hair coat. These will repel fleas. But if you think a flea collar is more fashionable, there are herbal varieties that are nontoxic to an animal.

RINGWORM

Cats appear to be nature's favored dispenser of ringworm, a highly contagious fungus condition that has nothing to do with worms.

The typical manifestation is an ugly round, hairless area on the skin, with or without scales and crust, and is usually seen in young animals.

A contaminated cat, whether showing the signs or not, can and does pass on the infection to other animals and people as well. Felines, in fact, are the main source of ringworm infection in humans.

"It's been estimated that, as far as children are concerned, 10 to 30 percent of the ringworm of the scalp is due to the cat," says Cornell's Dr. Danny Scott. "So we're not talking about an insignificant public health phenomenon at all."[9]

Many cats who carry this fungus are totally asymptomatic. Anywhere from 10 to 90 percent of a given cat population, depending on whose survey you read, says Scott.

In an article on feline skin conditions in *Persian Quarterly,* Scott adds a note of caution about using griseofulvin (Fulvicin), an oral drug commonly used in ringworm treatments.

"Beware of Fulvicin and its side effects," he says, especially when treating pregnant queens. "It causes all kinds of fetal abnormalities, affecting the heart, skeleton, eyes, brain and everything else."[10]

The treatment of ringworm is a tremendous problem. Just ask any cattery owner who's had it.

You cannot cure ringworm with vitamins and minerals. But you can keep feline resistance high with a solid supplementation program. Cattery owners do tell me my program minimizes the incidence of ringworm.

I have said before how important it is to maintain animals on the program. I'll say it again. Once off, resistance drops and a cat becomes more susceptible to harmful organisms. I know of several cases where supplemented young cats were sold to individuals who did not follow the program, and in a few months' time the animals were wearing the telltale patches of ringworm.

EAR MITES

In my practice I have not seen many cases of ear mites, but I have seen many cases where people *think* their cats have ear mites. The typical signs are head shaking, ear scratching, and the appearance of a dark discharge in the ear canal. A few shakes and some shadow in the canal and people rush out to buy an insecticide.

If you suspect ear mites, bring your cat to a veterinarian. This parasitic condition should be diagnosed professionally. I have treated many animals for general ear inflammations who were originally brought in for ear mites.

An insecticide in a cat's ear can cause irritation.

Another word about ear mites: If they are in the ear, they are very likely elsewhere on the body, so the whole cat will have to undergo treatment. And if one your cats has the critters, you can be fairly sure other animals in your household have it as well.

Leave mites for a veterinarian to diagnose and treat.

SKIN ALLERGIES

"Roscoe" was a neutered male cat who was doing fine until his owners changed carpeting in the house. Then suddenly "Roscoe" started itching like crazy and losing his hair.

Just like people, a cat can be allergic to anything he eats, drinks, touches, or inhales. Substances that cause an allergic reaction are called allergens. They are found among the creations of Mother Nature and likewise among the unnatural creations of modern technology. They can be mold spores from mildewed material and fungus, house dust, pollens, fumes from a gas heater, a flea bite, food, food additives, insecticides, pollutants in the air, and, as in the case of poor "Roscoe," the carpeting on the floor.

There is some evidence that cooked food can make cats more susceptible to allergies.

During the thirties and forties, Dr. Francis M. Pottenger, Jr., a California doctor, conducted a ten-year study with cats and found a relationship between cooked meat and a lowered threshold of allergic resistance. Compared with cats fed raw meat, the animals given cooked meat developed skin lesions and allergies that became "progressively worse from one generation to the next."[11]

Cats evolved on raw food, primarily raw meat. Today, however, a substantial part of the average cat's diet is highly processed, highly cooked, and chemically treated commercial food and it is likely this kind of diet has upset natural metabolic activity and led to some irregularities in digestive, enzyme, and hormonal function.

I believe the chemical blitz of our technological age has far outpaced the ability of our bodies—both humans and pets—to adapt. It seems as if everytime I pick up a newspaper or medical journal I read how this or that chemical is dangerous to health or causes genetic defects.

Allergy experts tell us that a healthy individual or animal can be exposed to pollens and molds and environmental chemicals without seeming to suffer. The body's manner of adaptation is complex and not completely understood. Yet gradually or suddenly, at any point in life, genetic weakness or inadequate nutrition can topple the biochemical barricades. Allergic problems can then develop anywhere in or on the body.

Once-tolerated substances are now allergens producing cellular death in the system. As cells die, they release a toxin called histamine, which enters the bloodstream and performs all sorts of biochemical mischief. You are familiar with the term *antihistamine*. This is a medicine taken to counter the effects of an allergic reaction.

Histamine has a tendency to irritate skin tissue. A cat thus affected will begin scratching or licking the area or will develop bumps, rashes, or swelling. This initial situation is made worse by further rubbing, biting, scratching, and licking. The skin becomes damaged, and infection can set in.

What vitamins and minerals can do for this kind of potential trouble is to maintain a strong resistance to allergens. Both vitamin C and pantothenic acid, for instance, are essential in the production of the adrenal hormone, cortisone. This substance is secreted into the bloodstream and acts as an antiinflammatory and antihistamine agent.

Ascorbic acid is the natural antihistamine—produced in the liver and used by mammals for millions of years. The liver is supposed to increase ascorbic acid production when an animal is under stress, but this response is sluggish in most cats. Perhaps long ago, when the cat provided for himself, vitamin C production was more efficient. But domestication, the cooked diet, and the proliferation of chemicals have probably disabled this natural process.

By supplementing, we are correcting this disability.

I have used vitamin C alone to treat and prevent many allergy cases in animals. But I prefer to use the whole team of vitamins and minerals. I want the effect of pantothenic acid. I want vitamin E involved as well since it, too, has proved effective against allergies. In tests with both laboratory animals and humans, Japanese dermatologist Dr. Mitsuo Kamimura has demonstrated that vitamin E supplementation reduces or eliminates swelling caused by injected or topically applied allergens.[12]

In my experience, the reactions of allergic cats and dogs on a good program are greatly minimized. In many cases, the allergy symptoms disappear.

The case of "Roscoe," the carpet-sensitive cat, is a good example. I first put the animal on short-term steroids, and he seemed to hold his own against the carpet. A week or so later when the medication ran out. "Roscoe" started scratching again.

When his owners returned, I told them about the dangers of prolonged steroid use and suggested they try the vitamin and mineral program.

"Look," I said, "you love your cat and probably love your new carpet, too, and don't want to sacrifice either one. So try the vitamins. I cannot assure you they will eliminate the problem, but they will certainly stimulate the animal's immune system so he can better cope with the carpet."

They agreed. Three weeks later they called to say the scratching and hair fallout had lessened greatly.

As long as "Roscoe" was maintained on the program, the allergy was under control. Whenever the supplements ran out and were not soon replenished, the allergy would flare up again.

Skin rashes and itchy, scratchy skin can be signs of a food allergy. The problem most frequently is seen around the ears and eyes, on the feet, and on the underside. This is where most of the histamine irritation occurs.

Dr. Alfred J. Plechner, a West Los Angeles veterinarian who specializes in food and immune problems, says that many food-related allergies are not being diagnosed by veterinarians.

"I am seeing a lot of referrals after classic therapy has not worked," he says. "In my opinion, perhaps 20 percent of the problems in regular veterinarian practices are food based."

Plechner singles out beef and tuna as the major offenders in cats.

"These poor animals are screaming. Day after day they get beef and tuna in one form or another because that is essentially what's out there on the market shelves. Beef and kidney. Liver and kidney. Chicken and tuna. Tuna and kidney. Ad nauseam.

"Cats can be allergic to beef and fish no matter what form these foods come in: kibble, meal, biscuits, bones, rawhide or chewsticks."

Food insensitivity is not necessarily limited to skin problems, Plechner points out. Animals can and do develop diarrhea, vomiting, convulsions, hyperactivity, and a whole range of serious diseases.

Other allergenic offenders for pets are wheat, wheat germ, wheat germ oil, corn, corn oil, peas, beans, nuts, eggs, milk and milk products, shellfish, chocolate, fresh fruit, tomatoes, grapes, pineapples, mushrooms, yeast, foods containing yeast, spices, and additives used in food preparations.[13]

Anything can cause an allergic response, says Plechner. He has found, for instance, that many animals will react to dry food products because of the multiplicity of allergens they contain. He has even incriminated B complex vitamins and brewers' yeast, although in my practice I have rarely encountered this. Still, I should point out that many humans are allergic to yeast, and since B complex vitamins are usually prepared from yeast, this could indeed be a source of allergic irritation. An alternative to both brewers' yeast and yeast-based B vitamins, if an allergy does exist, is rice. Schiff, a leading vitamin manufacturer, markets a line of B complex products using rice as the nutrient source. If you believe your cat is allergic to yeast, then this may offer a solution. You can find these products at health-food stores.

Of the meat products fed to dogs and cats, Plechner has found lamb to be the least allergenic.

The best approach to a suspected food allergy situation is to change the diet and put the animal on a vitamin and mineral program. The importance of changing the diet is this: If day after day the cat is eating substances that are allergenic, then the vitamins and minerals can do only so much. The stress can be greater than the protection.

For information on special food products for allergic pets, write or call the following companies: Cornucopia Products, manufactured by Veterinary Nutritional Associates, 229 Wall Street, Huntington, NY 11743, telephone (516) 427-7479; Nature's Recipe, manufactured by Earth Elements, Inc., P.O. Box 5249, Orange, CA 92667, telephone (213) 531-1172; Lick Your Chops, the first health-food store for pets in the country, 1863 Commerce Street, Yorktown Heights, NY 10598, telephone (914) 962-4599.

Let me add a word of caution: Any time your animal develops diarrhea, vomiting, or a chronic skin problem, which can be signs of allergy but also of other conditions, consult a veterinarian. The veterinarian can treat the symptoms and, if an allergic response is suspected and he is not set up for allergic testing, he may be able to refer you to a specialist.

SHEDDING

Nature has endowed the cat with a built-in cooling system: shedding. Come warmer weather, the heavy winter coat starts dropping off.

Many of our domestic animals have a problem of year-round shedding. This may be the consequence of an indoor existence or a poor diet, or both.

Constant shedding is not normal. After two or three weeks it should stop.

A vitamin and mineral program eliminates or minimizes this problem. I discovered this happy fact as a by-product of using nutritional therapy for other conditions.

21

Tumors

Among cats, dogs, and humans, the feline has the lowest rate of cancer incidence: 155 cases per 100,000 population, compared with 271 for humans and 381 for dogs.

But the numbers are misleading. While fewer cats develop cancer, the cancer they do have is more likely to be fatal.[1]

The most common form of cancer in cats is a deadly malignancy of the blood and lymphatic system called lymphosarcoma. It is caused by none other than the feline leukemia virus, the infamous perpetrator of so much suffering in cats.

According to a 1971 survey by the National Cancer Institute of 488 feline tumors, lymphosarcoma is malignant 97 percent of the time.[2] A malignancy means a rapidly spreading mass of abnormal cells that invades nearby tissue, disrupts vital bodily functions, and often causes death.

There is no effective treatment for lymphosarcoma, especially once it becomes advanced. The administration of chemotherapy is of benefit in some cases, however, the mortality rate is high.

Symptoms of lymphosarcoma include weight loss, lethargy, vomiting, diarrhea, fever, difficult breathing, and increased thirst. Cats with this condition develop masses in different parts of the body along with swellings of the lymph nodes.

Following lymphosarcoma, the skin is the next most common site of feline tumors. Malignancies here run at around 40 percent, according to the 1971 survey. Many of the skin tumors appear around the ears, nose, and eyes, where the fur is thin and the skin receives more exposure to damaging solar rays. All-white or white-faced cats tend to be at higher risk for facial tumors.

Tumors of the oral cavity are also common. Almost 70 percent of them are malignant. The tongue, gums, and palate are frequent sites. These growths present a particular problem because they are hidden from sight and are usually not detected until they are well advanced. Often the cancer has spread to other areas of the body by the time it has been diagnosed.

Symptoms of oral cancer are drooling, foul breath, clawing at the face, bleeding from the mouth or nose, labored breathing and eating, and swelling around the lips or gums.

Other frequently encountered tumors involve the digestive system (75 percent malignant) and the mammary glands (90 percent malignant).

The risk of tumors in cats increases with age. There is no apparent breed disposition, however in one survey of 132 mammary cancer cases, Siamese cats had twice the risk for this form of tumor than other breeds.[3] For lymphosarcomas, male felines are said to be more susceptible than females.[4]

In addition to the leukemia virus and solar radiation, other possible causes of cancer in cats are: X rays, certain chemicals, radioactive elements, foods, drugs, and changes in hormonal function. These are also the same factors that affect humans.

Feline tumors tend to be highly malignant in nature. Early detection and treatment is extremely important, and many cases can be successfully resolved if handled promptly. If any of the early warning signs are observed, an animal should be taken to a veterinarian at once.

Dr. Anita Henness, a Garden Grove, California, veterinarian who specializes in cancer of small animals, says one problem in dealing with feline tumors is that "cats are laid back. They don't complain, so they don't get treatment as soon as they should."

It is therefore important for cat owners to be especially observant, she says. Animals should be examined once a month for any abnormalities such as swellings or lumps, chronic bleeding, bad odors, difficulty in eating or swallowing, and persistent weight loss or fatigue.[5]

VITAMIN AND MINERALS
AGAINST CANCER

The late cancer expert Dr. Hardin Jones of the University of California once said, "It is not the cancer that kills the victim; it's the breakdown of the defense mechanism that eventually brings death."[6]

If there is one thing I have learned during my twenty years of practice, it is the fact that strong bodily defenses are dependent on good nutrition. An optimally healthy immune system means optimal protection against all serious diseases, including cancer. Animals maintained on a vitamin and mineral program and eating good-quality food have the robust internal defenses to neutralize viruses, chemicals, pollutants, additives, and abnormal cell growths involved in this disease process.

Briefly, let's survey some of the major vitamins and minerals with reputations for cancer protection:

• **Vitamin A.**

Since 1925, researchers have connected vitamin A deficiency with cancer. This vitamin helps prevent tumors by protecting the vital nucleic acid inside epithelial tissue, the top layer of cells that form the lining of the skin, glands, and internal systems and organs. The vitamin also influences normal cellular proliferation and keeps mucous membranes healthy. Supplementally, vitamin A has been repeatedly shown to reduce many experimentally induced cancers in animals.[7]

• **B complex vitamins.**

Tumors have been induced in mice as a result of withholding several of the B vitamins. In one research project, liver and brewers' yeast, primary sources of B vitamins, protected laboratory rats who were fed a banned food coloring agent known to cause liver cancer.[8] In another test, B complex supplementation to a normal rodent diet was shown to increase resistance to connective tissue malignancies.[9]

• **Vitamin C.**

The National Cancer Institute has known of the cancer-killing power of vitamin C since 1969. At that time a team of researchers found megadoses of ascorbic acid to be highly lethal against tumor cells in laboratory experiments. The researchers also described the vitamin as "remarkably nontoxic."[10]

Unfortunately, mainstream medicine has not pursued this promising lead but concentrated instead on toxic chemotherapeutic drugs.

Dr. Linus Pauling in the United States and Dr. Ewan Cameron in Scotland were the first to demonstrate the effectiveness of vitamin C on cancer patients. In an ongoing trial begun during the seventies, they administered 10 grams or more daily to terminally ill cancer patients. They found this resulted in a fourfold extension of survival time compared to other similarly ill patients who did not receive the vitamin. Some of the vitamin C patients were still alive eight years after initiation of the therapy.[11]

The work of Pauling and Cameron has been confirmed by Japanese studies with terminal cancer patients, individuals who had been informed by their physicians they could not be treated any longer by conventional forms of therapy and who were expected to die shortly. Patients who received large doses of vitamin C survived up to fifteen times longer than those who were given small doses or none at all. In all these studies, vitamin C was found to markedly reduce pain and dependence on painkilling drugs, while at the same time increasing poor appetites, stimulating mental alertness, and promoting a sense of well-being.[12]

Pauling and Cameron believe the influence of vitamin C is felt on several fronts.

For one, it maintains the strength of collagen. The stronger this intercellular cement, the greater is the resistance of tissues to the infiltration and spread of tumors.

In the case of malignancies caused by viruses, and in the feline this is a paramount factor, high doses of vitamin C have a proven deterrent ability. In one experiment with a common viral tumor in chickens, researchers at the University of California observed a "substantial reduction in virus replication after addition of ascorbic acid." Furthermore, the vitamin seems to render the virus less infectious, they said.[13]

And yet another ability of vitamin C is to detoxify chemical agents such as nitrites that are known to cause cancer.

The risk for tumors in domestic animals increases with age, and we have seen how an animal produces less of his own vitamin C as he ages. Is there a connection between age-related tumors and this diminished natural ability to make vitamin C? I think so. Supplementation offers a compensating degree of protection in my opinion.

• **Vitamin E and Selenium.**

These two nutrients, along with vitamin C, are the body's natural antioxidants. They protect the cells against the harmful effects of peroxidation. They all contribute to immune system health in general and improve resistance to cancer in particular.

In a test with these three antioxidants, biochemist Richard Passwater reported reducing chemically caused cancer in rodents to about 10 percent of the expected level. "The antioxidants slowed the aging process as a secondary factor and prevented cancer as a primary factor," he wrote in his excellent book *Cancer and Its Nutritional Therapies.*[14]

Irish veterinarian N. H. Lambert used vitamin E for many years in his practice. He found it rendered tumors more operable or even made surgery unnecessary, increased the life-span for as long as five years in otherwise doomed animals, and contributed to a marked improvement in general health and appetite after surgery. Lambert used up to 200 International Units of vitamin E daily.[15]

Dr. Gerhard Schrauzer of the University of California at San Diego reduced the incidence of breast cancer in susceptible female mice from 82 percent to 10 percent merely by adding tiny amounts of selenium to the animals' drinking water.[16]

• **Zinc.**

Experiments with zinc have overwhelmingly shown that this vital mineral is required by every aspect of the immune protective system. Deficient animals become more susceptible to chemical carcinogens. High levels of zinc have been found to decrease tumor incidence.[17]

VITAMIN THERAPY

In my practice I do not see many feline tumors. I believe this may have something to do with the supplementation program my regular clients administer to their animals. When I do have a case, I will either remove the tumor surgically, if that is feasible, or recommend a veterinarian specializing in cancer.

The problem with cancer is that all too often by the time we veterinarians are consulted, an animal has an advanced case with a poor outlook for survival. The best a nutritional program can do in these cases is to minimize suffering and pain.

Once a tumor is removed, I certainly recommend an animal be put on vitamins and minerals. This will help in healing and offer protection for the future.

I have read letters to the editors in popular nutrition magazines describing successful home treatment of pet tumors—particularly dogs—with vitamins and minerals. This does not surprise me. However, any such attempt should be conducted under the guidance or at least with the knowledge of a skilled veterinarian who can monitor progress.

Dr. Robert Goldstein of Yorktown Heights, New York, specializes in small-animal tumors within his general holistic veterinary practice. He has developed a vitamin and mineral therapy program using massive doses of the nutrients I have just discussed.

Goldstein says it is essential to treat tumors as early as possible. In his practice, many of the animals have been referred to him by other veterinarians after chemotherapy has failed against malignant tumors.

"By then these animals are usually too far gone," he says. "The best we can do with vitamins is to increase the quality of their life in the time remaining to them."

Goldstein says he has had good results using nutritional therapy to clear up benign fatty tumors and skin tumors.

22

Worms

A woman rushed into my office with a prostrate kitten seven weeks old. The animal was dehydrated from diarrhea, had a potbelly, subnormal temperature, rough hair coat, and a mucous-like jelly oozing out its rear end.

The cat had been sick for a few days, the woman said. She produced a small vinyl wrapper containing a worm which she said she pulled out of the kitten's rectum.

I told her the animal clearly had a heavy infestation of worms and probably was too weak to cope with a chemical deworming agent.

I tried to administer fluids, but the kitten was too far gone and soon died. Autopsy revealed an intestinal tract riddled with roundworms.

This case was typical of many I have treated. A cat owner notices an animal is not normal for a few days yet delays veterinary treatment thinking the cat might get over whatever is bothering it. When a worm is sighted, the cat is finally brought in.

Anytime a kitten develops any sign of illness, it is imperative to see your veterinarian immediately. A small kitten is very vulnerable and is soon a dead kitten. I have seen many young cats over the years so riddled with parasites that there was no way they could survive. The parasitic stress saps their defense mechanisms, leaving them wide open to bacterial and viral infections.

Nationally, roundworms appear to be the most common intestinal parasite afflicting cats. An infected queen commonly passes larvae to her kittens during nursing. Cats of all ages also pick up worms directly from contaminated dirt or water.

Upon pregnancy, a queen should always be examined for worms. This can prevent serious problems later on.

It is a wise practice also to routinely check the kitty litter. Tapeworms can often be detected in the droppings. They appear as little pieces of rice. Sometimes they can be observed as small white balls around the rectum hairs. Obviously, whenever you make such an observation, see your veterinarian.

In my practice I frequently treat tapeworm infestations during the summer. Fleas feed on tapeworm eggs which are then ingested by cats as they bite and crush the insects harassing them. Inside the intestines the eggs develop into adults and feed right along with the cat. They can grow up to five feet long. A cat with a thriving case of tapeworms will eat excessively to make up for what the worms are eating. The hair coat will be rough. A potbelly is often present and sometimes diarrhea.

Deworming has always been a problem due to the weakened state of the animal. The deworming chemical is essentially a poison supposed to kill the parasites. But it may also kill a weakened cat, especially a kitten.

Happily, there is a product available now for tapeworm elimination that is not at all toxic. It is called Dronsit. It lowers the resistance of the worm to the digestive process. The cat's own juices disintegrate the parasite.

Vitamins and minerals cannot prevent an animal from becoming infected with intestinal parasites. However, they can minimize the effects of the worms, compensate for lost nutrition, and also offer a degree of protection against the chemical stress of toxic deworming compounds.

Carolyn Bussey, a Washington State breeder, routinely steps up the amount of vitamin C and E to her kittens whenever she has any deworming to be done. She uses Piperzine for three days, adding at the same time 250 milligrams of vitamin C and 25 International Units of E per kitten in the food to protect the animals from the toxin.

You may want to try garlic as a worm preventive. Garlic is an old remedy for intestinal parasites, used by the ancient Chinese and Hindus among others. Both fresh garlic cloves as well as tablets and powder can be effective. Garlic and parsley tablets can be crunched up and added to the food. The parsley neutralizes the garlic odor.

Garlic is also a natural antibiotic.

Reference Notes

Chapter One

1. "Crazy Over Cats," *Time* magazine, December 7, 1981, p. 72.
2. Ibid., p. 77.
3. Lyle A. Baker, "Veterinary Corner," *International Academy of Preventive Medicine Bulletin,* Winter 1980, p. 3.
4. Robert Wilson, before the U.S. Senate Select Committee on Nutrition and Human Needs, quoted in "Scientist Tells Senate of Critical Need for More Nutrition Training Programs," *DVM,* November–December 1978, p. 1.
5. Paul M. Newberne, "Problems and Opportunities in Pet Animal Nutrition," *Cornell Veterinarian,* April 1974, pp. 159–160.

Chapter Two

1. David Kronfeld, "Peculiarities of Cat Nutrition—Feeding Commercial Cat Foods and Home-Cooking for Cats," *Cat Fanciers' Association Yearbook 1980,* p. 460.
2. Jean Burden, *The Woman's Day Book of Hints for Cat Owners,* Fawcett Columbine, New York, 1980, p. 83.
3. "Cat Food," *Consumer Reports,* September 1972, pp. 560–565.
4. Ibid., p. 563.
5. "Nutrient Requirements of Cats," National Research Council, National Academy of Sciences, Washington, D.C., 1978, p. 1.
6. Stanley N. Gershoff, "Nutritional Problems of Household Cats," *Journal of the American Veterinary Medical Association,* March 1, 1975, p. 455.
7. "Vitamin Assurance for Pet Foods," *Roche Animal Nutrition and Health Manual 102,* Hoffmann-La Roche, Inc., Nutley, N.J.

8. Kronfeld, op. cit., p. 463.

9. Frances Sheridan Goulart, "Bone Appetit—Rating Pet Foods," *Consumers Digest,* November-December 1979, p. 7.

10. J. P. Greaves, cited in Gershoff, p. 455.

11. Phyllis Lehmann, "More Than You Ever Thought You Would Know About Food Additives," part III, *FDA Consumer,* June 1979, p. 12.

12. Marshall Mandell, *Dr. Mandell's 5-Day Allergy Relief System,* Thomas Y. Crowell, New York, 1979, p. 140.

13. Newberne, op. cit., p. 164.

14. Goulart, op. cit., p. 8.

15. Jacqueline Verrett and Jean Carper, *Eating May Be Hazardous to Your Health,* Anchor Press/Doubleday, Garden City, N.Y., 1975, p. 53.

16. James G. Fox and George W. Boylen, Jr., "Analysis of Lead in Animal Feed Ingredients," *American Journal of Veterinary Research,* January 1978, p. 168.

17. W. C. Edwards et al., "Lead, Arsenic and Cadmium Levels in Commercial Pet Foods," *Veterinary Medicine/Small Animal Clinician,* November 1979, p. 1609.

18. John D. Rhoades, "Lead Poisoning in Small Animals," *DVM,* August– September 1980, p. 17.

19. Lester Hankin et al., "Lead Content of Pet Foods," *Bulletin of Environmental Contamination and Toxicology,* May 1975, pp. 630– 632.

20. James G. Fox et al., "Lead in Animal Foods," *Journal of Toxicology and Environmental Health,* January 1976, pp. 461– 467.

21. Edwards, op. cit., pp. 1611– 1612.

22. Alfred J. Plechner, "Food Mediated Disorders," *California Veterinarian,* June 1978.

23. Francis M. Pottenger, Jr., "The Effect of Heat-Processed Foods and Metabolized Vitamin D Milk on the Dentofacial Structures of Experimental Animals," *American Journal of Orthodontics and Oral Surgery,* August 1946, pp. 467– 485.

24. Gustavo D. Aguirre, "Retinal Degeneration Associated With the Feeding of Dog Foods to Cats," *Journal of the American Veterinary Medical Association,* April 1, 1978, pp. 791– 796.

Chapter Three

For general reading on vitamin C and its medical applications, see Dr. Irwin Stone's book, *The Healing Factor: Vitamin C Against Disease,* Grosset & Dunlap, New York, 1972.

1. "Nutrient Requirements of Cats," National Research Council, National Academy of Sciences, Washington, D.C., 1978, p. 16.

2. I. B. Chatterjee, "Evolution and the Biosynthesis of Ascorbic Acid," *Science,* December 21, 1973, p. 1272.

3. J. V. Lacroix et al., "Ascorbic Acid Blood Levels in the Dog," *North American Veterinarian,* May 1942, p. 329.

4. Brian Leibovitz and Benjamin Siegal, "Ascorbic Acid, Neutrophil Function and the Immune Response," *International Journal of Vitamin Nutrition Research,* vol. 48, 1978.

5. Fred R. Klenner, "The Treatment of Poliomyelitis and Other Virus Disease with Vitamin C," *Southern Medicine and Surgery,* vol. 111, 1949, pp. 209–214.

6. Fred R. Klenner, "Significance of High Daily Intake of Ascorbic Acid in Preventive Medicine," *Journal of the International Academy of Preventive Medicine,* Spring 1974.

7. Akira Murata, "Virucidal Activity of Vitamin C," *Proceedings of the First Intersectional Congress of the International Association of Microbiological Societies,* Tokyo, 1975, pp. 431–436.

8. Edward J. Calabrese, quoted in "Make Vitamin C Your Shield Against Pollution," *Prevention,* April 1982, p. 18.

9. Work of I. B. Chatterjee, cited in Dr. Carl C. Pfeiffer's *Zinc and Other Micro-nutrients,* Keats Publishing, New Canaan, Conn., 1978, p. 180.

10. Irwin Stone, *The Healing Factor: Vitamin C Against Disease,* p. 155.

11. Pfeiffer, op. cit., p. 180.

12. J. J. Doyle, "Effects of Low Levels of Dietary Cadmium in Animals," *Journal of Environmental Quality,* April–June 1977, pp. 111–115.

13. M. R. Spivey Fox et al., "Cadmium Toxicity Decreased by Dietary Ascorbic Acid Supplements," *Science,* September 4, 1970, pp. 989–991.

14. W. C. Edwards et al., op. cit., pp. 1609–1612.

15. Sidney S. Mirvish, "Blocking the Formation of N-Nitroso Compounds With Ascorbic Acid in Vitro and Vivo," presented at the Second Conference on Vitamin C, New York Academy of Sciences, October 9–12, 1974. Melvin Greenblatt, "Ascorbic Acid Blocking of Aminopyrine Nitrosation," *Journal of the National Cancer Institute,* April 1973, p. 1055. I. A. Wolff and A. E. Wasserman, "Nitrates, Nitrites and Nitrosamines," *Science,* July 7, 1972, p. 15.

16. Steven R. Tannenbaum, "Nitrate and Nitrite: Origin in Humans," *Science,* September 28, 1979. A detailed description of a study conducted by Tannenbaum showing the protective ability of vitamin C against nitrosamine formation appears in *Prevention,* April 1982, pp. 19–20.

17. W. J. McCormick, "Ascorbic Acid as a Chemotherapeutic Agent," *Archives of Pediatrics,* April 1952, p. 152.

18. I. B. Chatterjee, op. cit., p. 1271. Natarjan Subramanian et al., "Role of 1-Ascorbic Acid on Detoxification of Histamine," *Biochemical Pharmacology*, vol. 22, no. 13, 1973, p. 1671. Sherry Lewin, *Vitamin C: Its Molecular Biology and Medical Potential*, Academic Press, London, 1976, p. 84.

19. W. M. Ringsdorf, Jr., and E. Cheraskin, "Vitamin C and the Metabolism of Analgesic, Antipyretic, and Anti-inflammatory Drugs," *Alabama Journal of Medical Sciences*, vol. 16, no. 3, 1979, p. 219.

20. E. Cameron and L. Pauling, "Vitamin C and Cancer," *International Journal of Environmental Studies*, vol. 10 (1977), p. 303.

21. Linus Pauling before the U.S. Senate Subcommittee on Health, quoted in *A Physician's Handbook on Orthomolecular Medicine*, Roger J. Williams and Dwight K. Kalita, editors, Pergamon Press, New York, 1977, p. 48.

22. Ibid., p. 48.

Chapter Four

1. *The Complete Book of Vitamins*, by the staff of *Prevention* magazine, Rodale Press, Emmaus, Pa., 1977, p. 311.

2. Lon D. Lewis quoted in "Clinical Manifestations of Nutritional Deficiencies," *DVM*, July 1981, p. 48.

3. "Nutrient Requirements of Cats," National Research Council, National Academy of Sciences, Washington, D.C., 1978, pp. 8–12.

4. Erwin DiCyan, *Vitamins in Your Life and the Micronutrients*, Fireside Books, New York, 1974, p. 40.

5. Benjamin E. Cohen et al., "Vitamin A–Induced Nonspecific Resistance to Infection," *Journal of Infectious Diseases*, May 1974, p. 597.

6. Satoshi Innami et al., "Polychlorobiphenyl Toxicity and Nutrition," *Journal of Nutrition Science and Vitaminology*, vol. 20, 1974, p. 363.

7. "Defense Against PCBs," *DVM*, January 1980, p. 62.

8. D. Bennett, "Nutrition and Bone Disease in the Dog and Cat," *Veterinary Record*, April 17, 1976, p. 318.

9. Kronfeld, op. cit., p. 462.

10. Patricia P. Scott, as quoted in a chapter on the nutritional requirements of cats in the *Basic Guide to Canine Nutrition*, Gaines Professional Services, White Plains, New York, 1977, p. 86.

11. Gershoff, op. cit., p. 457.

12. R. B. Baggs et al., "Thiamine Deficiency Encephalopathy in a Specific-Pathogen-Free Cat Colony," *Laboratory Animal Science*, vol. 28, no. 3, 1978, pp. 323–325.

13. Roger J. Williams, *Nutrition Against Disease*, Bantam Books, New York, 1978, pp. 146–47. Richard B. Pelton and Roger J. Williams, "Effect of

Pantothenic Acid on the Longevity of Mice," *Proceedings of the Society for Experimental Biology and Medicine,* December 1958, p. 632.

14. Adelle Davis, *Let's Get Well,* Harcourt, New York, 1965, p. 160.

15. I. Szorady, "Pantothenic Acid and Allergy," *Acta Paediatrica,* Budapest, vol. 4, 1963, p. 73.

16. Paul M. Newberne and Vernon R. Young, "Marginal Vitamin B_{12} Intake During Gestation in the Rat Has Long Term Effects on the Offspring," *Nature,* March 23, 1973, pp. 263–264.

17. Claudia J. Carey and James G. Morris, "Biotin Deficiency in the Cat and the Effect on Hepatic Propionyl CoA Carboxylase," *Journal of Nutrition,* February 1977, pp. 330–334.

18. J. P. W. Rivers and T. L. Frankel, "Vitamin D in the Nutrition of the Cat," *The Nutrition Society Proceedings,* December 1979, p. 36A. Gershoff, op. cit., p. 456.

19. N. H. Lambert, "Clinical Experiences With Vitamin E in Dogs and Cats," *Proceedings of the Third International Congress on Vitamin E,* September 1955, pp. 617–619.

20. Herbert Bailey, *Vitamin E—Your Key to a Healthy Heart,* ARC Books, New York, 1971, p. 35.

21. Ibid., pp. 40–49.

22. Mohammad G. Mustafa, "Influence of Dietary Vitamin E on Lung Cellular Sensitivity in Rats," *Nutrition Reports International,* June 1975, pp. 473–476.

23. Eileen Mazer, "Make Vitamin C Your Shield Against Pollution," *Prevention,* April 1982, pp. 20–22.

24. Ching K. Chow et al., "Influence of Dietary Vitamin E on the Red Cells of Ozone-exposed Rats," *Environmental Research,* vol. 19, 1979, pp. 49–55.

25. Ching K. Chow, quoted by Kerry Pechter, "Vitamin E—A Protector Comes of Age," *Prevention,* February 1982, p. 57.

26. Cheryl F. Nickels, "Protective Effects of Supplemental Vitamin E Against Infection," *Federation Proceedings,* June 1979, p. 2134.

27. Patricia Curtis, *The Indoor Cat,* Perigee Books, New York, 1981, p. 38.

28. "Nutrient Requirements of Cats," op. cit., pp. 8–9.

29. Scott, op. cit., p. 90.

30. Tadashi Suzuki et al., "Effect of Dietary Supplementation of Iron and Ascorbic Acid on Lead Toxicity in Rats," *Journal of Nutrition,* vol. 109, 1979, p. 982.

31. N. P. Singh, "Intake of Magnesium and Toxicity of Lead," *Archives of Environmental Health,* May 1979.

32. Sharon Faelten, *The Complete Book of Minerals for Health*, Rodale Press, Emmaus, Pa., 1981, pp. 112–113.

33. Ibid., p. 86.

Chapter Six

1. R. J. Williams, *Nutrition Against Disease*, op. cit., p. 53.

2. Fred Hale, "Pigs Born without Eyeballs," *Journal of Heredity*, March 1933, p. 105.

3. R. J. Williams, *Nutrition Against Disease*, op. cit., pp. 60–61.

4. E. Cheraskin, W. M. Ringsdorf, Jr., and J. W. Clark, *Diet and Disease*, Keats Publishing, New Canaan, Conn., 1968, pp. 111–113.

5. Williams, *Nutrition Against Disease*, op. cit., p. 55.

6. "Nutrient Requirements of Cats," p. 1.

7. Martin Zucker, "Childbirth Made Easier With Vitamin C," *Let's Live*, October 1979, pp. 22–30.

8. F. G. Darlington and J. B. Chassels, "A Study on the Breeding and Racing of Thoroughbred Horses Given Large Doses of Alpha Tocopherol," *The Summary*, February 1956, pp. 2–10.

Chapter Seven

1. A. E. Axelrod et al., "Effects of Pantothenic Acid, Pyridoxine and Thiamine Deficiencies Upon Antibody Formation," *Journal of Nutrition*, vol. 72, 1960, p. 325.

2. Adelle Davis, op. cit., p. 120.

3. Archie Kalokerinos, *Every Second Child*, Thomas Nelson (Australia) Ltd., Melbourne, 1974.

4. Mary Herron, "Clinical Forum," *Feline Practice*, May 1977, p. 19.

5. Joseph T. Hart, "A New Approach to Sidereal Sleeplessness," *The Journal of Orthomolecular Psychiatry*, vol. 10, no. 3, 1981, p. 214.

Chapter Eight

1. Richard H. Pitcairn, "What's Beneath Behavior Problems?", *Prevention*, November 1980, p. 150.

2. James O'Shea and Seymour Porter, "Double-Blind Study of Children With Hyperkinetic Syndrome Treated With Multi-Allergen Extract Sublingually," *Journal of Learning Disabilities*, April 1981, pp. 189–190.

3. Bennett A. Shaywitz et al., "The Effects of Chronic Administration of Food Colorings on Activity Levels and Cognitive Performance in Normal and Hyperactive Developing Rat Pups," *Annals of Neurology*, August 1978, p. 196.

4. William B. Buck, "Clinical Toxicosis Induced by Insecticides in Dogs and Cats," *Veterinary Medicine/Small Animal Clinician,* August 1979, p. 1119.

5. Ibid.

6. K. Chatterjee et al., "Studies on the Protective Effects of L-Ascorbic Acid in Chronic Chlordane Toxicity," *International Journal for Vitamin and Nutrition Research,* vol. 51, no. 3, 1981, pp. 254–265.

Chapter Nine

1. Milton Scott, "Advances in Our Understanding of Vitamin E," *Federation Proceedings,* August 1980, p. 2737.

2. L. H. Chen, "The Effect of Age and Dietary Vitamin E on the Tissue Lipid Peroxidation of Mice," *Nutrition Reports International,* December 1974, pp. 339–344. See also A. L. Tappel, "Will Antioxidant Nutrients Slow Aging Processes?" *Geriatrics,* October 1968, pp. 97–105.

3. Edda Gabriel et al., "Influence of Age on the Vitamin E Requirement for Resolution of Necrotizing Myopathy," *Journal of Nutrition,* July 1980, pp. 1372–1379.

4. Denham Harman et al., "Free Radical Theory of Aging," *Journal of American Geriatrics Society,* vol. 25, no. 9. 1977, pp. 400–406.

5. N. H. Lambert, op. cit., pp. 611–617.

6. Jacob E. Mosier, "General Considerations for Nutritional Supplementation of the Geriatric Dog and Cat," paper distributed to veterinarians by A. H. Robbins Co., Richmond, Va.

7. Ibid.

8. Personal communication from I. B. Chatterjee.

9. I. B. Chatterjee, "Aspects of Ascorbic Acid Biosynthesis in Animals," *Annals of the New York Academy of Sciences,* April 21, 1961, pp. 50–51.

10. Ewan Cameron et al., "Ascorbic Acid and Cancer: A Review," *Cancer Research,* March 1979, pp. 663–681.

11. Mosier, loc. cit.

12. Ibid.

Chapter Fourteen

1. Murray B. Gardner, "Prevalence of FeLV Infection, Immunity and Disease in FeLV-Infected Multiple Cat Households," *Friskies Research Digest,* Spring 1980, p. 14.

2. Chris K. Grant et al., "Natural Feline Leukemia Virus Infection and the Immune Response of Cats of Different Ages," *Cancer Research,* March 1980, pp. 823–829.

3. William D. Hardy, Jr., "Current Status of FeLV Diseases," *Friskies Research Digest,* Summer 1979, p. 3.

4. Niels C. Pedersen, as quoted in "Feline Infectious Diseases Analyzed at AAHA Session," *DVM,* July 1981, p. 44.

5. Hardy, op. cit., p. 2.

6. Pedersen, loc. cit.

7. G. D. Norsworthy, "The Feline Leukemia Virus Associated Diseases," *Feline Practice,* May 1977, pp. 34– 36.

8. Wendell O. Belfield, "Vitamin C in Treatment of Canine and Feline Distemper Complex," *Veterinary Medicine/Small Animal Clinician,* April 1967, pp. 346– 348.

9. Sharon Faelten, op. cit., pp. 175– 77.

10. Jennifer L. Rojko et al., "Influence of Adrenal Corticosteroids on the Susceptibility of Cats to Feline Leukemia Virus Infection," *Cancer Research,* September 1979, pp. 3789– 3791.

Chapter Fifteen

1. Margaret Reister, "The Deadly Threat of FIP," *Cat Fancy,* February 1980, p. 11.

2. Niels C. Pedersen, "Feline Infectious Peritonitis: Something Old, Something New," *Feline Practice,* May 1976, p. 43.

3. Ibid., p. 44.

4. Pedersen, as quoted in *DVM,* loc. cit.

Chapter Sixteen

1. Guy H. Palmer, "Feline Upper Respiratory Disease: A Review," *Veterinary Medicine/Small Animal Clinician,* October 1980, p. 1557.

2. J. G. Lane, "Rhinitis and Sinusitis in the Cat," in *Current Veterinary Therapy VI,* W. B. Saunders, Philadelphia, Pa., 1977, pp. 228– 233.

3. W. C. Edwards, "Ascorbic Acid for Treatment of Feline Rhinotracheitis," *Veterinary Medicine/Small Animal Clinician,* July 1968, pp. 696– 698. See also Wendell O. Belfield and Irwin Stone, "Megascorbic Prophylaxis and Megascorbic Therapy: A New Orthomolecular Modality in Veterinary Medicine," *Journal of the International Academy of Preventive Medicine,* vol. II, no. 3, 1975.

Chapter Eighteen

1. Aguirre, op. cit., p. 795.

2. Aguirre, as quoted in *Cats* magazine, March 1981, p. 25.

Chapter Nineteen

1. Carl A. Osborne, "War on FUS, Feline Enemy #1," *DVM*, November/December 1981, p. 41.
2. K. C. Bovee et al., "Recurrence of Feline Urethral Obstruction," *Journal of the American Veterinary Medical Association*, vol. 174, no. 1, 1979, pp. 93–96.
3. Osborne, op cit., p. 41.
4. Thomas B. Follis, "Feline Urologic Syndrome—A Research Update," *Insights from Purina Research*, 1978, p. 3.
5. W. J. McCormick, as quoted in Stone, op. cit., p. 143.

Chapter Twenty

1. Frank Král and B. Novak, *Veterinary Dermatology*, Lippincott, Philadelphia, 1953, quoted in Mark Morris, *Nutrition and Diet in Small Animal Medicine*, Mark Morris Associates, Denver, 1960, p. 31.
2. Danny W. Scott, "Feline Skin Problems," *The Persian Quarterly*, Fall 1981, p. 40.
3. Joan O. Joshua, "The Use of Biotin in Certain Skin Diseases of the Cat," *The Veterinary Record*, February 7, 1959, p. 102.
4. Lacroix et al., op. cit., pp. 329–331.
5. Lewis, loc. cit.
6. Lambert, op. cit., pp. 617–20.
7. M. J. Burns in *Auburn Veterinarian*, Spring 1980, as quoted in *Veterinary Medicine/Small Animal Clinician*, February 1981, p. 153.
8. Lewis, op. cit., p. 49.
9. Danny W. Scott, loc. cit.
10. Ibid., pp. 40–41.
11. Pottenger, loc. cit.
12. Mitsuo Kamimura, "Anti-inflammatory Activity of Vitamin E," *Journal of Vitaminology*, vol. 18, 1972, pp. 204–209.
13. Plechner, loc. cit.

Chapter Twenty-One

1. Carol McGraw, "Veterinary Care Extends to Treatment of Cancer," Los Angeles *Times*, September 16, 1981, p. 23.
2. William A. Priester and Nathan Mantel, "Occurrence of Tumors in Domestic Animals: Data from 12 United States and Canadian Colleges of Veterinary Medicine," *Journal of the National Cancer Institute*, December 1971, pp. 1333–1344.

3. Howard M. Hayes, Jr., et al., cited in "Epidemiologic Features of Feline Mammary Carcinoma," *Veterinary Medicine/Small Animal Clinician,* August 1981, p. 1122.

4. Howard M. Hayes, "The Comparative Epidemiology of Selected Neoplasms between Dogs, Cats and Humans," *European Journal of Cancer,* vol. 14, 1978, pp. 1299–1308.

5. McGraw, loc. cit.

6. Jones, as quoted in Richard A. Passwater's *Cancer and Its Nutritional Therapies,* Keats Publishing, New Canaan, Conn., 1978, p. 18.

7. U. Saffiotti et al., "Experimental Cancer of the Lung," *Cancer,* May 1967, p. 857. Raymond J. Shamberger, "Inhibitory Effect of Vitamin A on Carcinogenesis," *Journal of the National Cancer Institute,* September 1971, p. 667.

8. Kanetmatsu Sugiura, "On the Relation of Diets to the Development, Prevention and Treatment of Cancer," *Journal of Nutrition,* vol. 44, 1951, pp. 345–559.

9. Roger Williams, "Concept of Genetotrophic Disease," *Nutrition Reviews,* September 1950, p. 257.

10. L. Benade et al., "Synergistic Killing of Ehrlich Ascites Carcinoma Cells by Ascorbate and 3-Amino-1,2,4-triazole," *Oncology,* vol. 23, no. 1, 1969, pp. 33–43.

11. Nathan Horowitz, "Now Japanese Report 6-Fold Survival Jump in Terminal Cancer with Ascorbate Megadoses," *Medical Tribune,* July 22, 1981, p. 1.

12. Ibid. Ewan Cameron and Linus Pauling, "Supplemented Ascorbate in the Supportive Treatment of Cancer," *Proceedings of the National Academy of Sciences,* September 1978, pp. 4538–4542.

13. M. J. Bissell et al., "Ascorbic Acid Inhibits Replication and Infectivity of Avian RNA Tumor Virus," *Proceedings of the National Academy of Sciences,* May 1980, pp. 2711–2715.

14. Passwater, op. cit., p. 129.

15. N. H. Lambert and Eileen Parkhill, "Preliminary Clinical Report on the Treatment of Tumors in Cats and Dogs With Vitamin E," *Veterinary Record,* May 2, 1959, pp. 359–362.

16. Passwater, op. cit., p. 140.

17. Eric R. Braverman and Carl C. Pfeiffer, "Essential Trace Elements and Cancer," *Journal of Orthomolecular Psychiatry,* vol. 11, no. 1, 1982, pp. 28–37.

Index

Vitamins, specific (*cont.*):
  B₁ (thiamine), xi, 21, 61–65, 79, 91,
    140–141
  B₂ (riboflavin), 61, 65, 91, 104
  B₃ (niacin), xi, 61, 65–66, 104, 141
  B₅ (pantothenic acid), 45, 61, 66–68,
    91, 100, 104, 123, 132, 141,
    208–209
  B₆ (pyridoxine), 45, 61, 67, 58, 104,
    141
  B₉ (folic acid), 55, 61, 67, 68–69,
    91, 104, 141
  B₁₂ (cobalamin), 61, 69–70, 79, 91
  biotin, 61, 70–71, 91, 104, 201
  C, xi–xii, 5–7, 32, 37–54, 55, 60, 67,
    79, 81, 104, 109, 111, 120, 121,
    123, 126, 132, 133, 190, 192–193
    administering, 155–158
    age fighter, 138–140
    analgesic, 52–53
    antihistamine, 51, 208–209
    and cancer, 214–216
    cats poor producers of, 39–42, 93,
      172, 197
    choosing and buying, 148–150
    and collagen, 51–52, 116–117,
      139, 145–146, 215
    and detoxification, 48–51, 53, 128–
      130, 139, 172, 215
    and deworming, 219
    as a do-it-all, 55–56
    dosages, 151–154
    and exposure to cold, 132
    and FUS, 196–198
    and immunity, 42–48, 181
    and kidney degeneration, 144
    megadoses, 46–47, 53–54
    and pregnancy, 92–94, 96, 98, 99
    preventive and therapeutic, 38
    and skin conditions, 201
    and sudden infant (kitten) death,
      106–107

    and viral diseases, 45–46, 168–
      175, 179–182, 184–185
    and zinc, 49
    (*See also* Ascorbic acid; Sodium
      ascorbate)
  D, 55, 71, 78, 98
  E (tocopherol), 7, 34, 51, 55, 72–76,
    79, 81, 105, 109, 120, 145, 172,
    190, 201–202
    age fighter, 134–138, 140
    and allergies, 209
    and cancer, 216
    choosing and buying, 148
    and deworming, 219
    dosages, 151–154
    and pregnancy, 92, 95–96, 99
  H (biotin), 61, 70–71, 91, 104, 201
  P, 149
Vomiting, 31, 64, 82, 130, 143, 144,
  165, 196, 210, 211, 212

Water, drinking, 133, 146, 196
Weakness, 4, 66
  (*See also* Lethargy)
Waterproofing, 131–132
Weight loss, 66, 69, 70, 80, 99, 141,
  165, 166, 177, 212, 213
White blood cells, 44, 82, 104, 105,
  141, 165, 166, 173, 175, 184
Wilson, Robert, 11
Williams, Roger J., 66–67, 91, 92
Worms, 101, 103, 127–128, 144, 158,
  218–219
  nontoxic deworming, 219
Wounds, healing of, 81–82, 101, 118–
  120, 134–135, 141, 202

Yeast, brewers', 64–65, 66, 100, 109,
  204, 210
Yogurt, 109
Young, Vernon, 69

Zinc (*see* Minerals)

About the Authors

Dr. Wendell O. Belfield is director of the Bel-Mar Orthomolecular Veterinary Hospital in San Jose, California, a clinic specializing in disease prevention and treatment of small animals through nutrition. He is a member of the Santa Clara Valley Veterinary Medicine Association and a fellow of the International College of Applied Nutrition. He has published numerous papers in professional journals. He has been a veterinarian for twenty years.

Martin Zucker is a free-lance journalist who has written extensively about health, nutrition and fitness for national publications. He is a former Associated Press newsman.